The R[ough]

Montenegro

written and researched by

Norm Longley

ROUGH GUIDES

NEW YORK • LONDON • DELHI

www.roughguides.com

Contents

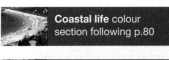

Coastal life colour section following p.80

The Great Outdoors colour section following p.144

◄◄ Boats on the Black Lake, Žabljak ◄ Sveti Stefan

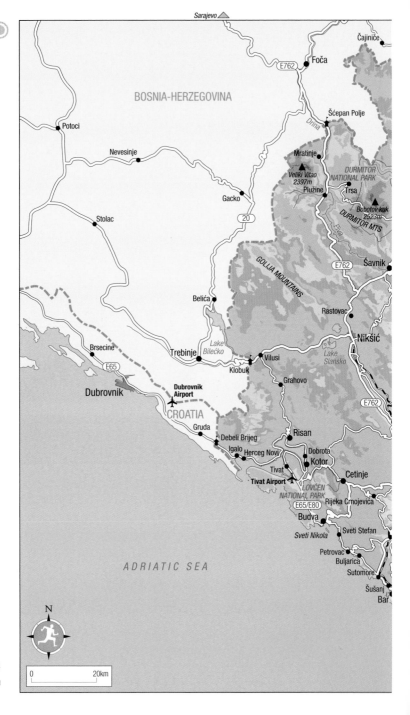

Sarajevo

Čajiniče

E762 Foča

BOSNIA-HERZEGOVINA

Šćepan Polje

Drina

Potoci

Nevesinje

Mratinje

Veliki Vitao
2397m

DURMITOR
NATIONAL PARK

Plužine

Trsa

Gacko

20

Bobotov kuk
2523m

DURMITOR MTS

Piva

Stolac

Šavnik

E762

GOLIJA MOUNTAINS

Belića

Rastovac

Nikšić

Lake
Slansko

Brsecine

Lake
Bilećko

Trebinje

Vilusi

E65

Klobuk

Grahovo

Dubrovnik
Airport

Dubrovnik

E762

CROATIA

Gruda

Risan

Debeli Brijeg

Igalo

Dobrota

Herceg Novi

Kotor

Tivat

Cetinje

Tivat Airport

LOVĆEN
NATIONAL PARK

Rijeka Crnojevića

E65/E80

Budva

Sveti Stefan

Sveti Nikola

Petrovac

Buljarica

ADRIATIC SEA

Sutomore

Šušanj

Bar

N

0   20km

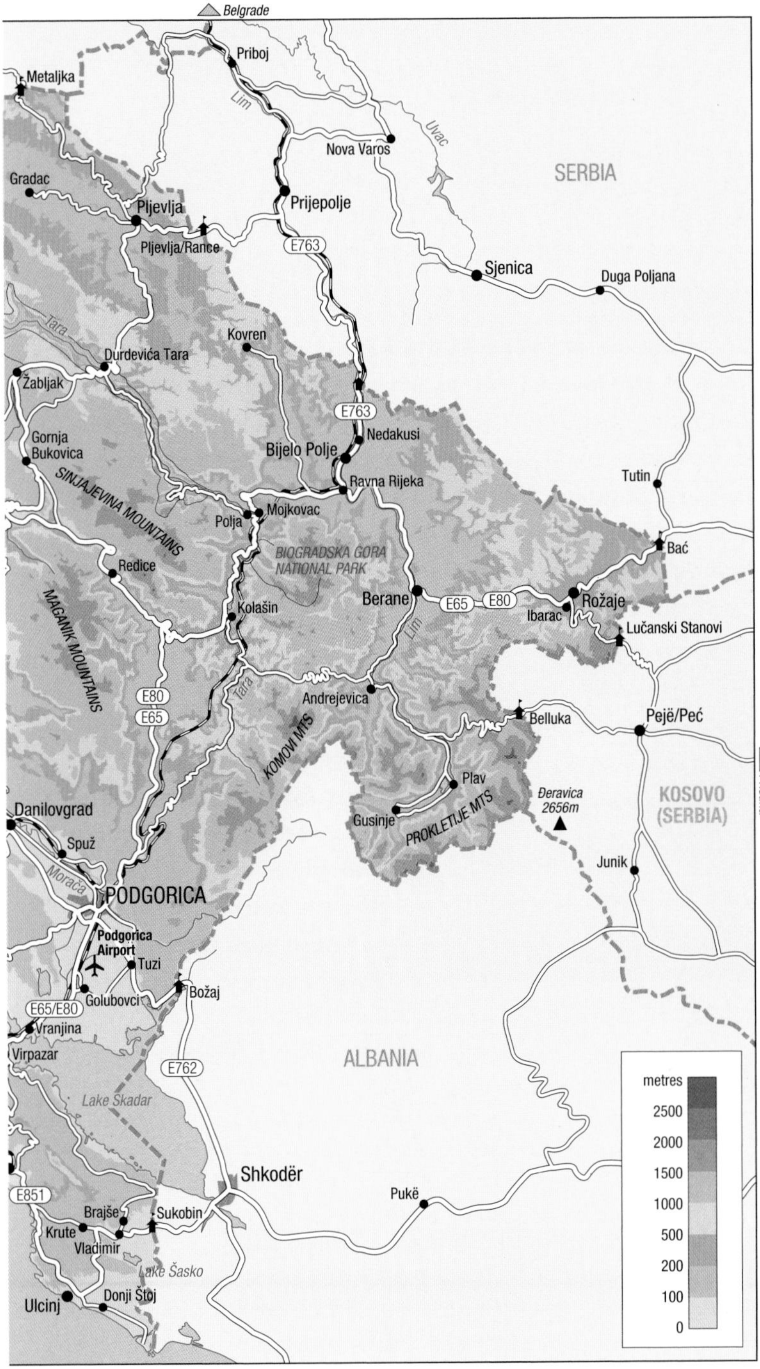
Belgrade
Priboj
Metaljka
Lim
Uvac
Nova Varos
SERBIA
Gradac
Pljevlja
Prijepolje
Pljevlja/Rance
E763
Sjenica
Duga Poljana
Tara
Kovren
Durdevića Tara
Žabljak
E763
Nedakusi
Gornja
Bukovica
Bijelo Polje
Tutin
Ravna Rijeka
SINJAJEVINA MOUNTAINS
Polja
Mojkovac
Bać
BIOGRADSKA GORA
NATIONAL PARK
Redice
Berane
E65
E80
Rožaje
Ibarac
MAGANIK MOUNTAINS
Kolašin
Lučanski Stanovi
Lim
Tara
Andrejevica
E80
E65
Belluka
Pejë/Peć
KOMOVI MTS
Pristina
Plav
Đeravica
2656m
KOSOVO
(SERBIA)
Danilovgrad
Gusinje
PROKLETIJE MTS
Spuž
Junik
Morača
PODGORICA
Podgorica
Airport
Tuzi
Golubovci
Božaj
E65/E80
Vranjina
Virpazar
ALBANIA
E762
Lake Skadar
metres
2500
2000
1500
1000
500
200
100
0
Shkodër
E851
Pukë
Brajše
Sukobin
Krute
Vladimir
Lake Šasko
Ulcinj
Donji Štoj

Introduction to

Montenegro

Boasting one of the most dramatic stretches of coastline in all of Europe, as well as some of the continent's wildest and most beautiful mountains, tiny Montenegro is likely to confound most visitors' expectations. Nearly 300km long, its stunning Adriatic coastline is liberally sprinkled with historic towns, lively beach resorts, secluded coves and comely white-stone fishing villages, all punctuated by strips of fine sand and pebble beaches. The remote,

often inhospitable interior, meanwhile, displays an outstanding array of snow-dusted peaks, crystal-clear lakes and rivers and deep forests and canyons. The whole adds up to a diverse landscape quite extraordinary for such a small country.

Yet the variety that Montenegro manifests stretches beyond its physical attributes. The country lies on one of Europe's great historical fault lines, where the Catholic West meets Orthodox East, with Islam thrown in for good measure: it's a heritage that imbues it with a remarkable cultural heterogeneity. Montenegro has been subject to numerous invaders and occupiers over the centuries, each of which has left an imprint of sorts. Foremost were the Ottomans, whose centuries of occupation left an Islamic legacy still evident in the many mosques in the capital, Podgorica, and the northern and easternmost settlements of the country. The Venetians, meanwhile, controlled much of the coastal region during roughly the same period, leaving their mark in the fine Baroque palaces and churches that remain all along the seaboard; this Mediterranean influence is also evident in the

▲ Herceg Novi

Fact file

• With an **area** of around 14,000 square kilometres (roughly the size of Northern Ireland) and a **population** of only 600,000, Montenegro is one of Europe's smallest countries. The country's official **language** is Montenegrin, which is essentially a variant of Serbian.

• In Montenegrin the country's **name** is Crna Gora ("Black Mountain"), a translation of which into the Venetian language during the Middle Ages formed the Western name for the country.

• Montenegro is an **ethnically diverse** country, comprising 43 percent Montenegrins, 32 percent Serbs, 8 percent Bosnians, 5 percent Albanians and the rest made up of other ethnicities. In terms of **religion**, around 75 percent are Orthodox, 18 percent Muslim, 4 percent Catholic and others representing around 3 percent.

• On June 3, 2006, Montenegro became an **independent republic**, having been part of a Yugoslav federation in some form or other since 1918. The constitution sets in place a **parliamentary system of government**, elected every four years, with the prime minister at its head; the president is head of state.

• **Tourism** is comfortably the fastest growing sector of the Montenegrin economy, with tourist arrivals increasing by around thirty percent year-on-year since 2004. Montenegro's most important **exports** are aluminium, agriculture and textiles.

• Montenegrins are often held to be the **tallest** people in Europe, with an average male height of around 6ft 1in (185cm).

olive groves and vines scattered along the coastal hinterland. The Orthodox faith, meanwhile, arrived with the great medieval dynasties of the Serbs, who bequeathed a marvellous ecclesiastical heritage of monasteries bursting with colourful frescoes and glittering iconostases.

Until recently, Montenegro had broken free from the yoke of foreign rule only once, during a short-lived spell of independence in the late nineteenth century. It then spent much of the twentieth century locked into a less than satisfactory Yugoslav federation, in all its many guises, though it managed to avoid the widespread

Most visitors make an immediate beeline for the magical Montenegrin seaboard, with its multiplicity of enticing resorts and superb beaches.

7

∎

carnage that accompanied the break-up of the federation in the 1990s. A relatively painless divorce from Serbia in 2006 resulted in the country's long-desired goal of independence, and it now has its sights firmly set on membership of the European Union.

Independence has coincided with a dramatic upsurge in visitor numbers, recalling the halcyon days of the 1970s and 1980s when Montenegro was one of the hottest destinations in all of Yugoslavia, attracting not only large numbers of package tourists but also celebrities and movie stars. Today, investment is pouring in, primarily from the Russians, who have pumped vast sums of capital into the many construction projects along the coast, mainly in the form of high-end hotels, while the littoral's popularity as a property hotspot for foreigners shows no signs of abating. And though much of the interior lags some way behind the coast in terms of its tourist infrastructure, its potential is immense, with plans afoot to develop the region into a prime ecotourism destination.

Where to go

With few significant towns or cities to speak of, the bulk of your time in Montenegro is likely to be spent either along the coast or in the mountainous interior. Most visitors make an immediate beeline for the magical Montenegrin seaboard, with its multiplicity of enticing resorts and superb beaches. The most popular destination is **Budva**, which features a fabulously appealing old town, some fine beaches and the coast's hottest nightlife. Further south, **Petrovac** boasts a gorgeous beach, beyond which lie the port

▼ Budva beach

8

▼ Piva Canyon

town of **Bar**, with the absorbing ruins of Stari Bar nearby, and bustling **Ulcinj**, close to the Albanian border and thus manifesting a strong Muslim heritage. North of Budva, the upper part of coast is dominated by the stunning **Gulf of Kotor**, Europe's southernmost fjord, throughout which are scattered numerous towns and resorts; best of these are **Kotor**, whose delightful Old Town is dominated by Venetian-inspired architecture, and **Perast**, once the seafaring capital of the Adriatic. Of the resorts hereabouts, **Herceg Novi**, just a few kilometres south of the Croatian border, is well worth a visit, especially given its proximity to the **Orjen Massif**, where there's gentle rambling, and the lovely **Luštica peninsula** a short boat ride away; meanwhile more modern **Tivat**, home to one of the country's two international airports, is currently reinventing itself as a major marina.

The modestly sized capital, **Podgorica**, is first and foremost a business and commercial centre – though you'll likely pass through, you're equally unlikely to want to linger. Nearby are the country's one-time royal capital, **Cetinje**, whose fine museums and architecture warrant a day-trip, and the industrial but personable town of **Nikšić**, Montenegro's only other sizeable centre; on the way there you can stop at **Ostrog Monastery**, Montenegrins' premier place of pilgrimage. Nature reasserts itself in fine style just south of Podgorica at **Lake Skadar**, the largest inland body of water in the Balkans and setting for hundreds of thousands of migrating birds during spring and autumn.

The further inland you go, the more spectacular the scenery becomes. This is nowhere more evident than around **Durmitor**, Montenegro's largest national park, which harbours magisterial peaks, alpine lakes and the sinuous **Tara River Canyon**, whose sheer valley walls carved through by a furious, foaming river make it the country's single most dramatic phenomenon. Durmitor lends itself perfectly to a whole host of active pursuits: as well climbing and hiking, there are excellent rafting and fishing on the Tara River, and, in the winter, skiing in the mountain resort of **Žabljak**.

▼ Sheep in Durmitor National Park

There's more wonderful mountain scenery, and more opportunities for adventure thrills, in the **Bjelasica** mountain range across to the east. At its heart is lovely **Biogradska Gora National Park**, dotted by glacial lakes and tracts of virgin forest. The one major resort in this part of the country – catering particularly to winter-sports enthusiasts – is **Kolašin**, which lies close to **Morača Monastery**, bedecked with marvellous Byzantine-era frescoes. By comparison, the northern and easternmost inland regions are much less visited, which is itself part of their attraction. There's very little tradition of tourism hereabouts but there are some rewarding places to visit: chief amongst these is the appealing little town of **Plav**, known for its beautiful blue lake; Plav is also the jumping-off point for the wild **Prokletije** mountain range bordering Albania, which offers more outstanding hiking.

When to go

To experience the full range of what Montenegro has to offer, the best time to visit is broadly between April and September. Montenegro's climate follows three distinct patterns: the coast has typically **Mediterranean** weather, with very warm summers – temperatures regularly hover around the mid- to upper thirties – and mild winters; while the interior manifests a **sub-alpine** climate, characterized by warm summers but bitterly cold winters – temperatures can drop to as low as minus fifteen or twenty degrees – with occasionally heavy rainfall and much snow. The relatively flat area of land between the coast and mountains (roughly from Lake Skadar up to Podgorica and beyond to Nikšić) has a more **continental** climate, with fairly hot, dry summers and cold winters, often with snow.

The **coast** is a pleasant place to be at any time of the year but it can get uncomfortably congested in July and August, when temperatures and crowds reach their peak; moreover, accommodation is at its most expensive during this period, with rates almost doubling in some places. Hence June and September are the optimum months for a visit, when the weather is still reliably hot and there's far less pressure on facilities. Between late October and early April some hotels close but you may well pick up excellent rates from those that do stay open.

While the mountainous **interior** is at its most temperate from late April to September – and these are the best months for hiking, climbing and rafting – the possibilities for skiing between late November and early April mean that a visit can be enjoyed almost any time of year. Moreover, the mountains receive a fraction of the numbers that hit the coast, so you're unlikely to have to worry about crowds.

Average daily temperatures (°C)

	Jan	Feb	Mar	Apr	May	Jun	Jul	Aug	Sep	Oct	Nov	Dec
Budva												
max	7	8	12	16	21	25	28	28	25	19	13	8
min	-1	1	3	7	11	14	17	17	13	9	5	1
Kolašin												
max	0	2	5	10	15	18	21	21	18	12	6	2
min	-7	-5	-3	1	5	8	10	10	7	3	-1	-5
Podgorica												
max	9	5	11	19	24	28	31	31	27	21	15	11
min	1	3	5	9	13	17	20	19	16	11	6	3
Ulcinj												
max	10	11	14	18	23	27	31	30	27	21	16	11
min	2	3	5	9	13	16	19	19	15	11	7	4
Žabljak												
max	-1	0	4	8	13	16	19	20	16	11	5	0
min	-8	-7	-4	0	4	7	9	9	6	2	-2	-6

things not to miss

It's not possible to see everything Montenegro has to offer in one trip – and we don't suggest you try. What follows is a selective taste of the country's highlights: historic sights, natural wonders, fun activities and great food and drink. They're arranged in five colour-coded categories, which you can browse through to find the very best things to see, do and experience. All highlights have a page reference to take you straight into the guide, where you can find out more.

01 Perast Page **55** • A postcard-perfect Venetian town complete with crumbling palaces and ornate churches. Whilst here, visit the fabulous Our Lady of the Rocks sited just offshore.

02

Njegoš Mausoleum, Lovćen National Park Page 122 • Cloaked in beech and oak, Lovćen affords some lovely rambling, though most people come to view this mausoleum of Petar Petrović Njegoš, Montenegro's most celebrated historical figure, from where there are unsurpassed views down to beautiful Kotor Bay.

03 Kotor's Old Town Page 60 • Sprinkled with Venetian-Gothic architecture, pretty little churches and quaint squares, Kotor's venerable Old Town is one of the coast's must-see destinations.

04 Kayaking Page 51 • One of the most fun ways to explore the hidden coves and beaches of Kotor Bay is from a sea kayak.

05 Cetinje Page 112 • Nestled amongst picturesque limestone mountains, Montenegro's one-time royal capital contains some absorbing museums and lovely architecture, including this impressive monastery.

13

06 Rakija Page **32** • A typically powerful Balkan brandy, Montenegro's throat-busting national drink should be tried at least once.

07 Ostrog Monastery Page **129** • Dramatically and improbably sited high up in the rock face, seventeenth-century Ostrog Monastery is the country's most important place of pilgrimage.

08
Lake Skadar
Page **107** • Not only is this beautiful lake the Balkans' largest body of water, but it also offers some of the finest birdwatching in southeastern Europe.

09
Tara Canyon
Page **141** • Sheer valley walls and a thrashing river have conspired to produce Montenegro's most amazing natural wonder. Don't miss the vertiginous Tara Bridge either.

10 Boka Nights

Page **59** • Montenegro's noisiest and most colourful annual spectacle sees a flotilla of boats line Kotor's harbour, before an explosion of fireworks lights up the bay.

11 Gulf of Kotor

Page **45** • Embracing a series of bays, most impressively Kotor, Europe's southernmost fjord is the Adriatic's most arresting natural feature.

13 Whitewater rafting

Page **143** • The fabulous, foaming Tara River is a first-class venue for this most thrilling of adrenaline-fuelled adventure sports.

12 Njeguši ham

Page **122** • Enjoy a slice or two of this fabulously tasty delicacy from the eponymous village – perfect with a drop of the excellent Vranac red wine.

14 Stari Bar

Page **84** •
Take a leisurely
stroll around
these ancient,
crumbling ruins,
which date back
to pre-Roman
times.

15 Budva Page **69** •

The coast's liveliest
and most atmospheric resort boasts a
delightful Old Town, great beaches and sizzling
nightlife.

16 Hiking in Durmitor

Page **142** • One of Europe's
least spoilt mountain ranges, these wild
peaks are Montenegro's prime hiking
destination, with trails to suit walkers of
all abilities.

17 Fish restaurants Page

54 • Choose from any number of
fabulous fish restaurants along the coast,
such as *Catovića Mlini* in Morinj, where
you can take your pick from the day's
freshest catch.

Basics

Basics

Getting there

Flying is the easiest way to reach Montenegro, with direct flights from the UK, although there are presently no direct flights from North America, Australasia or South Africa. Travelling overland from the UK is a long haul, and you'll save little, if anything, by taking the train, although with a rail pass you can take in Montenegro as part of a wider trip. Driving there will involve a journey of some 2300km from Britain, an absorbing trip but one best covered slowly.

Airfares are highest from June to August, and drop during the "shoulder" seasons – March to May and September to October. The best prices are found during the low season, from November to February, excluding Christmas and New Year when prices are hiked up and seats are at a premium.

You can often cut costs by going through a **specialist flight agent**, who in addition to dealing with discounted flights may also offer student and youth fares and travel insurance, rail passes, car rentals, tours and the like. Some agents specialize in **charter flights**, which may be cheaper than scheduled flights, but departure dates are fixed and withdrawal penalties are high.

Flights from the UK and Ireland

Flying to Podgorica **from the UK** takes approximately two and a half hours. Montenegro Airlines operates one flight a week from London Gatwick to the capital, **Podgorica**, and twice-weekly flights from London Gatwick to **Tivat** on the coast. However, as tourism takes off things are quite likely to change – during the summer months in particular the number of flights is likely to increase – so it's always worth checking on the latest situation. Expect to pay around £150–170 return in low season, £180–220 in high season.

A good, and slightly cheaper, alternative is to fly into **Dubrovnik**, just across the border in Croatia, to which there are more frequent services; both British Airways and Croatia Airlines operate flights between London Gatwick and Dubrovnik, while Thomsonfly fly to Dubrovnik from London Gatwick, Luton and Manchester. Doing it this way, fares can be obtained from as little as £100 in low season, rising to around £180 in high season. From Dubrovnik there are straightforward onward connections by bus into Montenegro (see box, p.23). Another cheaper possibility is to fly with easyjet to **Split**, though this is about four hours (by bus) further up the coast from Dubrovnik. You could also fly into **Belgrade** in Serbia with either British Airways or JAT (Yugoslav Airlines), from where there are regular onward flights (with JAT) to both Podgorica and Tivat.

Some package-tour operators (see p.21) specialize in **charter flights**, which may be cheaper than any scheduled flights. Balkan Holidays offer summer flight-only deals from London Heathrow to Tivat, as well as flights from London Gatwick, Manchester and Birmingham to Dubrovnik. Holiday Options have flights from both London Heathrow and Gatwick to Tivat, as well as to Dubrovnik from several UK airports.

There are no direct scheduled flights to Montenegro **from Dublin or Belfast**, but Aer Lingus do operate a service from Dublin to Dubrovnik. Alternatively, fly to London and take an onward connection.

Flights from the USA and Canada

There are no direct flights **from the USA or Canada** to Montenegro, so you'll have to use one of the national carriers to fly you into a major European hub and continue the journey from there. From the east coast of the US expect to pay around US$750 in low season and US$1100 in high season; and from the west coast around US$1000 in low season and US$1500 in high season. An alternative is to fly with a European carrier into the capital city of a country close to Montenegro, such as Budapest, in Hungary, from where you can get a connecting flight to Podgorica. Malev, the Hungarian carrier, flies direct from New York's JFK to Budapest, and offers similar fares. It also schedules direct flights from Toronto, with fares from around Can$900 in low season and Can$1300 in high season.

Flights from Australia and New Zealand

There are no direct flights to Montenegro **from Australia or New Zealand** so you'll have to change airlines, either in Asia or Europe, although the best option is to fly to a Western European gateway city, such as London, Paris or Frankfurt, and get a connecting flight from there. A standard return fare from the east coast of Australia to Podgorica, via London with Qantas, is around Aus$2200 low season and Aus$2700 high season. The same routings apply for flights from New Zealand, with a standard return fare from Auckland to Podgorica, via London, from around NZ$3000.

Flights from South Africa

There are no direct flights to Montenegro **from South Africa** so you'll have to change airlines at one of the major European gateways. A standard return fare from Johannesburg to Podgorica via Frankfurt or Vienna (with South African Airways or a leading European airline) is around ZAR10,000 in low season or ZAR12,000 in high season.

Airlines

Aer Lingus UK ☎0870 876 5000, Republic of Ireland ☎0818 365 000, US and Canada ☎1-800-IRISH-AIR; ⓦwww.aerlingus.com.
Air Canada US and Canada ☎1-888/247-2262, ⓦwww.aircanada.com.
Air France UK ☎0870 142 4343, US ☎1-800-237-2747, Canada ☎1-800-667-2747, Australia ☎1300 390 190, South Africa ☎0861 340 340; ⓦwww.airfrance.com.

Air New Zealand Australia ☎0800 132 476, New Zealand ☎0800 737 000; ⓦwww.airnz.co.nz.
American Airlines US and Canada ☎1-800-433-7300, ⓦwww.aa.com.
Austrian Airlines UK ☎0870 124 2625, Republic of Ireland ☎1800 509 142, US and Canada ☎1-800-843-0002, Australia ☎1800 642 438; ⓦwww.aua.com.
British Airways UK ☎0844 493 0787, Republic of Ireland ☎1890 626 747, US and Canada ☎1-800-AIRWAYS, Australia ☎1300 767 177, New Zealand ☎09/966 9777, South Africa ☎011/441 8600; ⓦwww.ba.com.
Croatia Airlines UK ☎0870 410 0310, US ☎1-973-884-3401, Australia ☎03/9699 9355, New Zealand ☎09/837 9897; ⓦwww.croatiaairlines.hr.
easyJet UK ⓦwww.easyjet.com.
JAT UK ☎020/7629 2007, US ☎1-212/6891-677, Canada ☎1-416/920 4222, Australia ☎02/9268 0305; ⓦwww.jat.com.
Lufthansa UK ☎0871 945 9747, Republic of Ireland ☎01/844 5544, US ☎1-800-3995-838, Canada ☎1-800-563-5954, Australia ☎1300 655 727, New Zealand ☎0800 945 220, South Africa ☎0861 842 538; ⓦwww.lufthansa.com.
Malev Hungarian Airlines UK ☎0870 909 0577, Republic of Ireland ☎0818 555 577, US ☎1-800-223-6884, Canada ☎1-866-379-7313; ⓦwww.malev.hu.
Montenegro Airlines ⓦwww.montenegroairlines.com.
Quantas Australia ☎13 13 13, New Zealand ☎0800 808 767; ⓦwww.qantas.com.
SkyEurope UK ⓦwww.skyeurope.com.
South African Airways South Africa ☎011/978 1111, ⓦwww.flysaa.com.
Swiss UK ☎0845 601 0956, Republic of Ireland ☎1890 200 515, US and Canada ☎1-877-3597-947, Australia ☎1300 724 666, New Zealand ☎09/977 2238, South Africa ☎0860 040 506; ⓦwww.swiss.com.
Thomsonfly UK ☎0871 231 4869, ⓦwww.thomsonfly.com.
United Airlines US ☎1-800-864-8331, ⓦwww.united.com.
Virgin Atlantic US ☎1-800-821-5438, ⓦwww.virgin-atlantic.com.

Agents and operators

Online booking

ⓦwww.expedia.co.uk (in UK), ⓦwww.expedia.com (in US), ⓦwww.expedia.ca (in Canada)
ⓦwww.lastminute.com (in UK)
ⓦwww.opodo.co.uk (in UK)

Fly less – stay longer! Travel and climate change

Climate change is perhaps the single biggest issue facing our planet. It is caused by a build-up in the atmosphere of carbon dioxide and other greenhouse gases, which are emitted by many sources – including planes. Already, **flights** account for three to four percent of human-induced global warming: that figure may sound small, but it is rising year on year and threatens to counteract the progress made by reducing greenhouse emissions in other areas.

Rough Guides regard travel as a **global benefit** and feel strongly that the advantages to developing economies are important, as are the opportunities for greater contact and awareness among peoples. But we also believe in travelling responsibly, which includes giving thought to how often we fly and what we can do to redress any harm that our trips may create.

We can travel less or simply reduce the amount we travel by air (taking fewer trips and staying longer, or taking the train if there is one); we can avoid night flights (which are more damaging); and we can make the trips we do take "climate neutral" via a carbon offset scheme. **Offset schemes** run by climatecare.org, carbonneutral .com and others allow you to "neutralize" the greenhouse gases that you are responsible for releasing. Their websites have simple calculators that let you work out the impact of any flight – as does our own. Once that's done, you can pay to fund projects that will reduce future emissions by an equivalent amount. Please take the time to visit our website and make your trip climate neutral, or get a copy of the *Rough Guide to Climate Change* for more detail on the subject.

ⓦ www.roughguides.com/climatechange

ⓦ www.orbitz.com (in US)
ⓦ www.travelocity.co.uk (in UK), ⓦ www .travelocity.com (in US), ⓦ www.travelocity .ca (in Canada), ⓦ www.travelocity.co.nz (in New Zealand)
ⓦ www.travelonline.co.za (in South Africa)
ⓦ www.zuji.com.au (in Australia)

General agents and operators

ebookers UK ☏ 0871 223 5000, ⓦ www .ebookers.com; Republic of Ireland ☏ 01/431 1311, ⓦ www.ebookers.ie. Low fares on an extensive selection of scheduled flights and package deals.
North South Travel UK ☏ 01245/608 291, ⓦ www.northsouthtravel.co.uk. Friendly, competitive travel agency, offering discounted fares worldwide. Profits are used to support projects in the developing world, especially the promotion of sustainable tourism.
STA Travel UK ☏ 0871 2300 040, US ☏ 1-800-781-4040, Australia ☏ 134 782, New Zealand ☏ 0800 474 400, South Africa ☏ 0861 781 781; ⓦ www.statravel.com. Worldwide specialists in independent travel; also student IDs, travel insurance, car rental, rail passes and more. Good discounts for students and under 26s.
Trailfinders UK ☏ 0845 058 5858, Republic of Ireland ☏ 01/677 7888; ⓦ www.trailfinders.com. One of the best-informed and most efficient agents for independent travellers.

Specialist operators

Adventures Abroad UK ☏ 0114/247 3400, USA ☏ 1-800-665-3998; ⓦ www.adventures-abroad .com. Active and cultural tours of Croatia, which also include a couple of days in Montenegro, visiting Kotor and Cetinje.
Balkan Holidays UK ☏ 0845 130 1114, ⓦ www .balkanholidays.co.uk. One and two-week summer beach holidays in Bečići, Budva, Kotor, Petrovac and Sveti Stefan, as well as charter-flight-only options.
Bosmere Travel UK ☏ 01473/834094, ⓦ www .bosmeretravel.co.uk. Montenegrin specialists offering tailor-made trips including accommodation (hotels and apartments), transport, excursions and activities.
Concorde Republic of Ireland ☏ 01/872 7822, ⓦ www.concordetravel.ie. Adriatic specialists with holidays in several coastal resorts – Budva, Bečići, Kotor and Sveti Stefan – as well as charter flights.
Exodus UK ☏ 0845 863 9600, ⓦ www.exodus .co.uk. Eight-day hiking tour (moderate to challenging) taking in Durmitor and Biogradska Gora, as well as a visit to Kotor. They also offer an eleven-day, two-country (with Bosnia-Herzegovina) cultural tour: the Montenegro leg takes in Kotor, Perast, Cetinje and Durmitor. In the Republic of Ireland, contact Worldwide Adventures (☏ 01/679 5700).
Explore Worldwide UK ☏ 0845 013 1537, ⓦ www .explore.co.uk. Nine-day walking/cultural tour,

incorporating hiking in the Durmitor, rafting on the Tara River and visits to Ostrog Monastery, Kotor and Lovćen National Park.

Holiday Options UK ☏ 0870 420 8386, ⓦ www .holidayoptions.co.uk. Major operator offering coastal resort holidays in both family and luxury accommodation. Also offers two-centre holidays with Dubrovnik and charter flights.

Inghams UK ☏ 020/8780 4433, ⓦ www.inghams .co.uk. Another major operator offering coastal (Budva and Petrovac) and mountain (Kolašin) package holidays, from four to seven nights in high-quality hotels.

Original Travel UK ☏ 020/7978 7333, ⓦ www .originaltravel.co.uk. Three-day coastal breaks to Sveti Stefan and Miločer.

Ramblers Holidays UK ☏ 01707/331 133, ⓦ www.ramblersholidays.co.uk. Eight-day walking tour (moderate difficulty) of the coastal region; based in Budva, the tour comprises walks between resorts and up into the hills above.

By train

Travelling **by train** to Montenegro is likely to be considerably more expensive than flying, and the shortest journey takes about 36 hours. However, it can be an enjoyable way of getting to the country, especially if you plan to stop off in other parts of Europe along the way.

A standard second-class **return ticket**, incorporating Eurostar, will cost around £350. Eurostar trains depart more or less hourly (roughly 6am–7.30pm) from London St Pancras through the Channel Tunnel to Paris Gare du Nord (1hr 50min) and Brussels (2hr). Arriving in Paris, you take a train to Vienna and change there for the next leg to Belgrade. Alternatively, from Brussels pick up a connection to Cologne, before boarding a train for Vienna and then the onward leg to Belgrade. In Belgrade, you need to change again for the last leg to Podgorica. Tickets are usually valid for two to three months and allow for unlimited stopovers.

The best printed source for **timetables** is Thomas Cook's red-covered *European Rail Timetable*, which details schedules of the main Montenegrin train service; the same publisher also produce the useful *Rail Map of Europe*. Online, the best resource is ⓦ www.bahn.de (see below).

Rail passes

If you're taking in Montenegro as part of a wider trip, then you might consider the **InterRail Pass** (ⓦ www.interrail.net). These are only available to European residents (or those who have been resident in a European country for at least six months), and you will be asked to provide proof of residency before being allowed to buy one. They come in over-26 and (cheaper) under-26 versions, and cover thirty countries, of which Montenegro is one.

There are now two types of pass. The old zonal pass has been replaced with a **Global Pass**, covering all thirty countries (one month of continuous use costs €599 for over 26s/ €399 for under 26s; 22 days continuous €469/€309; 10 days in 22 €359/€239; 5 days in 10 €249/€159). InterRail Passes do not include travel between Britain and the Continent, although holders are eligible for discounts on rail travel in Britain and Northern Ireland and cross-Channel ferries, as well as reduced rates on the London–Paris Eurostar service The other InterRail scheme, the **One-Country Pass** (formerly the Eurodomino pass) does not cover Montenegro but does include Serbia (8 days in one month costs €119 for over 26s/€77 for under 26s; 6 days in one month €99/ €64; 4 days in one month €69/€45; 3 days in one month €49/€32), which means that if you wish to travel between Belgrade and Montenegro, you only need to purchase the portion of the ticket covering travel in Montenegro.

Non-European residents qualify for the **Eurail Pass** (ⓦ www.eurail.com), which must be bought before arrival in Europe (or from RailEurope in the UK). Neither Eurail's Global Pass nor their One-Country Pass include either Montenegro or Serbia, but their **Select Pass** includes both. The pass allows travel in three (from €207), four (from €232) or five (from €255) bordering countries over a selected period of time (5, 6, 8, or 10 days within a two-month period).

Rail contacts

Deutsche Bahn ⓦ www.bahn.de. The German national rail website is the best source of international timetabling information.

European Rail UK ☏ 020/7619 1083, ⓦ www.europeanrail.com. Independent specialists offering a range of European rail tickets, including InterRail.

Europrail International Canada ☏ 1-888-667-9734, ⓦ www.europrail.net. Eurail and country passes.

Eurostar UK ☏ 0870 518 6186, outside UK ☏ +44/1233 617 575; ⓦ www.eurostar.com. High-speed train links from London St Pancras to Paris, Lille and Brussels.

The Man in Seat 61 ⓦ www.seat61.com. Excellent website detailing routes, timings and fares across Europe.

Rail Europe UK ☏ 0844 848 4064, ⓦ www .raileurope.co.uk; US ☏ 1-888-382-7245, Canada ☏ 1-800-361-7245, ⓦ www.raileurope.com; Australia 03/9642 8644, ⓦ www.raileurope.com.au; New Zealand 09/377 5415; South Africa ☏ 011/628 2319, ⓦ www.raileurope.co.za. Wide range of European passes, including InterRail, and Eurostar tickets.

By car

Driving to Montenegro, a distance of around 2300km from London, can be a pleasant proposition. However, it's really only worth considering if you are planning to travel around Montenegro extensively or want to make various stopovers en route. See p.25 for details of driving within Montenegro.

Getting there from neighbouring countries

Montenegro is easily reached overland from several neighbouring countries, none of which require visas.

From Croatia

Since there are regular flights to the city, one of the most convenient ways of reaching Montenegro is to fly into **Dubrovnik Airport**, just 30km from the border at Debeli Brijeg. Unless you wish to spend some time in Dubrovnik itself, 22km northwest of the airport, the easiest way to reach Montenegro is to take a taxi direct to Herceg Novi, which will set you back around €40. You can also hire a car at the airport and drive down into Montenegro from there – all the major car hire companies are represented.

Alternatively, if you do wish to explore Dubrovnik, you can either wait for a bus into the city (only Croatian Airlines' flights are met by buses), or take a taxi, which will cost around 240–260kn (€30–35). From the bus station in Dubrovnik, next to the harbour 4km west of the Old Town in Gruž, three buses a day make the hour-long journey to Herceg Novi, costing around €12. There are also direct services once to twice daily to Budva, Kotor and Tivat further along the coast.

It's a four-hour bus journey from **Split** to Dubrovnik, some 220km south, from where you can catch an onward bus to Herceg Novi; there are also a handful of services direct into Montenegro.

From Serbia

From **Belgrade** in Serbia, three daily trains make the journey through the Montenegrin interior, via Podgorica, to Bar on the coast. Two services run during the daytime; to Podgorica they cost €15 in second class, €30 in first class and take around 8hr. A third service runs overnight (11hr), and during the summer should be booked (at the train station) at least seven days in advance. The train has a sleeping car (*kolima za spavanje*): on top of the regular fare, expect to pay around €10 for a bed in a four- or six- bed cabin, €15 for a bed in a two-bed cabin and €35 for a single cabin.

Otherwise, there are eight daily buses from Belgrade to Podgorica (7–8hr) and the coastal towns of Budva, Tivat and Kotor, as well as to mountain towns including Brjelo Polje, Kolašin and Žabljak.

From Bosnia-Herzegovina

From Bosnia-Herzegovina, there are four buses (around €20) a day between the capital, **Sarajevo**, and Podgorica, via Nikšić, as well as services direct to the coast. It's a fabulously scenic journey, taking between six and seven hours.

For details of ferry crossings into Montenegro **from Italy**, see p.24.

Once across the Channel (see opposite), the fastest **route** (around thirty hours at a leisurely pace with plenty of stops) is through the Netherlands, Germany, Austria, and then down through Slovenia, Croatia and Bosnia-Herzegovina. Major border crossings are open 24 hours a day. Detailed printouts of the route can be obtained from the Michelin website (ⓦ www.viamichelin.com).

An alternative is to drive down to Bari in Italy (a distance of some 2000km), from where you can catch a **ferry** across to Montenegro. In this case, once across the Channel drive across France and Switzerland into Italy. **Montenegro Lines** operate ferries to Bar year-round from Bari (July to mid-Sept 6 weekly; rest of year 3 weekly; 9hr) and in the summer only from Ancona (July–Sept 2 weekly; 14hr), while **Azzurra Lines** operate a summer service between Bari and Kotor (June–Sept 1 weekly; 9hr). On Montenegro Lines, deck tickets in high season cost around €50 from Bari to Bar,

€60 from Ancona; cabins range from €70/€80 to €100/€115, and it costs €80/€90 to take on a car.

Ferry and Channel Tunnel contacts

Azzurra Lines ⓦ www.azzurraline.com. Bari to Kotor.
Eurotunnel UK ☎ 0870 535 3535, ⓦ www .eurotunnel.com. Drive-on, drive-off shuttle trains for vehicles from Folkestone to Coquelles, near Calais.
Montenegro Lines ⓦ www.montenegrolines.net. Bari and Ancona to Bar.
Norfolkline UK ☎ 0870 870 1020, ⓦ www .norfolkline.com. Dover to Dunkerque.
P&O Ferries UK ☎ 0871 664 5645, ⓦ www .poferries.com. Dover to Calais.
Sea France UK ☎ 0871 663 2546, ⓦ www .seafrance.com. Dover to Calais.
SpeedFerries UK ☎ 0871 222 7456, ⓦ www .speedferries.com. Dover to Boulogne.
Stena Line UK ☎ 0870 570 7070, ⓦ www .stenaline.co.uk. Harwich to Hook of Holland.

Getting around

Whatever mode of transport you use, travelling around Montenegro is rarely anything other than fabulously scenic. In the absence of a comprehensive rail network, buses offer a far quicker and more practical way of getting around, with regular services fanning out from Podgorica and shuttling up and down the coast. Driving is another attractive proposition, enabling you to visit anywhere you please, and in your own time.

By train

The Montenegrin **railway network** (željeznice Crne Gore) covers just 294km, running from the border near Bijelo Polje in the northeast of the country, down through Mojkovac, Kolašin and Podgorica to Virpazar on Lake Skadar, and then down to Bar on the coast. Because the route originates in Belgrade (see box, p.23), the line is extremely popular in the summer with vacationing Serbs visiting the coast.

Years of little or no investment, however, have left the system in a rather dilapidated state and it's neither particularly clean nor

particularly reliable – delays and inexplicable stoppages occur with maddening regularity, and it is quite normal for trains to arrive anywhere up to an hour after their scheduled time. That said, fares are incredibly cheap (see opposite), and the journey is one of the most spectacular in Europe. The country's only other rail line links Podgorica with Nikšić, though it was only carrying freight trains at the time of writing; there are however plans to reopen it to passengers, possibly by 2009. There are no rail links with any neighbouring country other than Serbia.

There are two **types of train**: *brzi* (fast) and

poslovni (slow) – though there's actually little distinction between the two, and the cost is the same regardless of which one you travel on. **Timetables** (*vozni red*) are displayed in stations and offices – arrivals (*dolazak*) are usually on a white board, departures (*odlazak*) on a yellow one – though don't expect trains to conform too closely to them. Otherwise, you could check out the network's website (ⓦwww.zeljeznica.me), though the site is somewhat erratic – in any case, you should always check at the station.

Fares are calculated by distance travelled, and are extremely low: a journey of 50km, for example, will cost around €2 in second class, €3.50 in first class (there's not much to distinguish between the two classes, save for the fact that the seats are bigger and more comfortable in first). Expect to pay around €3.50 in second class from Podgorica to Bar and €5 from Podgorica to Bijelo Polje. **Reservations** are not necessary. Details of main routes are summarized at the end of each chapter. For key terms, see p.189.

By bus

Montenegro's **bus network** consists of a well-coordinated array of private companies, and is far and away the best way to get around. By and large, services are cheap, clean and reliable, with buses rarely that full; the only downside is sometimes the lack of air-conditioning. A fairly comprehensive network of buses fans out from Podgorica, and there are also plentiful services along the coast, where a constant stream plies between all the major resorts, covering most other places en route. Inland, and particularly in mountainous regions, services are far more sporadic. Bus drivers are normally quite happy to drop passengers off at the roadside (for example if you want to see a particular attraction), though you do then face the problem of knowing when the next one might come along.

Fares are slightly higher than on the trains – expect to pay around €3 from Podgorica to Cetinje (30km), €5 from Podgorica to Bar or Budva (both 70km), €7 from Podgorica to Bijelo Polje (100km), and €8 from Podgorica to Žabljak (130km). If you don't have time to buy your ticket from the bus station counter, you can pay onboard.

Main bus routes are listed in the Travel details section at the end of each chapter.

By car

Driving in Montenegro is, on the whole, a highly appealing option. Away from the major coastal road, the roads are relatively traffic-free, and many routes are wonderfully scenic. That said, the state of the country's **roads** is highly variable. Montenegro has no highway, though plans are under way to construct a motorway linking the south and north of the country, and extending all the way to Belgrade, though this will take some years. The main roads are, generally speaking, in fairly good condition but minor roads are invariably poor, with many disintegrating and littered with potholes – this is particularly the case in the north of the country and around the mountain regions. Indeed, great care should be exercised if driving here (especially in winter), as the roads are often poorly surfaced and narrow in places. The road up the Morača Valley, from Podgorica to Kolašin, is particularly notorious, as is the road beyond to Žabljak.

More generally, Montenegrin **driving habits** often leave much to be desired, a particular danger being the tendency to overtake at absurdly risky moments. The accident rate here is quite high, as evidenced by the many (rather distracting) roadside memorials. The usual precautions apply when it comes to the potential for **theft**: never leave valuables inside the car and always lock it, even if you're just popping into a shop for five minutes.

Petrol stations (*benzinska pumpa*) can be found almost everywhere, though are less prominent inland and the further north you go towards the mountains; in these regions, make sure you fill up whenever you get the chance. Most cars now use lead-free petrol (*bezolovni*), though diesel (*dizel*) is widely available – expect to pay around €1.10 per litre of unleaded. Credit cards are accepted at most stations. Most service stations are open from around 7am to 8 or 9pm, and there are also quite a few 24-hour ones, usually located on the outskirts of larger towns.

Montenegro distance chart (km)

	Bar	Bijelo Polje	Budva	Cetinje	Herceg Novi	Kotor
Bar		194	38	67	103	59
Bijelo Polje	194		178	149	243	199
Budva	38	178		29	65	21
Cetinje	67	149	29		94	50
Herceg Novi	103	243	65	94		44
Kotor	59	199	21	50	44	
Nikšić	126	168	110	81	175	131
Pljevlja	250	112	234	205	299	255
Podgorica	76	118	60	31	125	81
Tivat	61	202	23	54	53	9
Ulcinj	26	226	64	93	129	85
Žabljak	234	95	218	189	283	239

Rules and regulations

The most important **rules** for driving in Montenegro are to drive on the right and overtake on the left side, and for traffic on a roundabout to give way to traffic entering from the left. Speed limits for cars are 50kph in built-up areas, 80kph on the open road. Drinking and driving is absolutely prohibited and severely punished; headlights must be on at all times; seat belts must be worn at all times; and it is forbidden to use a hand-held mobile phone while driving.

The **police** (*policija*) are ubiquitous and it's not unusual to be pulled over randomly – just make sure you have all your documents with you. They are not empowered to levy on-the-spot fines for road traffic offences (such as speeding, which they are particularly hot on), and instead you'll be issued with a ticket (typically €40–80) which you must pay at a local bank or post office. Make sure you have a national driving licence and third-party insurance. If you have an **accident**, you're legally obliged to await the arrival of the police.

You can get technical assistance and motoring information from AMSCG (Automobile Association of Montenegro; ☎081/225 493). In the event of a **breakdown**, call AMSCG's 24-hour breakdown service on ☎9807, whereupon an English-speaking operator will direct you to the nearest point of assistance.

Car rental

Renting a car is simple enough, provided you are 21 or older, and hold a valid national driving licence. You can order a car through rental agencies in your own country (see below), which sometimes works out cheaper than getting it once you arrive in the country, particularly if you book online. Most of the major car rental companies have branches in Podgorica (and Podgorica Airport) and the major coastal towns such as Budva, Herceg Novi and Tivat. **Costs** are not especially cheap: expect to pay around €40–45 for a day's hire (unlimited mileage) and €35–40 per day for seven days' hire or more. You may find that **local companies**, of which there are quite a few in Podgorica and along the coast, offer better deals; these are listed across the Guide. Credit cards are usually required for a deposit.

Car rental agencies

Avis UK ☎0844 581 8181, Republic of Ireland ☎021/428 1111, US ☎1-800-331-1212, Canada ☎1-800-879-2847, Australia ☎13 63 33, New Zealand ☎0800 655 111, South Africa ☎011/923 3660; ⊛www.avis.com.

Budget UK ☎0870 156 5656, US ☎1-800-527-0700, Canada ☎1-800-268-8900, Australia ☎1300 362 848, New Zealand ☎0800 283 438; ⊛www.budget.com.

Europcar UK ☎0845 758 5375, Republic of Ireland ☎01/614 2800, US and Canada ☎1-877-940 6900, Australia ☎1300 131 390; ⊛www.europcar.com.

	Nikšić	Pljevlja	Podgorica	Tivat	Ulcinj	Žabljak
Bar	126	250	76	61	26	234
Bijelo Polje	168	112	118	202	226	95
Budva	110	234	60	23	64	218
Cetinje	81	205	31	54	93	189
Herceg Novi	175	299	125	53	129	283
Kotor	131	255	81	9	85	239
Nikšić		146	50	134	158	86
Pljevlja	146		174	258	282	60
Podgorica	50	174		83	102	158
Tivat	134	258	83		87	242
Ulcinj	158	282	102	87		266
Žabljak	86	60	158	242	266	

Hertz UK ☎0870 040 9000, Republic of Ireland ☎01/870 5777, US and Canada ☎1-800-654-3131, Australia ☎13 30 39, New Zealand ☎0800/654 321, South Africa ☎021/935 4800; ⓦwww.hertz.com.

National UK ☎0870 400 4588, US ☎1-800-227-7368, Australia ☎0870 600 6666, New Zealand ☎03/366 5574; ⓦwww.nationalcar.com.

SIXT UK ☎0870 156 7567, Republic of Ireland ☎06/120 6088, US and Canada ☎1-888-749-8227, Australia ☎1300 660 660, South Africa ☎0860 031 666; ⓦwww.sixt.com.

By bike

Although **mountain biking** as an organized activity is still in its infancy here, there are many possibilities for genuinely wonderful biking in Montenegro's hills. The most exciting areas are Bjelasica and the Biogradska National Park, the Durmitor region and the Orjen mountain range on the Bosnian border. There are now quite a few places offering bike hire, which we've detailed in the relevant sections of the Guide. Given the mountainous terrain and the poor state of many of the country roads, you'll need to be fit and self-reliant however. Cycle shops are few and far between, although most village mechanics can manage basic repairs. Carry a spare tyre and a few spokes, and check carrier nuts regularly, as the potholes and corrugations will rapidly shake them loose.

Accommodation

Montenegro lags behind most other countries in the region in terms of both the range and quality of accommodation on offer. For the most part hotels here tend to be concentrated at the upper end of the scale and there's very little in the way of budget accommodation, a problem compounded by the almost complete absence of youth hostels. That said, there is a good spread of private rooms in most places and especially in the coastal resorts. The few campsites that do exist are fairly rudimentary.

Accommodation price codes

Hotels listed in this Guide have been price-coded according to the scale below. Prices given are for the cheapest **double room** available during peak season, including breakfast.

❶ Under €25
❷ €25–35
❸ €35–45

❹ €45–55
❺ €55–65
❻ €65–80

❼ €80–95
❽ €95–120
❾ Over €120

Hotels and pensions

Montenegro's **hotels** are a mixed bunch, running the gamut from Communist-era, breeze-block monstrosities to plush, top-end establishments. That said, many of the state-run hotels – of which there are still quite a few, both along the coast and inland – are gradually being upgraded or completely refurbished. Along the coast in particular, many hotels have been heavily invested in with foreign (particularly Russian) finance. There is however a dearth of hotel accommodation – of any description – throughout much of inland Montenegro, and less still of any real quality.

Although still few and far between, there is a growing number of smaller, guesthouse or **pension**-style places, many of which offer much better value than hotels of a similar price. These are typically found in smaller towns or rural areas, such as Virpazar on Lake Skadar.

Hotels use the traditional five-star grading system for classification, although this often gives only the vaguest idea of **price**, which can fluctuate wildly according to the locality and season. Along the coast, room rates are typically graded according to the month, with the lowest prices out of season (Oct–March). Rates increase gradually from April onwards and reach a peak during July and August when they can be almost double the low-season price. During this period, it's safest to make advance hotel **reservations**. During the off-season, some of the better places become pretty good value, though note that a fair proportion of places, especially the lower-end ones, close between late September/early October and late April/early May. Conversely, in ski resorts such as Žabljak and Kolašin, most hotels up their prices over the winter period (Dec–Feb), and even more so over the Christmas and New Year period.

Although ratings are widely used, they are not always indicative of the quality of a place, particularly at the lower end of the scale, where standards can, and do, vary tremendously. The plushest four- and five-star hotels (mostly confined to Podgorica and the coast) offer all the luxuries one would expect of such establishments, while three-star hotels can be unpredictable in terms of both quality and cost; you should, however, expect a reasonable standard of comfort, as well as a private bathroom and TV, in most. Generally speaking, whatever the category of hotel, most have air-conditioning, a real boon given the often sweltering summer temperatures.

One particular problem that has traditionally beset many hotels along the coast during the summer is **water shortages**, though this is slowly being remedied. In some of the most basic places you may find that hot water is only available for a few hours a day, so check before deciding to take a room.

Private rooms and apartments

Your best bet if you're looking to sleep on the cheap is a **private room** (*privatno soba*), which is usually just a room in someone's home. These are in plentiful supply, particularly in the coastal resorts and, to a lesser extent, in mountain areas. Rooms are usually well furnished, if very basic, with shared shower and toilet facilities. Expect to pay anywhere between €8 and €20 per person per night depending upon the location and season; if you stay longer than three nights, you can usually negotiate a slightly lower price. Some, though not many, places may also offer breakfast, which may or may not be included in the quoted price.

Tourist offices often have good listings of private accommodation, and they can often

Addresses in Montenegro

Montenegrin addresses are usually written with just the name of the street, followed by the number, though the street name is sometimes prefixed with **ulica** (street) or **bulevar** (boulevard) – for example, Ulica Njegoševa 45, or Bulevar Sv Petra Cetinjskog 20. *Put* means "road", or "way". Some street signs are written in Cyrillic, which can be confusing for visitors – the Cyrillic alphabet is given in the Language section (see p.188). In this Guide, however, all street names are transcribed into the Roman alphabet.

In some places, houses do not have a number – this is denoted by the acronym **bb** (*bez broj*, meaning "without number"). Conversely, in some smaller villages and, for example, Kotor's Old Town, houses simply have a number and no street name.

Streets, boulevards and squares (**trg**), are commonly named after national heroes like Petar Njegoš or King Nikola (Podgorica's Njegoševa and Bulevar Kralja Nikole respectively), or after the date of an important event, such as Oktobarske revolucije. Some streets and squares are still named in deference to Tito, though most have now been renamed.

advise on places though they do not usually book them. Alternatively, look out for signs reading "**sobe**" (rooms) – again these are more prevalent in tourist areas. You may also be approached by landladies waiting at bus or railway stations – it's perfectly fine to take a room in this way, though be sure to establish both the price and location beforehand.

Some tourist offices and agencies, particularly along the coast, can also organize **apartments**, which can be rented either on a daily basis or for longer. Expect to pay anywhere between €50 and €80 per day. Generally speaking, you can expect the quality to be pretty high, with the majority of places being extremely clean, modern and well furnished, with all the standard mod cons.

Mountain huts

Montenegro has a limited number of **mountain huts** (*planinarski dom*), mostly confined to the Durmitor and Bjelasica mountain areas. Open during the summer months only (April/May to Sept), most huts are fairly basic affairs, with few amenities beyond running water, electricity and occasionally the provision of basic refreshments, such as soups and hot and cold drinks. However, they're generally very friendly and serve as useful places to pick up information about trails and the weather. The majority of huts are fairly isolated and accessible only by mountain tracks or footpaths. Beds cost about €2–3, and there is usually

no need to book in advance, though you can if you wish. Details of individual huts are listed throughout the guide.

Scattered across the mountains are small wooden cottages called **katuns**, which essentially function as shepherd's huts. They are not part of an organized system, so you'll just have to take a chance as and when you come across one: some offer basic shelter (there will be no facilities) or a spot for camping but little else.

Camping

Montenegro's few **campsites** are almost all confined to the coastal resorts and mountain areas, and are generally open between May and September. Many of them are posted as *autocamps*, which basically means that there's access for vehicles. As a rule, most sites are pretty rudimentary, with few amenities beyond basic toilet and shower facilities. Water shortages can hit campsites especially hard, while along the coast overcrowding is a major drawback. You'll generally pay about €3 per person per night, plus around €5 for a car.

In addition to organized campsites, in parts of the mountains there are certain designated **camping areas**, though these are few and far between. However, providing you don't light fires in forests, leave litter or damage nature reserves, officialdom tends to turns a blind eye to tourists **camping wild**; at worst they may tell you to move along.

Food and drink

In common with other Balkan countries, Montenegrin cuisine is overwhelmingly dominated by meat, though the coastal region offers plentiful opportunity to indulge in some excellent fish and other seafood. Many inland dishes manifest a heavy Turkish strain, while others reflect the country's Austrian influences. Along the coast, Mediterranean, and in particular Italian, flavours dominate.

Breakfasts and snacks

Breakfast (*doručak*) in your average hotel typically consists of bread or rolls with jam or marmalade as an accompaniment, fresh juice and cereal with milk or yoghurt. Only in the better hotels will you receive a full buffet, with cooked food (typically eggs in various guises, along with smoked or skinless sausages), pastries or croissants and fresh fruit. Breakfast is usually washed down with a large coffee or a cup of tea.

The most common **street snacks** are the ubiquitous *čevapčići* (rissoles of spiced minced meat usually served in groups of five), *pljeska-vica* (basically an oversized hamburger) and *ražnjići* (shish kebab). All of these are available from street stalls or kiosks (usually around €2), but you'll equally find them on restaurant menus countrywide. Also popular is *burek*, a greasy, flaky, Turkish-style pastry filled with cheese (*sa sirom*), meat (*sa mesom*) and occasionally apple (*sa jabukom*); it's best eaten with a glass of thick yoghurt (*jogurt*). Pizza slices, topped with cheese and salami and smothered in ketchup, are another common staple. Montenegrin ice cream (*sladoled*) is particularly good, and is sold on the streets almost all year round.

For bread (*hleb*), find the nearest **bakery** (*pekara*), which is also the best place to grab a pastry or croissant, particularly if your hotel or lodging does not provide breakfast. **Supermarkets** (*samoposluga*) are good places to stock up on sandwich and picnic ingredients, such as bread, cheese (*sir*) and salami (*salama*). Alternatively, ask the delicatessen counter to make you up a sandwich – they will normally oblige. Fresh fruit and vegetables are available in supermarkets too, but if possible try and get these provisions from a **market** (*pijaca*). Usually operating

Monday through to Saturday, these are found in most towns and cities (less frequently in the villages), and typically offer decent-quality seasonal produce, alongside hams, cheeses and olives (*maslina*) – these last are particularly good along the coast.

Restaurants

Restaurants (singular: *restoran*) vary in style and in quality, from the down-at-heel to the very smart. Generally speaking, the classier, more contemporary establishments are to be found in Podgorica and the more popular coastal resorts. In these areas, as elsewhere throughout the country, you'll also come across a more traditional-style establishment known as a **konoba**, a rustically themed inn with folksy decor. Similar in style, but generally only found in the more remote northern parts of the country, is a **savardak**, a cosy, alpine-style lodge serving basic but hearty, meat-heavy dishes. There is no shortage of restaurants along the coast, the overwhelming majority of which, not surprisingly, are seafood establishments, many invariably decked out with nautical-style paraphernalia. By way of contrast there is a general paucity of places to eat in many of the towns of the interior, in which case hotel restaurants are usually your best bet. Almost non-existent in Montenegro are foreign restaurants: even in the capital it's virtually impossible to track down a genuine ethnic eatery – and don't bother with Chinese restaurants.

Most restaurants open at 10.30 or 11am and close around 11pm, though many of those in the coastal resorts stay open until midnight, sometimes even later, during the summer. As a rule, eating out is cheap: you should be able to get a decent two-course meal with a glass of beer or wine for between €8 and €12 in Podgorica and along the coast, while inland, and particularly in the north, you can expect to pay around a third less for the same.

Inevitably, standards of **service** vary depending upon the type of establishment you are dining in, but it's generally pretty efficient and welcoming. You'll find that most restaurants in the capital and along the coast have **menus** in English, less so inland, though waiting staff – most of whom have a reasonable level of English – are happy to translate. Whatever you settle on, it's always worth enquiring *šta imate danas* ("What do you have today?") before studying the menu too seriously.

The concept of no **smoking** in Montenegrin restaurants is almost non-existent, though many places claim to have a no-smoking section – usually just a handful of tables in one part of the restaurant.

Montenegrin cuisine

Generally speaking, menus vary little in whatever type of restaurant you eat, and are invariably dominated by meat dishes, principally pork (*svinjetina*), lamb (*jagnjetina*) and beef (*govedjina*); along the coast, you're more likely to encounter fish (*riblja*).

Starters

Traditional **starters** (*predjela*) include *pršut*, a delicious air-dried ham (the best of which hails from the tiny village of Njeguši under Mount Lovćen), a rich array of different broths (*supa*), typically veal, beef or chicken, and *čorba*, a thick soup of Turkish origin. The fish variety (*riblja čorba*) is especially tasty.

Main dishes and local specialities

Alongside the most popular grilled meat dishes – *čevapčići*, *pljeskavica* (best enjoyed stuffed, with cheese and mushrooms) and *ražnjići* (see opposite) – the most common **main dishes** (*gotova jela*) are: *sarma* (cabbage leaves stuffed with minced meat and rice, often served with *kajmak* – see below); less commonly, *japrak* (grape leaves with the same filling); *pasulj* (a thick bean soup with pieces of bacon or sausage); *podvarak* (roast meat with sauerkraut); and the gut-busting *karađorđe snicla*, a breaded veal cutlet, rolled and stuffed with cheese.

Whilst all the above are pretty much Balkan staples, there are plenty of authentic Montenegrin foods to enjoy, with domestic **cheeses** (*sir domaći*) to the fore. *Njeguški sir* is the most renowned: preserved in oil, it's typically served with the equally delicious air-dried ham from the same village. In a similar vein, there's *cicvara* (stewed corn meal in salted cheese) and *kačamak* (buttered potato, corn meal and cheese), while the ever popular *kajmak* (a thick sour cream) is often served as an accompaniment to grilled meat dishes.

Montenegrin **meat dishes** include Njeguški steak, a generous slab of veal stuffed with Njeguški ham and cheese, while a favoured inland treat, particularly in the Durmitor region, is lamb cooked in milk (*jagnjetina u mlijeku*) in order to make it softer and more succulent. Many of these meat-based dishes are prepared using a traditional form of cooking known as *ispod sač* (under the coals), whereby the food is placed in a large dish and covered with a bell-like metal lid (*sač*); the dish is then smothered in hot embers to be baked. Also popular inland are *kobasice*, extremely flavoursome and often quite strong-tasting dried or smoked sausages.

You'll normally be offered a choice of **accompaniments** with your main course: chips aside, boiled potatoes (*kuvan krompir*) or roast potatoes (*pečen krompir*), rice (*pirinač*), pasta (*testenina*) and vegetables are the most common, whilst you will almost always be asked if you'd like a salad (*salata*; see p.32).

Fish and seafood dishes

The Montenegrin coast presents limitless opportunities to sample some of the finest, freshest **seafood** going. The most common dishes are: squid (*ligne*), usually served fried (*pržene lignji*) or stuffed (*punjene lignji*); scampi (*škampi*); mussels (*dagnje*), which are terrific in a *bouzzara* sauce (oil-fried onions and tomatoes); and octopus salad (*salata od hobotnice*), which is usually served as a starter. Oysters (*ostrige*), lobster (*jastog*) and crab (*rak*) are also popular staples, though

For a comprehensive glossary of **food and drink terms**, see p.192.

more usually found in slightly more upmarket establishments. In many places you'll come across a range of excellent freshly caught **fish**, such as sea bass (*brancin*), sea bream (*orada*), mullet (*cipal*) and John Dory (*kovač*) – you can always ask the waiter to bring you a selection of the day's catch. There's also terrific freshwater fish available – from Lake Skadar – in the form of carp (*krap*), which is usually fried or smoked, and eel (*jegulja*), best served grilled.

Vegetarian dishes

Vegetarians will have a dull time in a country where voluntarily doing without meat is simply beyond comprehension. Even in the better restaurants, options tend to be rather meagre and predictable, with pizza, salads and egg or cheese-based dishes being the main possibilities. Local dishes worth trying – whether as a starter or a main – are *srpska salata* (tomato, cucumber, onion and peppers on a bed of lettuce), *šopska salata* (similar but topped with grated soft cheese), *gljive na žaru* (grilled mushrooms), *gibanice* (layered cheese pie) and *zeljanica* (cheese pie with spinach). More traditional options might include *raštan* (cabbage mixed with potatoes and spices) or *prebanac*, oven-cooked white beans served with onion. You can try asking for something *bez meso, molim* ("without meat, please"), but you're unlikely to get very far.

Cakes and desserts

Montenegrin **cakes and desserts** are sticky and very sweet. Most menus feature pancakes (*palačinke*) with various fillings, as well as the Turkish-influenced baklava (sweet pastry with chopped walnuts and syrup) and strudel (pastry filled with apple or rhubarb). Ice cream is never far from the menu either.

Drinking

Drinking generally takes place in **cafés** (singular: *kafić*), most of which tend to double up as bars. They offer coffee and other non-alcoholic beverages alongside the full range of alcoholic drinks but very few serve food of any description. Most places open around 10 or 11am and close around 11pm or midnight, though in the capital and

in the more popular coastal resorts, it's not unusual for cafés to stay open until 1 or 2am, often later in the summer. Generally speaking, most cafés are relaxed, welcoming places and receptive to children, although, like many restaurants, they can get quite smoky.

Few Montenegrins get by without a strong cup of **coffee** (*kafa*) to kick-start the day, traditionally served Turkish-style (black, thick and with grinds at the bottom), though you'll find instant coffee (with milk is *kafa sa mlijekom*) and decent espresso and cappuccino in most cafés; coffee is often accompanied by a glass of water whether from the tap (*voda*) or mineral water (*mineralna voda*). **Tea** (*čaj*) is usually served straight (with lemon is *sa limunom*). **Fruit juices** (*voćni sok*) come in various guises, including *gusti* (a natural dense pulp), and flavours, such as orange (*narandža*) or apricot (*kajsija*).

The national alcoholic drink is **rakija**, a ferociously powerful brandy that is served neat; the most common variety is the plum-flavoured *šljivovica*. *Loza*, the grape-based variety is no less popular – you will invariably be offered a glass of one or the other if invited into someone's home. Another popular drink is **pelinkovac**, a bittersweet aperitif-type liquor based on wormwood.

Montenegrin domestic **beer** (*pivo*) is amongst the best in the Balkans. Most notable is the hoppy Nikšićko, from Nikšić, which comes in both light (Nik Gold or Nik Cool) and dark (*tamno*) forms; it's best sampled in its draught version (*točeno pivo*). Otherwise, imported continental-style lagers, such as Stella Artois and Heineken, are widespread.

Montenegro produces a good, though not particularly extensive, range of both red (*crna*) and white (*belo*) **wines** (singular: *vino*). The best of these is Vranac, a dry, dark ruby-red variety primarily cultivated in the Crmnica region in between Lake Skadar and the coast. Its full and fairly intense taste makes it an excellent complement to smoked and grilled meats and strong, mature cheeses. In pride of place amongst the whites is Kŕstac, a fruity, light tipple from the same region. *Špricer* (white wine with soda or sparkling mineral water) is a refreshing alternative on hot summer days.

The media

Given the country's size, it's little surprise that it has fewer newspapers in circulation than just about any other European country. Its television coverage, meanwhile, is similar to that of the rest of Eastern Europe.

Newspapers and magazines

During the Milošević era, the Montenegrin print media always managed to maintain greater press freedom than its sister republic, thanks in part to the Montenegrin government's overtures to the European Union seeking independence. Today, there are three major daily **newspapers**: the pro-government *Pobjeda* ("Victory"); the independent-minded *Vijesti* ("Independent"); and *Dan* ("Day"), a socialist rag. There is just one English-language publication currently in print, *The Montenegro Times* (Ⓦwww.themontenegrotimes.com), a reasonably well-informed weekly newspaper available from most kiosks; you can also pick it up free from most hotels. Western newspapers are almost impossible to track down, though the classier hotels may sell previous day's editions, which are inevitably heavily marked up in price.

Television, film and radio

Montenegrin **television** offers the standard diet of news, soaps and game shows, and is rarely turned off in many homes and bars. The state channel, RTM (Radio Television Montenegro), isn't too bad, offering a reasonable mix of independent news and documentaries, while several commercial channels do the soap/quiz/sport thing to varying degrees of success. Many people also now have access to cable TV, offering the standard foreign channels – BBC World, CNN, MTV and so on. Any decent hotel should have TV with cable or satellite TV, though Italian channels, as well as those from countries of the former Yugoslavia, still dominate the airwaves.

Like many of the foreign-language programmes on Montenegrin TV, films at the **cinema** are shown in their original language with Serbian subtitles.

There are plenty of state and private **radio** stations, but for news most listeners tune into foreign stations, especially the BBC World Service (Ⓦwww.bbc.co.uk/worldservice), Radio Canada (Ⓦwww.rcinet.ca) or Voice of America (Ⓦwww.voa.gov).

Festivals

Montenegro packs in plenty of annual festivals, ranging from jamborees of art, music and theatre to sporting events and the odd religious celebration. The majority of festivals take place along the coast, and in particular in resorts such as Budva, Herceg Novi and Kotor, the latter boasting an impressive roster of events.

Festivals specific to particular places are listed throughout the Guide; the following is an overview.

February to April

Mimosa Festival Herceg Novi (Feb). Heralding the beginning of spring, this colourful festival celebrates the mimosa, with a carnival and an exuberant parade of the eponymous flower. See p.47.

Days of St Tripun Kotor (early Feb). Religious celebration dedicated to Kotor's patron saint, featuring folk and choral music performances, folkloric dances and a town centre parade. See p.59.

Masked Ball Kotor (mid-Feb). Procession of masked troupes through the Old Town, loosely based on the Venetian equivalent. See p.59.

Montenegro Dance Festival Kotor and Tivat (mid-April). Week-long dance jamboree with participants competing for prizes in all forms of dance, from ballet to hip-hop and ballroom to tap. See p.59.

A Tempo Podgorica (late April). Classical music gathering in the capital's National Theatre featuring both domestic and overseas artists. See p.105.

May and June

Lim Regatta Plav (late May). White-water rafting regatta on the River Lim, with competing teams from all across the region. See p.157.

International Folklore Festival Budva (early June). Enchanting folkloric singing, starring groups from across Eastern Europe performing on a large stage by the Old Town walls. See p.70.

Mediterranean Song Music Festival Budva (late June). The country's largest pop music festival is a lively celebration of Mediterranean song, which also pulls in some big-name acts from the former Yugoslavia such as Goran Bregovič. See p.70.

July

Morača River Dives Podgorica (mid-July). Spectacular and daring plunges from the city's Vezirov Bridge. See p.105.

Children's Theatre Festival Kotor (mid-July). Exclusively for kids, this is a terrific programme of artistic and theatrical performances and workshops in the Old Town. See p.59.

Fašinada Perast (July 22). A flotilla of around fifty boats make its way out to the Island of Our Rock to pay homage to the church. See p.57.

International Summer Carnival Kotor (late July). Similar to February's Masked Ball but a larger affair, with concerts, regattas and exhibitions. See p.59.

Guitar Festival Nikšić (late July). Week-long programme of guitar-related events: concerts, competitions, lectures and symposiums. See p.131.

August

International Folklore Festival Cetinje (Aug). Folklore exhibitions, concerts, plays and author readings constitute Cetinje's annual festival.

Montenegro Film Festival Herceg Novi (early Aug). The country's premier film fest, showcasing the best of the region's new movies in the atmospheric setting of the Kanli Kula (Blood Tower). See p.47.

Refresh Kotor (early Aug). Cracking four-day DJ-fest featuring some of the hottest stars of the European electronic music scene. See p.59.

Boka Nights Kotor (second or third Sun of Aug). The coast's single most impressive spectacle, incorporating a dazzling fireworks display from a flotilla of barges in the bay. See p.59.

Petrovac Jazz Festival (late Aug). Montenegro's main jazz festival is an intimate affair taking place on the town's lovely beach and featuring mostly Eastern European acts, plus also the occasional UK or US artist. See p.80.

October to December

International TV Festival Bar (late Oct). One of the largest media gatherings in the Balkans, this unusual festival incorporates TV and documentary screenings, with representation from organizations worldwide, including the BBC.

Days of Wine and Bleak Virpazar (mid-Dec). Wine- and food- (fish soup) tasting, alongside small-scale concerts and poetry to celebrate the maturing of the wine.

Sports and outdoor activities

With the country's geography dominated by mountains, lakes and coastline, it's little surprise that the possibilities for outdoor pursuits are endless. Montenegrins love their sports, and although public facilities are extremely limited for would-be participants, a number of team sports are well attended at professional level.

Spectator sports

Not surprisingly, Montenegro's sporting prowess has traditionally been closely wed to that of Serbia, its footballers and other sporting stars having previously competed as part of a Serbia and Montenegro and, before that, Yugoslav, team. Following independence in 2006, all that changed and now the country proudly boasts its very own representation, which culminated in sending its first-ever team (albeit very modest, with competitors in just four sports) to the Beijing Olympics in 2008 – unfortunately, no medals were won at this first attempt. Although Montenegro possesses some excellent individual sportsmen and -women, the country's athletes have traditionally been strongest in team sports, notably basketball, handball, volleyball and water polo.

For such a small country, Montenegro has produced some outstanding **footballers** over the years, with many of those who represented Yugoslavia (or Serbia and Montenegro) having hailed from here. Arguably its greatest-ever footballer was **Dejan Savićević**. Born in Titograd (Podgorica) in 1966, Savićević began his club career at Budućnost, in Podgorica, before making his name at Red Star Belgrade in Serbia, where he helped the team win the European Cup in 1991. An illustrious career at AC Milan was crowned by a magnificent performance in the 4–0 crushing of Barcelona in the 1994 European Cup. A much less distinguished, and very brief, tenure as coach of the national team (Serbia and Montenegro) followed.

Montenegro's other most gifted footballer was **Predrag Mijatović**, another native of Podgorica, who also started out at Budućnost before moving to Belgrade's FK Partizan. This was followed by a move to Valencia, and then a lucrative contract at Real Madrid – his finest moment was scoring the winning goal for Real in the 1998 final against Juventus, which sealed the club's first European Cup for 32 years.

Watching domestic football is unlikely to be as exhilarating, with a terribly weak national game routinely dominated by the two Podgorica-based clubs, Budućnost and Zeta; matches are usually played on Saturdays from August to May, with a break from November to February. Tickets for league games cost roughly €2–3, which you can get at the ground itself. Check with the local tourist office to find out when games are scheduled.

Football aside, other team sports are extremely popular, and it's always worth trying to catch a **basketball**, **handball** or **volleyball** match if you can; they are usually free to attend. Club matches, particularly those featuring teams participating in European league fixtures, are of a pretty high standard.

Outdoor activities

The prime area for outdoor pursuits is the country's mountainous interior, in particular its **national parks**, which provide extensive opportunities for hiking, rambling and, to a lesser extent, mountain biking. Its biggest national park, Durmitor, not only has an extensive network of walking trails but is also the country's most important ski resort and its centre for white-water rafting.

Lake Skadar is a totally different environment, attracting a spectacular array of winged fauna during the spring and autumn migrations, thus lending itself perfectly to some unique bird-watching opportunities, not to mention some excellent fishing. The **coast**, meanwhile, presents possibilities for such adventurous pursuits as sea-kayaking, windsurfing and diving.

For more on all these activities, see *The Great Outdoors* colour section.

Travel essentials

Costs

Montenegro remains a good-value destination on the whole. As anywhere else, your biggest expenditure is likely to be on accommodation (see p.27), where there is a relative lack of budget accommodation and costs for what is available are on a par with Western European countries. Eating out, however, remains very affordable (see p.30), even in the better places, and public transport is extremely cheap (see p.25). Museum admission charges too are extremely low, the typical fee being €1–2. Expect to pay for car rental (see p.26), however, what you would pay in most other European countries.

If you're on a tight budget (camping or staying in private accommodation, buying food from a supermarket and using public transport), count on spending around £22/€28/$38 per day. Those on a moderate to mid-range budget (cheap to mid-range hotel, meals out plus car hire) can expect to spend around £70/€90/$125. If you're on a higher level of spend (the best hotels and restaurants, plus car hire), count on spending upwards of £100/€130/$180.

Costs vary according to where you are in the country, however. Along the coast, and to a lesser degree in Podgorica, they are appreciably higher than elsewhere, and you can expect to pay almost double for a cup of coffee or a meal in somewhere like Budva or Kotor than you would in one of the inland towns.

Crime and personal safety

Montenegro is a safe country and it's unlikely that you'll have any problems. Violent crime against tourists is almost non-existent and petty crime rare, while a few common-sense precautions should minimize the risk of theft. To call the **police** dial ☏92.

Montenegro was fortunate enough to remain on the periphery of the Balkan wars of the 1990s, and there is no danger to travellers from mines. However, if you are travelling into Kosovo, you may come across areas, particularly along the border, that were mined – these are clearly marked and sealed off.

Culture and etiquette

Although most kinds of attire are permitted when visiting churches, more modest **clothing** should be worn when visiting monasteries, and you should try and abstain from wearing beachwear or shorts – though some monasteries do supply overalls. Shoes should be removed when visiting any of the country's mosques.

Although **tipping** is not obligatory, it is polite to offer between five and ten percent in restaurants and when taking a taxi. In common with much of the Balkans, **smoking** is widespread, and despite the fact it was officially banned in public places in 2004, this is not enforced – little (if any) regard is given to non-smokers in restaurants, though it's always worth asking if the place has a no-smoking section.

The few **public toilets** that do exist (many are of the rather awkward "squat" variety) are generally pretty awful; expect to pay around €0.40, which guarantees you a sliver of paper, but you'd do well to carry your own supply. *Muški* means men and *ženski* means women.

Female travellers should have no reason at all to feel threatened, and should just follow the normal precautions.

Electricity

In Montenegro the current is 220 volts. A standard continental adaptor enables the use of 13-amp, square-pin plugs.

Entry requirements

Citizens of the EU, US, Canada, Australia and New Zealand can enter Montenegro with just a **passport** and may stay in the country for up to ninety days. For those nationalities that do require a visa (tourist visas last for 90

Rough Guides travel insurance

Rough Guides has teamed up with Columbus Direct to offer you **travel insurance** that can be tailored to suit your needs. Products include a low-cost **backpacker** option for long stays; a **short break** option for city getaways; a typical **holiday package** option; and others. There are also annual **multi-trip** policies for those who travel regularly. Different sports and activities (trekking, skiing, etc) can usually be covered if required.

See our website (ⓦ www.roughguides.com/website/shop) for eligibility and purchasing options. Alternatively, UK residents should call ☎0870 033 9988, Australians should call ☎1300 669 999 and New Zealanders should call ☎0800 559 911. All other nationalities should call ☎+44/870 890 2843.

days), which includes South Africans, applications can be made to any Montenegrin consulate abroad in person or by post.

Montenegrin embassies abroad

UK 11 Waterloo Place, London, SW1Y 4AU ☎020/7863 8806.
USA 1610 New Hampshire Ave, Washington DC 2009 ☎01 202 234 6108.

Gay and lesbian travellers

In common with many Balkan countries, tolerance of the gay community in Montenegro is low. The majority of the population remains largely unsympathetic, and there are very few, if any, manifestations of gay life, even in the larger centres of population. Moreover, there is currently no nationwide gay or lesbian organization.

Health

No **vaccinations** are required for Montenegro, although having hepatitis A, polio and typhoid boosters would be wise if you're planning to stay in more remote areas for any length of time. Avoid any contact with stray dogs, as there's a very slight risk of **rabies**. There is a reciprocal health agreement between Montenegro and the UK, though citizens of other countries will have to pay for any treatment.

Summers can be blisteringly hot, particularly in the capital and the coastal region, so make sure you take a high-factor **sun cream**, while you might wish to consider bringing **insect repellent** if you're visiting Lake Skadar. Conversely, inclement weather in the mountainous regions, particularly at higher altitudes, can present potential dangers – take appropriate clothing, sufficient provisions and equipment, and keep an eye on the weather.

Tap water is pretty much safe to drink everywhere, though bottled water (*mineralna voda*) is widely available.

In case of minor complaints, go to a **pharmacy** (*apoteka*), where the staff usually speak a reasonable level of English. Normal opening hours are Monday to Friday 8am–8pm and Saturdays 8am–3pm, though most have an emergency number displayed in the window if you require anything outside these times. To call an **ambulance** dial ☎94.

Insurance

Before travelling to Montenegro, you'd do well to take out an **insurance policy** to cover against theft, loss and illness or injury. Before paying for a new policy, check whether you are already covered by your home insurance policy or private medical scheme. A typical travel insurance policy usually provides cover for the loss of baggage, tickets and – up to a certain limit – cash, as well as cancellation or curtailment of your trip. Most of them exclude dangerous sports unless an extra premium is paid: in Montenegro, this could mean, for example, skiing or trekking.

Internet

Internet access is readily available in just about every town in Montenegro – with the curious exception of the capital, Podgorica – although connections in some places can be dreadfully slow. Expect to pay around €1 per hour online. **Wi-fi** is becoming increasingly widespread, and certainly in the better hotels this is now almost a standard facility. The useful site ⓦwww.kropla.com gives details of how to plug your laptop in when abroad.

Laundry

Launderettes are just about non-existent, so it's a choice of doing it yourself or paying your hotel to do it for you – even then, only the classier hotels offer such a service.

Living in Montenegro

Opportunities for working in Montenegro are relatively few, though there are some possibilities for **teaching English**. International House (ⓦwww.ihworld.com) offers TEFL training and recruits for teaching positions – they have a branch in Podgorica at Vaka Djurovica, Sjeverna Tribina ulaz 1 sprat 1 (☎069 747 747, ℮cambridge@t-com.me). Otherwise, the Oxford Centar in Podgorica, 64 PC Krusevac (☎020/234 425; ℮oxford-centar@t-com.me) sometimes has teaching vacancies – they also have a centre in Bar. The TEFL website (ⓦwww.tefl.com) is always worth a look.

Mail

Most **post offices** (*pošta*) are open Monday to Friday from 8am to 7pm, and on Saturdays from 8am to noon, although some of those in the smaller towns close around 3 or 4pm on weekdays and do not open at all on Saturday. Sending a postcard home from Montenegro should cost around €0.70, and take about five days to Britain, two weeks to North America and Australasia. Buy stamps at the post office.

Maps

Nearly all the best **maps** of Montenegro are published outside the country, but they are available through most good map outlets, such as Stanfords in the UK.

The best **country map** is the 1:250,000 offering by the Hungarian publishers Gizimap, which illustrates all road and rail connections, as well as the country's topography, national parks, campsites and other places of interest. A good, and very detailed, coastal map is the 1:100,000 Črnogorsko primorje (Montenegrin coast) map by the Slovenian publishers Kod & Kam.

If you're taking in Montenegro as part of a wider pan-Balkan trip, there are plenty of maps incorporating the country, such as Gizimap's 1:500,000 Serbia and Montenegro map, a 1:600,000 map of Slovenia, Croatia, Bosnia-Herzegovina and Montenegro by Freytag & Berndt and a third map featuring the same countries by Michelin.

Local **city** or **town maps** produced by the tourist offices are variable – in some cases there aren't any at all – but usually suffice for navigating your way around town.

Unfortunately decent **hiking maps** are hard to come by, though you may find the odd one in the local tourist office.

Money

Although it's not part of the European Union, Montenegro's unit of currency is the **euro** – coins come in denominations of 1c, 2c, 5c, 10c, 20c, 50c, €1 and €2, with notes as €5, €10, €20, €50, €100, €200 and €500. At the time of writing the exchange rate was £1: €1.25 and US$1: €0.70. For current rates, check the websites ⓦwww.xe.com or ⓦwww.oanda.com. The euro is also the currency used in neighbouring Kosovo.

Banks (*banka*) are generally open Monday to Friday between 9am and 6 or 7pm and on Saturdays between 9am and noon. **ATMs** are now widespread, and even in the smaller towns you'll have no problem tracking one down. **Credit cards** are accepted just about everywhere, including hotels, restaurants, shops and petrol stations.

By far the most recognized **travellers' cheques** are American Express, whether sterling or dollars. Although it may not be required in all instances, make sure you have your passport when changing travellers' cheques (or cash). Also note that, in some banks, you may have to show the receipt from the issuing bank, or another cheque to prove continuity of serial numbers.

Opening hours and public holidays

Shops are generally open from 9 or 10am to 7 or 8pm Monday to Saturday, with department stores and some food stores opening from 8am to 9 or 10pm Monday to Saturday and from 8am to 1pm on Sunday. If you're trying to sort out flights or car rental, be

Calling home from abroad

Note that the initial zero is omitted from the area code when dialling the UK, Ireland, Australia, New Zealand and South Africa from abroad.
UK international access code + 44 + area code.
Republic of Ireland international access code + 353 + city code.
US and Canada international access code + 1 + area code.
Australia international access code + 61 + city code.
New Zealand international access code + 64 + city code.
South Africa international access code + 27 + city code.

aware that some offices are closed by 4pm.

Museum opening times can vary greatly, but are generally Tuesday to Sunday from 9am to 5pm or 10am to 6pm. For the opening hours of post offices and banks see opposite and for pharmacies, see p.37.

Public holidays in Montenegro are: January 1 (New Year); January 7 & 8 (Orthodox Christmas); Easter, April 27 (Statehood Day); May 1 & 2 (Labour Day); May 9 (Victory Day); November 29 (Republic Day).

Phones

Public payphones are almost non-existent, so if you want to make a call (local or international) you're best off heading to a post office, where you can call from one of the booths – you make the call and pay afterwards. International calls made this way cost about €1 a minute to Britain, and around €2 to North America and Australasia. Calls are most expensive from 7am to 7pm Monday to Friday and 7am to 3pm on Saturday, and cheapest from 11pm to 7am daily.

The main **mobile phone** providers in Montenegro are ProMonte and Monet, with numbers designated by the prefixes ☏067 or ☏069. Coverage throughout the country is pretty good, even in mountainous regions. Calling a mobile from within Montenegro, you must dial all the numbers; calling from abroad, you need to drop the "0". For further information about using your phone in Montenegro, check with your provider.

The **international dialling code** for Montenegro is +382.

Shopping

Montenegro is hardly a shopper's paradise, although there are several items that might make for interesting **gifts**. Beautifully painted **icons** can be bought from most souvenir shops, but the better ones are to be found in the country's many churches and monasteries. Some monasteries also cultivate their own **foodstuffs**, which they sometimes have for sale. Food worth looking out for includes olives and olive oil from the traditional growing areas around Bar, as well as the air-dried ham and cheeses from the village of Njeguši (see p.122).

Alcohol can be a great gift, and **rakija**, whether *šljivovica* or the grape-based *loza*, makes for a terrific present. Both types can be purchased from most supermarkets, though if you can get your hands on a bottle of the homemade stuff, then so much the better. Montenegrin wine, and in particular its most popular variety, Vranac, is another possibility, and can be picked up cheaply at supermarkets.

Otherwise, there's **embroidery and lacework** from the area around Kotor, the latter being the country's traditional lacemaking centre – look out for embroidered tablecloths and covers.

Time

Montenegro is one hour ahead of GMT, six hours ahead of Eastern Standard Time and nine ahead of Western Standard Time. It is also ten hours behind Australian Eastern Standard Time and twelve hours behind New Zealand. Clocks go forward one hour for the summer at the same time as other European countries (from the last Sunday in March to the last Sunday in October).

Tourist information

The **Montenegrin Tourist Board** has a UK office at 20 Hanover Street, London W1S 1YR and a useful website (☏www.montenegro.travel). Within Montenegro there is a reasonable spread of **tourist offices**, though these are largely confined to towns in the coastal and mountain resorts. In many of the inland towns the local tourist board (which is usually just a small administrative office that oversees tourism for that town or region) may be the only source of (very limited) information.

Opening times can be somewhat erratic, but generally speaking most tourist offices are open between 9am and 6pm daily in the summer (roughly May–Sept), sometimes later in some of the coastal resorts. Out of season they are normally open Monday to Friday between 8am and 4pm.

Travellers with disabilities

Very little attention has been paid to the needs of the disabled in Montenegro, and there's little sign of any change in attitude. Getting around is a major problem, as **public transport** is often poorly accessible, and cars with hand controls are rarely available from the car rental companies. The only place where facilities for disabled people are likely to be anything like comprehensive are in some of the classier **hotels**, where there should be a degree of level access and some awareness of the needs of wheelchair users. Around half a dozen **beaches** have disabled access.

Make sure you carry a **prescription** for any drugs you need, including the generic name in case of emergency, and spares of any special clothing or equipment, as it's unlikely you'll find them in Montenegro.

Travelling with children

Children are readily accepted – indeed welcomed – in public places throughout Montenegro, and from a practical point of view, travelling with youngsters is easy enough. Most of the better **hotels** are well disposed to catering for kids; those under twelve may often share an adult's bed for free, or pay half of the adult cost for an extra bed in the room. Most **restaurants** of a decent standard should be able to provide highchairs for younger children and babies. **Car rental** firms generally provide child or baby seats for a small extra charge, though you should check this at the time of booking. In terms of **provisions**, you'll have few problems tracking down milk, baby food, nappies and suchlike, though you'd do well to stock up if you're heading further inland where there are far fewer shops.

Many of the coast's **beaches** are well suited for families with young children. Bečići, Rafailovići, Pržno, Velika Plaža and Kalardovo are all safe, with shallow waters and lifeguards, and some also have other facilities, such as changing areas and showers. Most beaches also have large umbrellas (*suncobran*) for hire.

Guide

Guide

The coast

BOSNIA-
HERZEGOVINA

SERBIA

CROATIA

KOSOVO
(SERBIA)

ALBANIA

ADRIATIC SEA

N

0   20km

CHAPTER 1 # Highlights

* **Sea kayaking** Don some rubber boots, grab a paddle, and go explore the hidden coves and beaches along the coastline around Herceg Novi. See p.51

* **Orjen Massif** This alluring karst landscape is criss-crossed with trails offering terrific walking opportunities. See p.52

* **Kotor** The coast's most historic town is a delightful tangle of narrow cobbled streets, pretty squares and Venetian-inspired architecture. See p.58

* **Budva** Great beaches, plenty to see and some invigorating nightlife combine to make this the coast's most exciting hangout. See p.69

* **Sveti Stefan** This glamorous island resort, now restored to its former glory, is the coast's showpiece landmark. See p.79

* **Petrovac** A gorgeous, arcing, red sandy beach is the defining feature of the coast's most attractive resort. See p.80

* **Stari Bar** Wander around the spectacular, crumbling ruins of ancient Bar. See p.84

* **Ulcinj** This chaotic and intriguing town has a distinct Muslim flavour, and also lies within range of some terrific beaches. See p.85

▲ Swimming off Sveti Stefan

1

The coast

Extending from the southern tip of Croatia down to the border with Albania, the Montenegrin **coast** is the country's real jewel. Blessed with abundant sunshine, warm water and endless strips of long sand and pebble beaches, this startlingly beautiful coastline packs in some of the most striking scenery of the entire Adriatic. The seaboard ribbon shelters shallow bays, rocky coves and white-stone fishing villages, alongside a dense concentration of traditional seaside resorts, all backed by steeply rising mountains and rolling green hills dotted with cypress trees and olive plantations. The coast also offers a rich complement of historical sights; almost all the principal seaboard towns fell into the hands of the Venetians, whose occupation left its mark, bestowing them with a rich architectural legacy.

During the 1980s, the Montenegrin coast was one of the hottest holiday destinations for tourists from the UK and elsewhere, but the wars and recession of the 1990s pretty much put paid to that and it was left to rely almost solely on domestic custom, principally visitors from neighbouring Serbia. The shoots of recovery are now well under way, however, manifest in the steady return of foreign visitors, alongside a massive influx of overseas, in particular British and Russian, investment in and around several of the larger resorts. And while this frenzy of construction, mainly in the form of medium- to large-scale luxury hotels, threatens in parts to destroy the charms that it was intended to exploit, for the most part the coast has thus far managed to avoid the worst excesses of mass tourism development.

The coast can be divided into three fairly distinct regions, namely the Gulf of Kotor, the Budva Riviera and the area south of here, which essentially comprises the towns of Bar and Ulcinj. Dominating the Montenegrin seaboard, the **Gulf of Kotor** (Boka Kotorska) is undoubtedly the single most impressive feature along the entire Adriatic coast, and in terms of sheer natural beauty is hard to beat anywhere in Europe. Massive green mountains sweep down into the clear blue waters, which are more a series of inland bays than a gulf, while behind rises the sheer, pale peak of Lovćen. **Kotor** – which is essentially its compact walled Old Town – is utterly charming, an enticing jumble of narrow stone-paved streets and cobbled squares packed with Venetian-inspired architecture and exquisite little churches. Nudging the Croatian border, the Gulf's major beach resort is lively **Herceg Novi**, from where you can embark on boat trips across to the **Luštica peninsula**, a thick thumb of land where you'll find some of the coast's most pristine beaches, or up to the **Orjen Massif**, with its terrific hiking possibilities. Further around the Gulf, **Risan** exhibits some superb Roman mosaics, while close by is the erstwhile naval base of **Perast**, a delightful spot from where boats whisk you over to the island of **Our Lady of the Rock**, serenely poised just offshore. The other key resort within

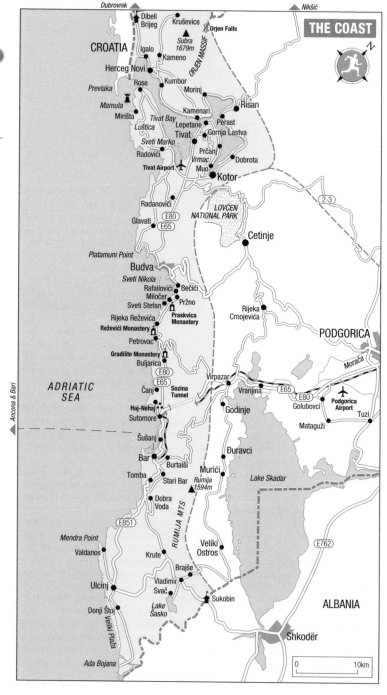

Dubrovnik

Nikšić

THE COAST

N

Dibeli Brijeg
Kruševice
Orjen Falls

CROATIA
Igalo
Kameno
Subra 1679m
ORJEN MASSIF

Herceg Novi
Kumbor
Morinj
Rose
Prevlaka
Kamenari
Risan
Mamula
Mirišta
Perast
Luštica
Lepetane
Gornja Lastva
Tivat Bay
Tivat
Sveti Marko
Prčanj
Radovići
Vrmac
Dobrota
Tivat Airport
Muo
Kotor

Radanovići
LOVĆEN NATIONAL PARK
(E80)
Glavati
(E65)
Cetinje

Platamuni Point

Budva
Sveti Nikola
Rafailovići
Bečići
Miločer
Pržno
Sveti Stefan
Rijeka Crnojevića
Rijeka Reževića
Praskvica Monastery
Reževići Monastery
Petrovac
PODGORICA
Gradište Monastery
Buljarica
(E80)
(E65)
Virpazar
ADRIATIC SEA
Čanj
Sozina Tunnel
Vranjina
(E65)
(E80)
Godinje
Golubovci
Podgorica Airport
Haj-Nehaj
Sutomore
Tuzi
Mataguži

Šušanj
Đuravci
Bar
Burtaiši
Murići
Tomba
Stari Bar
Rumija 1594m
Lake Skadar
Dobra Voda
RUMIJA MTS
(E851)

Mendra Point
Valdanos
Veliki Ostros
(E762)
Krute
Brajše
Vladimir
Svač
Sukobin
Ulcinj
Lake Šasko
ALBANIA
Donji Štoj

Veliki Plaža
Shkodër

Ada Bojana

Ancona & Bari

Moraća

0   10km

the Gulf is **Tivat**, which is the location for the country's second civilian airport and has grand designs on becoming home to the country's premier marina.

South of Tivat is **Budva**, a bristling, self-indulgent resort which can count on a stack of fine beaches and associated activities, a fabulously appealing old town and the coast's most animated nightlife. The stretch of coastline immediately south of Budva – commonly known as the Budva Riviera – embraces a multiplicity of smaller resorts such as **Bečići**, **Rafailovići** and **Pržno**, which all segue imperceptibly into one another, before the picture-postcard island retreat of **Sveti Stefan** hoves into view, images of which adorn much of the country's tourist literature. Edging further south, **Petrovac** is one of the coast's most seductive spots, a pretty, laid-back resort starring one of its finest beaches. From here it's a short hop down to **Bar**, terminus for ferries across from Italy, and within striking distance of the ancient ruins of **Stari Bar**. The coast's most southerly town – and only separated from the Albanian border by the immense twelve-kilometre-long stretch of **Velika Plaža** (Great Beach) – is **Ulcinj** which, thanks to centuries of Turkish rule and a majority Albanian population, remains overwhelmingly Muslim in character.

During July and August, the height of the summer season along the coast, many hotels ramp up their prices – in some cases almost doubling the normal rate – and the major coastal spots can get uncomfortably congested. For these reasons, the **best time to visit** is either side of those months (May, June and September) when there are some much better deals to be had. **Getting around** the region is easy enough – buses zip up and down the main coastal road with regular frequency, connecting all the major centres and most of the smaller resorts in between. The only part of the coast covered by train is the short stretch from Bar to Sutomore, where the line turns inland towards Lake Skadar and on to Podgorica.

Herceg Novi and around

Tumbling down a steep hillside at the mouth of the Gulf of Kotor, the town of **HERCEG NOVI** was once a favourite holiday spot for the bourgeoisie of nineteenth-century Vienna. Today, faded villas wallow in wisteria, bougainvillea, palms and orange trees as they explode from every inch of ground, and even now these streets hint at the genteel respectability of former times. Although it lacks the history and charm of Kotor, and the raw vigour of Budva, Herceg Novi has enough to rate a leisurely few days' exploration or relaxation. Moreover, it's just a short boat ride across to the **Luštica peninsula**, with its pretty beaches and coves, while the nearby **Orjen mountain range** offers some fabulous hiking possibilities. The town's proximity to the Croatian border also means that a sidetrip to Dubrovnik, just 50km north, can easily be done in a day.

Herceg Novi plays host to two important events, namely the **Mimosa Festival** (Praznik Mimoze) in February, which celebrates the coming of the spring flower with a range of cultural and sporting happenings and a major carnival parade; and the **Film Festival** (Filmski Festival) in September, which features a roster of national and regional films up in the atmospheric surrounds of the Kanli Kula above the Old Town.

Some history

Herceg Novi was founded by the Bosnian king, Tvrtvo, in 1382 to give Bosnia access to the sea. Its obvious strategic value ensured the town a stormy history and in a dizzying succession of rulers it changed hands over a dozen times, though most of what remains was built by the Venetians, Turks and Austro-Hungarians,

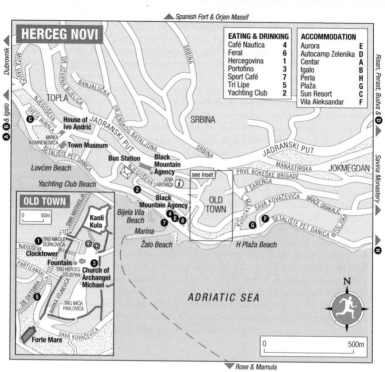

a mixed heritage that's left a ragbag of styles. Herceg Novi acquired its present name in the mid-fifteenth century during the reign of Duke (Herceg) Stjepan Vukšić Kosača – a Serb nobleman and one-time governor of Bosnia – who set about fortifying the town. It was conquered by the Turks in 1482 who, save for a brief interruption in 1538 when the Spaniards took over, ruled for a further two hundred years. In 1687, the Venetians pitched up, ruling until 1797, when the town was occupied by the Austrians. Following this, it was administered variously by the Russians, French and, eventually, the Austro-Hungarians who stayed until the end of World War I. Annexed to the province of Dalmatia by the Italians during World War II, Herceg Novi was finally liberated by Yugoslav Partisan forces in 1943, and thereafter incorporated into Montenegro. During the wars of the 1990s, the town and its region were heavily flooded with refugees from Bosnia-Herzegovina. Most of them have now returned, and today Herceg Novi is experiencing something of a property boom, with foreign investors snapping up large chunks of real estate in the hills above town.

Arrival and information

Herceg Novi's **bus station**, which fields both domestic services and buses to and from Dubrovnik, is on the main coastal road, Jadranski put, just a five-minute walk from the Old Town. A useful online resource is ⓦ www.hercegnovi.cc, while the local **tourist office** is at Jova Dabovića 12 (Mon–Fri 8am–4pm; ☏031/350 820, ⓔ info@hercegnovi.travel); it has rather limited information, but there's more comprehensive material available in summer when an information booth is posted down on Trg Nikole Đurkovića (July & Aug daily 8am–10pm). The **post office** is at Njegoševa 31 (Mon–Sat 7.30am–8pm), and there's **internet** access at a couple of places in the Old Town: one in the *Stari Grad* café next to the church, and another a few paces along in the PC Koloseum shop.

There's an excellent **travel agency**, Black Mountain, at Šetalište pet Danica 41 (☎031/321 968, 🌐www.montenegroholiday.com); they also have a small office next to the bus station. Black Mountain can arrange accommodation (hotels and apartments) and **car rental**, in addition to a multitude of activities, such as hiking, mountain biking, sailing, scuba diving and whitewater rafting, both locally and across the country. Another good local car rental company is Gorbis, Njegoševa 64 (☎031/322 085, 🌐www.gorbis.com).

Accommodation

For one of the coast's most prominent resorts, Herceg Novi boasts surprisingly little in the way of decent or varied **accommodation**. In addition to those in town, there are further, and generally much cheaper, options in neighbouring **Igalo**, a crowded little satellite resort 5km west of town, though these tend to be the older, state-run hotels, nearly all of which are in desperate need of investment. The places listed here cover Herceg Novi, Igalo and **Topla**, a suburb midway between Herceg Novi and Igalo. Herceg Novi also has a decent **campsite**, in the form of the *Autocamp Zelenika* (☎067 678 631; April–Oct), located at Sunčana obala bb some 3km east of town in the suburb of Zelenika. Your best bet if looking for some **private accommodation** is to contact the Black Mountain agency (see above).

Hotels

Aurora Šetalište pet Danica 42 ☎031/321 158, 🌐www.auroramontenegro.com. Occupying what was once the town's railway station, this small but handsome and perky hotel offers two double and four twin rooms, all brightly coloured and with sea-facing views. ❽

Centar Sava Ilića 7, Igalo ☎031/332 442, 🌐www.centar-igalo.com. This tower block is a typical state-run place, with small rooms furnished with low beds and careworn carpets – it is, however, just about the cheapest option going. Open April–Oct. ❹

Igalo Sava Ilića 2, Igalo ☎031/322 772. Almost identical to the *Centar*, this high-rise is somewhat dreary, but it's another cheap option. Open May–Sept. ❺

Perla Šetalište pet Danica 98 ☎031/345 700, 🌐www.perla.me. Pleasant, small hotel located on the quieter southern side of town, around 800m along from the harbour, accommodating smart, sunny rooms, a decent restaurant and its own bit of (concrete) beach. ❽

Plaža Sava Kovačevića 58 ☎031/346 151, 📧bokasale@t-com.me. Oversized glass building sloping down towards the water's edge, which conceals a warren of nicely sized, though rather characterless rooms. The hotel is due to be completely refurbished. ❼

Sun Resort Sv Bubala bb, Topla ☎031/355 000, 🌐www.hotelsunresort.hunguesthotels.com. Sited right above the water's edge, this is Herceg Novi's most polished hotel, a large complex which also comprises a series of villas and bungalows. The hotel rooms are colourfully decorated and neatly designed, while the bungalows are basically enlarged rooms with a living space. It also has two lovely pools (one for children) and a wellness centre. ❾

Vila Aleksandar Sava Kovačevića 64 ☎031/345 806, 🌐www.hotelvilaaleksandar.com. A small, quiet and intimate hotel on the seafront with comfortable, colourful rooms, most of which have balconies. ❼

The Town

Although Herceg Novi's sights are quite well dispersed, they are easily explorable on foot, as long as you don't mind a few steep paths and steps along the way. The personable **Old Town** core harbours several intriguing places of interest, while to the north and east of here respectively stand the old, tumbledown **Spanish Fortress** and serenely set **Savina Monastery**. Most things of an active or social nature take place along **Šetalište pet Danica**, a long, tidy promenade stretching all the way to Igalo.

The Old Town

The best place to start any exploration of the town is the small main square, Trg **Nikole Đurkovića**, to the east of which is the entrance to the **Old Town**, a tight, triangular wedge sloping steeply down to the seafront. Presaged by a **clocktower** (Sahat Kula), erected in 1850, is **Trg Herceg Stijepan**, a pristine little square framed by low, bright white-stone houses and spread with comely cafés. In the centre, and fronted by two huge palms, stands the **Church of St Michael Archangel** (Crkva Sv Mihaila Arhanđela). Looking much older than its one hundred years (it was built in 1900), this eclectic, creamy-white stone-block structure is immediately noticeable by its taper-thin towers and spiky turrets, while a dazzling gold mosaic is pressed inside the portal, itself framed by two chunky pillars intricately carved with twisted rope motifs. The high, sky-blue dome notwithstanding, the most striking aspect of the church's interior is the white marble altar, patterned with carved floral designs and displaying icons of revered saints. Just outside the church is the **Karača fountain**, a lovely stone structure from whence a cool stream of drinking water emerges.

Both the northern and southern extremes of the Old Town are framed by bulky fortifications, which were once links in the substantial city walls. To the north, up a set of steep steps, is the sixteenth-century **Kanli Kula** (€1), which appropriately translates as the "Bloody Tower" – although primarily a fortification system, this substantial stronghold also functioned as a prison during Turkish rule. Today, it's a fittingly dramatic venue for open-air theatrical productions, while the views over the bay and across to the Luštica peninsula (see p.53) are quite splendid. Leading from the southern portion of the square, Marka Vojnevića is a long, narrow street with tall, overhanging buildings concealing the odd shop or gallery – it winds up near the **Forte Mare** (Sea Fortress), a less imposing fortification than Kanli Kula, but which presented a no less formidable barrier to prospective invaders.

Along Šetalište pet Danica

A set of steps to the side of the Forte Mare spirals down to **Šetalište pet Danica**, the seafront promenade which runs the entire length of the coast to Igalo, some 5km distant. Unlikely as it seems now, between 1936 and 1967 the promenade was actually a railway line, as evidenced by the handsome looking former railway-station building opposite the marina, which today functions as a small hotel (see p.49), cinema and restaurant complex; as well as being a popular strolling spot, the promenade is where you'll find the town's liveliest restaurants, bars and cafés. The town doesn't possess much in the way of sandy or pebble **beaches** – instead the seafront consists of wide concrete platforms occasionally broken up by the odd rocky cove concealing a small pebbly area.

About 1km on from the marina, signs point upwards to the **town museum** (Grad muzej; daily 9am–5pm; €2) at Mirka Komnenovića 9, whose exhibits primarily focus upon the town's maritime heritage, with paintings, costume and navigational equipment comprising the bulk, though there is also a fabulous collection of icons on wood worth viewing. A short walk up from the museum, at Njegoševa 65, is the one-time **house of Ivo Andrić** (1892–1975). Widely regarded as the finest writer to emerge from any of the ex-Yugoslav countries in the twentieth century, the Bosnian-born author spun rich tales of life in that country under Ottoman rule, most famously in his 1961 Nobel Prize-winning work, *The Bridge on the Drina*. The house is now a drab restaurant, but you can pop your head in to view the upstairs room, which contains a selection of his books and photographs.

The Spanish Fort

High above town sits the sixteenth-century **Spanish Fort** (Tvrđava Španjola), so named by the Spanish who briefly occupied the area in 1538, although it was the

Turks who completed the job. Today its thick walls and huge circular bastions conceal a messy, graffiti-scrawled ruin, which was further damaged by the 1979 earthquake (see box, p.85). However, the steep twenty-minute walk is rewarded with splendid views over the town and the entrance to the Boka beyond – from behind Trg Nikole Đurkovića, walk up Sima Matavulja, through the underpass and then uphill along Srbina for about fifteen minutes, before turning left down an unnamed road; it's very poorly signposted.

Savina Monastery

A pleasant twenty-minute walk east of town – along Sava Kovačevića and Braće Grakalić – on a wooded hillock by the side of the road sits the **Savina Monastery** (Manastir Savina). Founded in the seventeenth century by refugee monks from Trebinje (in modern-day Bosnia-Herzegovina), the monastery has two adjacent churches, both dedicated to the Assumption. The larger of the churches is a cheerful meeting of Byzantine and Baroque, constructed of neatly trimmed white-stone blocks from the Croatian island of Korčula, which is renowned for its stone masonry, and featuring an elegant bell-tower with a beautifully carved stone rosette just above the porch. Otherwise featureless, the interior of this single-nave structure stars an extravagant, fifteen-metre-high iconostasis and an enormous, square gold chandelier. Although architecturally anonymous, the boxy smaller church is smothered in a layer of patchy, dark blue frescoes, thought to date from the fifteenth century, depicting great feast days as well as Christ's suffering. Above the interior entrance, a barely discernible inscription denotes that the church probably dates originally from 1030.

Sited high up on a hill above the monastery complex (it's a five-minute walk through the graveyard and up through the wood) is the tiny **Church of St Sava** (Crkva Sv Sava), which (according to conflicting historical sources) dates from either the thirteenth or fifteenth century. From here there are lovely views looking down over the monastery and out towards the bay. The two lower churches are fringed by renovated *konaks*, one of which contains the monastery's **museum**. Stuffed with gold and silver ornaments, its centrepiece is a thirteenth-century crystal cross that reputedly belonged to St Sava himself.

Eating

The town boasts a tight concentration of excellent **restaurants** along and close to the waterfront, which typically offer some fine seafood. Here, too, there are plenty of snack-type places.

Sea kayaking and other activities in and around Herceg Novi

One of the most enjoyable ways to explore the coastline around Herceg Novi during the summer months is from a **sea kayak** – it's easy to do and no experience is required. Kayak Montenegro (☏031/321 655, ⊛www.kayakmontenegro.com), who have a stand just beyond the *Sport Café*, offer kayaks for rent (€5 per hour or €15 for half a day for a single-seater, €7/€20 for a double-seater). They also organize tailor-made tours, both along the coast around Herceg Novi, and beyond, such as across to the Luština peninsula and down into the Bay of Kotor, while there's evening kayaking available, too.

Plenty of **other activities** can be arranged along the waterfront in Herceg Novi. A short way further down Šetalište pet Danica from Kayak Montenegro, the Water Sports Club (☏031/322 035) offers jet-skiing (€50 for 20min), waterskiing (€30 for 10min) and paragliding (€40 for one circuit of the bay). They also have bikes for hire (€15 per day).

Feral Šetalište pet Danica 47. By far the best place to eat along the promenade, this delightful taverna serves top-grade seafood, including some terrific shellfish dishes, such as mussels, oysters and scallops. Eat in the cosy, wood-furnished interior or out on the cool, well-shaded terrace.

Hercegovina Trg Nikole Đurkovića. Secreted away just off the main square opposite the market, this simple establishment, popular with locals, has some tasty grilled-meat dishes at rock-bottom prices.

Portofino Trg Herceg Stijepan. Cordial, welcoming place on the Old Town's main square, with a bright terrace and comfy red seating. The menu primarily comprises steak and fish, alongside good pasta and salad dishes.

Sport Café Šetalište pet Danica 34. Conspicuous glass building along the main promenade with a large raised terrace overlooking the marina. The food is more of the snack variety, such as pizza, pasta, salads and hot sandwiches.

Tri Lipe 28 Oktobra. So named after the large, leafy trees shading its popular stone terrace, the "Three Trees" is an informal eatery with an open kitchen dispensing the full range of Balkan grilled meats (*čevapčići, pljeskavica, kobasica*). The service is speedy and friendly, and takeaway is available around the clock.

Drinking

Most of Herceg Novi's drinking takes place along Šetalište pet Danica, where numerous **cafés and bars** jostle for custom. The most convivial are *Café Nautica*, which has a great range of continental draught beers, and the *Yachting Club* (℡031/324 014), around 300m further along, which also has a wine bar and nightclub, frequently staging live music in the summer. Opposite here, the *Sport Café* (see above) is a good place for a beer at sundown. Elsewhere, there is a cluster of sociable terrace cafés on both Trg Nikole Đurkovića and Trg Herceg Stijepan. In Igalo, the main promenade, Obala Nikole Kovačevića, is stacked with a raft of indistinguishable cafés and bars. Most of these places stay open until 1 or 2am at least.

Around Herceg Novi

The near vicinity of Herceg Novi offers plenty of opportunity for some active pursuits. Rearing up behind the town, the fabulous limestone shaft of the **Orjen Massif** presents some outstanding hiking possibilities, while across the water on the **Luštica peninsula** – accessible by regular ferry boats during the summer months – you can swim and snorkel among the beaches and coves.

The Orjen Massif

Looming over Herceg Novi and spilling over into neighbouring Bosnia-Herzegovina, the **Orjen Massif** is the highest mountain range along the entire Adriatic coast. It's a spectacular, jagged karst landscape, characterized by deep glacial valleys, fast-flowing streams, and innumerable fissures and sinkholes. Best of all, Orjen offers some truly excellent **hiking**, with a number of well-marked and challenging trails fanning out all across the range. One of the easiest and most enjoyable excursions from Herceg Novi is the hike up to the **Vratlo Pass** (3hr 30min; 1175m), via the village of Kameno and along the old Austro-Hungarian packhorse route. Sited on the pass is the *Planinarski dom za Vratlo*, currently the only functioning **mountain hut** on Orjen; a large facility, it has several dormitories, in addition to a kitchen, and you can also camp here. From the hut, you can press on into the heart of the massif to the peak of **Subra** (1679m), a further 6km on, which should take around two hours to reach – from here there are superb views of the Adriatic and Mount Lovćen down to the south.

The highest peak on Orjen is **Zubači kabao** (1894m), which is best reached via **Vrbanj** (1007m), itself 7km north of **KRUŠEVICE**, a pretty village of stone-built houses some 12km north of Herceg Novi – there are only a couple of buses a day from town to the village, so you're better off trying to hitch a lift or take a taxi. Once at Vrbanj, it's a two-hour walk along the old dirt road to the peak of **Orjen sedlo** (1590m), then a further ninety minutes or so to the summit of Zubački kabao. The whole round-trip from Kruševice to Zubački kabao should take approximately eight hours.

If you plan to stay at the mountain hut you should first contact the **Subra Montaineering Club** (☎032/344 112), who can also organize guides for climbing and caving in the mountains. The club also publishes the very useful *Guide to the Orjen Massif* (€10), which outlines a number of hikes and contains an excellent map – the best place to get it is the Black Mountain agency in Herceg Novi (see p.49).

The Luštica peninsula and Mamula

Some 6km out to sea from Herceg Novi and shielding the Gulf of Kotor from the open sea is the **Luštica peninsula**, a lush, sparsely inhabited thumb of land scattered with hilltop villages, olive groves and fig trees. Save for the boats that over the summer make the crossing from Herceg Novi to a couple of villages on the northern tip, and a few buses that make the trip from Tivat to one or two at the southern end (see p.69), there's little public transport to or around Luštica. However, if you have wheels, there are plenty of delightfully secluded coves and inlets to seek out.

Between June and September, passenger boats make the 45-minute trip between the harbour in Herceg Novi (€7 return) and the village of **ROSE** at the westernmost tip of the peninsula. There's a lovely little harbour here, a short walk to the north of which is a tidy sandy beach. Boats then continue down to **MIRIŠTA**, another comely village sited close to the **Blue Grotto** (Plava špilja), an atmospheric little cave which takes its name from the colours given off from the refraction of light within. To access the grotto, you must take one of the smaller boats that

▲ Mamula Fortress

❶

The Prevlaka peninsula

The **Prevlaka peninsula**, the slip of land at the entrance to the Gulf of Kotor, has been embroiled in a fairly rancorous dispute in recent times. After World War II, the peninsula was annexed to the Croatian republic, before its occupation by the Serb-dominated Yugoslav forces during the wars of the 1990s just as the siege of Dubrovnik was beginning to take hold. Despite repeated attempts by Croat forces to wrestle back territory, the Yugoslav military managed to retain control before both sides agreed to demilitarize the area in 1992. In 1996 an international observer mission, UNMOP, was set up to mediate the conflict; once they withdrew in 2002 the peninsula was returned to Croatia, with Montenegro taking control of the surrounding waters.

depart regularly from Mirišta beach. It's possible to both swim and snorkel inside the cave – if you wish to do the latter, contact the Black Mountain agency (see p.49), which also sells tickets for the boats to the peninsula from Herceg Novi.

Just offshore from Luštica sits the island of Lastavica, more commonly known as **Mamula** after the Austrian admiral, Lazar Mamula, who constructed the late nineteenth-century fort that stands on this small, circular sanctuary. Although ostensibly built as a fortress, hardly a cannonball was fired in anger, and in fact it saw more action during World War II when Italian forces commandeered it as a prison. Now in a long-term state of dilapidation, neither the fort nor the island is accessible, but you can get close-up views from the boats that make the trip from Herceg Novi to Rose and Mirišta.

South to Perast

From Herceg Novi, the main road runs south through several small resorts before reaching **Kamenari**, the dock for ferries shuttling across the narrow neck of water to Lepetane (see p.69). It's also an attractive little village in its own right, thanks to its cluster of neat, white stone-built houses lining the waterfront. Beyond here, **Morinj** houses one of the country's finest restaurants, while in **Risan** there's a superb collection of Roman mosaics to view. The undoubted highlight of this little corner of the Gulf, however, is **Perast**, with its illustrious seafaring heritage and beautifully sited **Our Lady of the Rock Island**.

Morinj

From Kamenari, a sharp turn north into the Bay of Risan brings you to **MORINJ**, where one of Montenegro's most highly regarded **restaurants** is located. Idyllically set in an old mill surrounded by lush vegetation, with a small brook and a sweet little duck-pond, the ⅃ *Čatovića Mlini* (daily 11am–11pm) offers seafood of the highest order, with a wide range of different sea and river fish garnished in exotically named sauces: the most eye-catching dishes are toadfish in saffron sauce, shrimp in *bouzzara* sauce (oil-fried onions and tomatoes) and lobster medallions, but there are plenty more to whet the appetite, including fish-based brown and black risottos. The smart summery terrace is the place to dine, though the cosy and classy stone interior serves just as well if it's on the chilly side. Signs along the main road clearly indicate the restaurant's whereabouts. Close by is the *Naluka* **campsite** (☎069 346 346; June–Aug), a good-sized site which has decent facilities including clean toilets and hot showers.

Risan

Beyond Morinj, the road loops around to the once-busy shipping port of **RISAN**, now a somnolent place comprising mostly newly built houses and weekend villas which slope down to a low-key waterfront interspersed with a handful of cafés. The one-time capital of the Illyrians, Risan is the oldest settlement in the Bay of Kotor – it was here around 228 BC that their queen, Teuta, committed suicide after her defeat at the hands of the Romans. Subsequently attached to the Roman province of Dalmatia, Risan (then called Risinium) was comprehensively destroyed by the Saracens in the ninth century.

The Villa Urbana

There remain some significant vestiges from the town's Roman past in the form of an outstanding assemblage of second- and third-century **mosaics** (Rimska mozaicima), housed in the **Villa Urbana** (May–Oct daily 8am–8pm; €2), located just up from the main road. Comprising a central courtyard, or atrium, with several side rooms, the site was initially excavated in 1930, revealing five separate mosaics, four of which are almost totally complete; most however were badly damaged during the 1979 earthquake (see box, p.85), as evidenced by the ruptures. On the west (sea-facing) side, a poorly conditioned mosaic features a stylized Roman rosette, representing either a flower or the sun. On the opposite side of the villa, in the former dining room, the first of the most intact mosaics manifests a series of black-and-white checked patterns – curiously, one corner of the room was left unornamented, which suggests that this may have been an area confined to servants. In the adjoining room, which has been identified as the living quarters, a beautifully detailed mosaic is impressed with sea-fauna and vine-leaf motifs – note here too, the seventh-century sarcophagus, in which a skeleton (since removed) was found. Beyond the third room – which also holds a large black-and-white checkerboard mosaic – is the site's star turn, a large square of terracotta tiles intermingled with coloured rosettes, in the centre of which is an extremely rare representation of a reclining Hypnos, the god of sleep – appropriately, this was the bedroom, or *dormitorium*.

Practicalities

Buses between Kotor and Herceg Novi stop off opposite the small cluster of shops on Risan's main road. Although there's little reason to stay, if you need or wish to overnight here, the unappealing-looking *Teuta* **hotel** (☎031/371 740, ✉onogost@t-com.me; ⑥) on the waterfront has some very ordinary accommodation. There's really nowhere to eat here, but if you're seeking refreshment, make for one of the pleasant terrace **cafés** spaced out along the waterfront.

Perast and around

Wedged into a narrow arc between the main coastal road and the water's edge, just 3km around the bay from Risan, is **PERAST**, as picturesque a place as any along the coast. The houses that run by the waterside are toytown Venetian Gothic, with a homely grandeur that recalls the town's magnificent past. For nearly half a millennium Perast was the muscle of Adriatic maritime strength, holding forth against repeated Turkish attacks when the rest of the Gulf had fallen. The sailors of Venice, and later Russia, came to the nautical school here and learned the skills of Perast's mariners, cartographers and engineers. At the peak of its powers, in the mid-eighteenth century, there were four shipyards here and a fleet of around a thousand ships. Eventually, earthquakes, political manoeuvring and simple age took away the town's pre-eminence and left it to a graceful retirement. Although

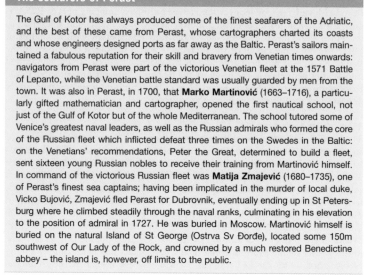

you can quite comfortably take in what Perast has to offer within a couple of hours, including **Our Lady of the Rock Island**, you'll probably want to linger a while longer.

Arrival, information and accommodation

Buses drop off along Obala Marka Martinovića, the main street that runs along the waterfront. In the absence of a tourist office, the best bet for any **information** is the museum (see below), though the website ⓦ www.perast.com is also a useful resource. There's a small **post office** (Mon–Sat 8am–2.30pm) next to the church.

Perast has a couple of extremely comfortable, though fairly expensive **hotels**, situated a couple of hundred metres apart on Obala Marka Martinovića. The small *Hotel Conte* (ⓣ 032/373 687, ⓦ www.hotel-conte.com; ⓞ), has three beautifully appointed rooms and a handful of well-furnished apartments, while *Vila Milinović* (ⓣ 032/373 556, ⓦ www.milinovic-perast.com; ⓞ) is slightly cheaper and marginally better value; zingy, lemon-yellow walls and thick, colourful rugs give its rooms a bright, homely feel, and each room has a DVD player and stereo. Both hotels also have good restaurants (see opposite). Aside from these options, you will also see the odd sign advertising **private rooms** (*sobe*).

The Town

Just about everything of note in Perast is sited along or near to Obala Marka Martinovića. Here, you'll find the most tangible remnants of the town's glory years, including the Baroque houses and palaces that once belonged to revered sea captains such as Marko Martinović, the most venerated of all Perast's naval heroes, and Matija Zmajević, admiral of the Russian Baltic fleet (see box, above) – unfortunately, many are now unidentifiable or stand idle. One that is still very much in use is the **Bujović Palace** (Palata Bujović), at the northern entrance to the town (it's one of the first buildings as you enter from Risan). Allegedly constructed from stone taken from a section of the old city walls in Herceg Novi, the palace was largely conceived in the Renaissance style, most evident in the superb arcaded porch and balustraded terrace above, atop which are two sculptures of lions, the symbol of the Venetian Republic. It now houses the **town museum** (Grad muzej; daily 9am–6pm; €2), with stern portraits of seafaring luminaries, furniture, books, flags and weaponry. In truth, though, it's a disappointing collection, with surprisingly little made of the town's naval exploits – the interior holds more of interest from an architectural perspective: as well as the balconied terrace, which you can reach via the second-floor gallery, note the beautifully trimmed, square stone portals as you enter each room.

At one time, the town possessed over a dozen churches, the most pre-eminent of which still remains. Standing on the square of the same name, the deceptively small **Church of St Nicholas** (Crkva Sv Nikole) was built from stone from Korčula (see p.51) and completed in 1616. Its single-nave interior features a wooden ceiling and richly carved, Baroque marble altars, while the adjoining treasury displays a rich horde of ecclesiastical objects, icons, vestments and suchlike. One of the most recognizable structures along the coast, the neighbouring 55-metre-high **belfry** (May–Oct daily 10am–6pm; €2) was completed in 1691, and had its clock brought here from Venice in 1730; it's worth clambering up the rickety steps of this lofty structure for the marvellous views out to the entrance of the Gulf. In front of the church are busts of both Martinović and Zmajević, and of the painter, Tripo Kokolja (see p.58).

Eating and drinking

Both the hotels in town boast pretty good **restaurants**, both specializing in seafood and comparable in price. *Conte* has the slight edge by virtue of its more varied menu, featuring an upscale take on dishes such as black risotto, mixed fish stew and lobster in olive oil and herbs, though *Vila Milinović* has an appealing covered-stone terrace that juts out into the water. In between these two, there's *Dardin*, which is good for pizzas, snacks and pastries. Both the *Conte* and *Vila Milinović* are the places to go to for a **drink**, be it a daytime coffee or a beer at sundown.

Our Lady of the Rock Island

Serenely poised some several hundred metres off shore, **Our Lady of the Rock Island** (Gospa od škrpjela) is one of the Montenegrin coast's showpiece landmarks. To trace its origins you have to choose your legend. In one, a sailor, shipwrecked in the Gulf, clung to a stone here one night, promising that if he survived he'd build a church to the Virgin on the rock. With morning came rescue, the sailor kept his word and dumped stones until the island rose. The alternative legend, a little less colourful, is that on July 22, 1452, two sailors found an icon of the Virgin and Child on the rock and took it to Perast; next day it was found that the icon had mysteriously made its way back to the rock, so the Perastians built it an island and fittingly grand church.

Each year on July 22, the island is the focus of a great **procession** – the Fašinada – in which a flotilla of around fifty boats brings stones and rock from the nearby mountains and dumps them into its surrounding waters. Rather more profanely, each May 15 local marksmen enjoy a game called *gadanje kokota* ("shooting the cock"), which involves tying an unfortunate rooster to a piece of wood and floating him out into the bay. The locals then blast away, and when the feathers settle someone is declared the best shot, thereby obliging the victor to buy a barrel of wine for the entire town.

Water taxis (May–Oct 9am–5pm, July & Aug till 7pm; €5) shuttle passengers from opposite the Church of St Nicholas to the island and back every half an hour, so you can stay for as long as you wish.

The church

Though severely battered and rebuilt over the years – most of the present-day incarnation postdates the 1667 earthquake – the **church** remains, and in the sea-blue and seaweed-green Baroque interior, you can still find the miraculous **icon**, held in a marble altarpiece of great value: for the green Italian marble the Perastians paid an equal weight of silver. A majestic piece of craftsmanship, the altar also incorporates red marble from Egypt and white marble from Siena. The icon was much revered by the Gulf's sailors, and round the walls are more than two thousand silver votive plaques featuring relief images of ships from the Gulf of Kotor, promised to the Virgin in moments of peril and given on safe return. There is much else to admire inside, not least a riot of artwork by Tripo Kokolja (1661–1713), a Croatian artist of outstanding repute – prominent amongst the seventy or so largely Baroque-inspired **paintings** that cover both walls and ceiling is the *Ascension of Lady Maria*, high up in the central ceiling panel. In the altar, meanwhile, four large canvases from the Genoese school vie for attention, alongside a beautifully cut, three-hundred-year-old Murano glass chandelier. The church **exterior**, too, reveals some eye-catching architectural detail, most notably the niche above the green bronze door which holds a miniature statue of the Virgin with Child and, just above this, a superbly carved stone rosette. Grafted onto the side of the church, the handsome, circular bell-tower is partitioned into three storeys and topped by several gun-barrel openings.

The museum

Next door to the church, a small but fascinating **museum** keeps a veritable treasure-trove of items garnered from shipwrecks or given as gifts to the church by sailors: there are vases from Japan, crosses and medallions, amphorae, figureheads and all manner of navigational equipment, as well as a fabulous collection of paintings depicting ships at sea. One particularly intriguing exhibit is an embroidered icon created by a local woman, Jacinta Kunić, in which she used seven different materials, including Chinese and Japanese silk, as well her own hair – given that it took her nearly thirty years to complete, it's little wonder that the colours vary between brown and grey.

Kotor and around

Squeezed into a small triangular wedge at the very end of a long, narrow bay, in the shadow of Mount Lovćen, the medieval walled town of **KOTOR** is indisputably the jewel in the coast's crown. A UNESCO World Heritage Site, it was once one of the busiest ports in Europe, both commercially and militarily, though today its picturesque natural harbour funnels mainly cruise ships. Kotor is essentially its compact **Old Town**, an enchanting warren of smooth stone-paved streets and irregularly shaped squares, many endowed with delightful names, such as Milk Square and Salad Square, reflecting the various trades or crafts that were once practiced there. Although the town can get swamped at the height of summer, particularly with large groups of day-trippers from the liners that dock here, its essential charms remain undiminished. Kotor is easily reached via buses plying the route between Herceg Novi and Tivat or Budva, though the most spectacular approach is from Cetinje, via Mount Lovćen (see p.122).

Some history

Although it had originally been colonized by the Greeks, Kotor first flourished in the twelfth century as the chief port of the Serbian state of Raška – it was, however, very much an independent commune, with a commercial power that came to rival that of Dubrovnik. Serbian rule lasted until 1371, when the town was taken over by the Austro-Hungarian king, Ludovic I, which was followed by a brief period of rule (1384–91) by King Tvrtvo of Bosnia. An independent state for thirty years thereafter, the golden years didn't last long, for the town's position was undermined by the Turkish conquests of the fifteenth century and forced to seek the protection of Venice in 1420, under whose aegis it remained until 1797, when it passed to the Austrian Empire. The period under Venetian rule witnessed a transformation in the city's appearance, with the construction of numerous churches and palaces, but was also marked by siege, earthquake and plague. After Venetian control, and save for a brief period in the early nineteenth century when it was assigned to Russia and then the Illyrian provinces, Kotor remained under the jurisdiction of the Habsburg Empire – under their rule, and especially during the latter part of the nineteenth century, the town underwent major social and cultural advancements, with the foundation of schools, libraries, workers' co-operatives and a National Guard.

As the main base of the Austro-Hungarian navy during World War I, Kotor was party to some of the fiercest sea-borne battles between local Montenegrin Slavs and Austro-Hungarians. At the conclusion of war, the town was assimilated into the new state of Yugoslavia and it assumed its current name – it had hitherto been called Cattaro. The massive earthquake of April 1979 (see box, p.85) reduced much of the Old Town to a smouldering heap, and it took a decade or so to restore it to its former glory.

Arrival and information

The town's **bus station** is a five-minute walk south of the Old Town on the road out towards Tivat – there's a left-luggage office here, too (daily 9am–9pm). There are no buses from Tivat airport to Kotor, so you'll have to rely on taking a taxi, which should cost no more than €20. **Ferries** from Bari dock at the harbour, located directly across the road from the Old Town. The **tourist office** (March–June, Sept & Oct 8am–7pm; July & Aug daily 8am–10pm; Nov–Feb Mon–Sat 8am–

Kotor's festival year

Kotor has the most diverse roster of **festivals** of any town along the coast, if not the entire country. First up, in February, is **Days of St Tripun** (Tripundanske Svečanosti), a day of folk dancing and church music in celebration of the eponymous saint, which is closely followed by the **Masked Ball** (Maskenbali), a colourful procession of masked troupes through the Old Town, culminating in a carnival concert on Trg od Oružja. The major spring event is the colourful **Montenegrin Dance Festival** (Crnogorski Plesni Festival) in April, a week-long programme incorporating just about every conceivable form of dance. The summer season kicks off in July with the **International Summer Carnival** (Internacionalni Ljetnnji Karneval; www.kotorkarneval.com), entailing all manner of theatrical and musical performances on stages throughout the Old Town. For kids, there's the popular **Children's Theatre Festival** (Dječiji Pozorišni Festival), a ten-day jamboree at the beginning of the same month, featuring improvised performances of theatre, music and poetry. Upping the tempo a notch or two, **Refresh** (www.refreshfestival.com), in either late July or early August, is a thumping four-day music bash attracting some of Europe's biggest-name DJs to the town's bars and clubs, as well as a host of bands performing up in the *Citadella*. The single biggest event of the year, however, is **Boka Nights** (Bokeljska noč), usually on the second or third Sunday of August, which sees the bay awash with a flotilla of boats and ends in a spectacular fireworks display.

4pm; ⓦwww.tokotor.com), located in a kiosk just outside the Sea Gate, offers some basic free maps, as well as some decent guidebooks on the Old Town (€5). There are two **post offices**, one next to the *Vardar* hotel just off Trg od Orujža, and another 200m along the road towards Prčanj (both Mon–Sat 7.30am–8pm), while there's **internet** access in a couple of Old Town cafés, namely *Forza* on Trg od Orujža, and *Evergreen* on Trg Bokeljske Mornorice. Cars are not permitted in the Old Town, but there's reasonably cheap **parking** (€0.80/hr) to the east of the Old Town walls, just beyond the Škurda River, and most hotels offer a porterage service. Note that there are almost no street names within the Old Town (Stari Grad), and each building is denoted just by a number. For good local **car rental** try M Rent-a-Car, 323 Dobrota bb (☎069 448 466, ⓔmrentacar@t-com.me), and Loading, 423 Stari Grad (☎067 342 777, ⓔloading@t-com.me).

Accommodation

Kotor has a limited, but very impressive, supply of **hotels**, almost all of which are located in the Old Town. Most of the places are very expensive, but a fifteen-minute walk north of town in the suburb of Dobrota is the large *Spasic–Masera* **hostel** (☎032/330 258; €15 per bed), accommodating multi-bed dorms, some with bathrooms.

Cattaro Stari Grad 232 ☎032/311 000, ⓦwww.cattarohotel.com. Occupying three separate but conjoined buildings – the Rector's Palace, Old Town Hall and Town Guard – this stylish outfit oozes class. Decorated in dark blues and sunny yellows, with pictures of naval heroes and famous sea battles adorning the walls, the large rooms are ranged along one side of a gorgeous, dark-wood-panelled corridor and all look out onto the Trg od Orujža; they also have large wall-mounted plasma screens, PCs and wi-fi. ❾

Marija Stari Grad 449 ☎032/325 062, ⓔhotel.marija.kotor@t-com.me. Sweet little hotel accommodating cosy, well-appointed rooms furnished with low-slung beds and painted in warm peach tones. Wi-fi available throughout. ❼

Rendezvous Trg od Mlijeka ☎032/323 931, ⓔrendezvouskotor@yahoo.com. Situated on the delightfully named Milk Square, this friendly little place has a variety of different-sized rooms, all of which are clean and modern if a little bit cramped. They're realistically priced, too. ❹–❻

Vardar Trg od Oružja ☎032/326 084, ⓦwww.hotelvardar.com. This warm, intimate establishment is the pick (and the most expensive) of the town's hotels: the bright, beautifully conceived rooms feature lots of smooth wood, sumptuous beds and large plasma TV screens, in addition to sparkling bathrooms. The hotel also possesses a lovely wellness centre comprising gym, sauna and Turkish bath. ❾

Vila Panonija Dobrota bb ☎032/334 893, ⓦwww.vilapanonija.com. An easy fifteen-minute walk north of the Old Town in the suburb of Dobrota, this restful villa, just a stone's throw from the water, possesses seven modern and tidily furnished double rooms; there's a triple available, too. ❼

Villa Duomo Stari Grad 385 ☎032/323 111, ⓦwww.villaduomo.com. Just a few paces along from Trg Bokeljske Mornarice, this sensitively restored building holds thirteen stunning apartments with marble-tiled flooring, elegant hand-crafted furnishings and bare-brick walls throughout. ❽–❾

The Old Town

Kotor's **Old Town** is a densely packed triangle of twisting streets and tiny squares framed to the west by the Gulf coast, to the north by the Škurda River, and the steep mountain slope of Sveti Ivan to the east. Dating originally from the fifteenth century and Venetian in style, the buildings throughout are fairly uniform – thanks partly to the extensive rebuilding that took place following the 1979 earthquake. Most are hewn from blocks of light cream stone with entrances framed by neatly cut square or semi circular stone portals.

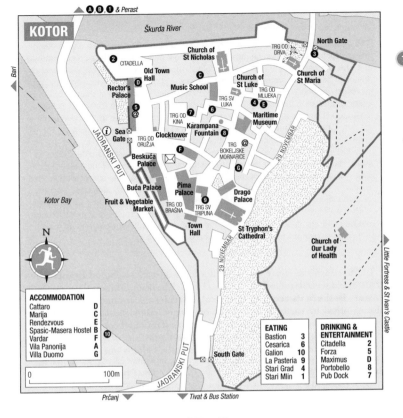

KOTOR

Škurda River

North Gate

Church of
St Nicholas

TRG OD
DRVA

CITADELLA

Old Town
Hall

Church of
St Maria

Rector's
Palace

Music School

Church of
St Luke

TRG OD
MLIJEKA

TRG SV
LUKA

Bari

Sea
Gate

TRG OD
KINA

Maritime
Museum

TRG OD
ORUŽJA

Clocktower

Karampana
Fountain

TRG
BOKELJSKE
MORNARICE

Beskuća
Palace

Kotor Bay

Buća Palace

Pima
Palace

Drago
Palace

N

Fruit & Vegetable
Market

TRG OD
BRAŠNA

TRG SV
TRIPUNA

Town
Hall

St Tryphon's
Cathedral

Church of
Our Lady
of Health

JADRANSKI PUT

29 NOVEMBAR

Little Fortress & St Ivan's Castle

ACCOMMODATION

Cattaro	D
Marija	C
Rendezvous	E
Spasic-Masera Hostel	B
Vardar	F
Vila Panonija	A
Villa Duomo	G

South Gate

EATING		DRINKING & ENTERTAINMENT	
Bastion	3	Citadella	2
Cesarica	6	Forza	5
Galion	10	Maximus	D
La Pasteria	9	Portobello	8
Stari Grad	4	Pub Dock	7
Stari Mlin	1		

0   100m

Prčanj   Tivat & Bus Station

JADRANSKI PUT

& Perast

Trg od Oružja and Trg od Brašna

In an outpouring of national fervour, the thick-set main town gate, known as the **Sea Gate** (Morska vrata), is inscribed with the date of Kotor's liberation (November 21, 1944) and one of Tito's many aphorisms – *Tuđe nećemo svoje nedamo*, which roughly translates as "What belongs to others we don't want, what is ours we'll never surrender." Note, too, on the wall, the relief of the winged lion with an open book, the symbol of the Venetian Republic. Easily missed in the vaulted passage is a splendid Gothic relief, with Virgin and Child, St Tryphon holding the town (see p.62), and St Bernard, revered poet and descendant of the Pima family (see p.62).

Through the gate is **Trg od Oružja** (Arms Square), the largest of the many squares dotted around the Old Town. By far the most conspicuous building here is the seventeenth-century **Rector's Palace** (Palata Kneževa), which shores up the square's western side. Featuring a fine balcony stretching its entire length, the former palace now comprises part of the very fine *Hotel Cattaro* (see opposite). Next door, the **Old Town Hall** (also called Napoleon's Theatre) accommodates the hotel's reception; it was one of the first theatres constructed in the Balkans and functioned as such until the late nineteenth century. Directly opposite the main gate the squat seventeenth-century **clocktower** stands faintly askew thanks to the many earthquakes that have shaken the town; just in front of it is a reconstructed medieval pillory.

A tour of the walls

The best way to get a perspective on the town and the bay is to take a walk along the old **fortress walls**, which meander for some 4.5km. More or less completed by the fifteenth century, the walls were originally conceived by the Byzantines around the ninth century as protection against the sea, and only later developed to hold off potential invaders. The walk itself is a fairly steep climb up a series of sharply inclining steps grafted onto the hillside. Starting from the steps behind the Church of St Maria on Trg od Drva (see p.64), pay the entrance fee (€3) and proceed up to the fifteenth-century **Church of Our Lady of Health** (Crkva Gospa od Zdravlja), 105m up. From here, it's a serpentine ascent up to the **Little Fortress** (Mala tvrđava), and then a little further on through more crumbling fortifications to **St Ivan's Castle** (Kaštel Sv Ivan), standing at 260m. At the top, take in the magnificent views of the flutter of red- and orange-coloured roofs of the Old Town and the bay quietly shimmering in the distance, before beginning the knee-jarring descent. It's a pretty strenuous workout, and you should allow a good ninety minutes to get to the top and back down again; if it's a warm day you're best off attempting it either in the morning or much later in the day – in any case, make sure you take some fluid, so you don't end up buying the expensive drinks from the vendors who wait at the top.

To the east of the square a narrow alley leads through to **Trg od Brašna** (Flour Square) and several studiedly elegant mansions. The first of these is the eighteenth-century **Beskuča Palace** (Palata Beskuča), which retains a magnificent stone portal distinguished by partly broken reliefs of winged saints and cherubs. The story goes that its owner was so aggrieved by the constant taunts of locals concerning the name of the house (which means "homeless") that, by way of riposte, he set out to build one hundred houses – unfortunately, he only got to (an admittedly respectable) sixty-eight before copping it. Immediately next door is the **Buća Palace** (Palata Buća) which, save for a couple of filled-in Gothic portals and a barely detectable coat-of-arms, betrays little evidence of a residence that once belonged to one of Kotor's most noble families. More stately is the Renaissance **Pima Palace** (Palata Pima) directly opposite, which has variously been the home of some of the city's greatest benefactors, including professors, poets, judges and lawyers. A fine vaulted loggia is topped by a badly weathered wrought-iron balcony, above which sits a second, longer balcony.

Trg Sv Tripuna and St Tryphon's Cathedral

From Trg od Brašna, a narrow alley leads to **Trg Sv Tripuna**, dominated by Kotor's most important ecclesiastical building, **St Tryphon's Cathedral** (Katedrala Sv Tripuna; €2), completed in 1166. Kotor came to have Tryphon as its patron saint in 890, when a passing merchant ship loaded with relics offered the townspeople a good deal on its most precious object, the head of the saint who had been put to death some six hundred years earlier. It was a bargain too good to miss, it would appear. Once you get past the fine front, added in the seventeenth century after an earthquake did away with the original, this twin-towered structure (one tower is is marginally shorter than the other) is predominantly Romanesque. Just inside is an intricately carved doorway, single survivor of the ninth-century rotunda on which the later church was built.

The sumptuous, light-filled interior is distinguished by neat columns of robust, reddish-brown pillars, a fine stone rib-vaulted ceiling and high Gothic–style window arches; note, too, how the walls and ceilings of the north aisle display the original brickwork. The church's standout architectural piece though is the **ciborium** straddling the altar, its red marble columns supporting a triangular awning crowned with an angel and richly decorated with bas-reliefs depicting scenes from the life of St Tryphon. On the wall behind are a superb silver altar-plate and the partial remains of an early fifteenth-century fresco of the Crucifixion. Up a flight of specially constructed steps on the north side of the church, the **treasury** is dominated by a superb medieval wooden crucifix and a silver chest in which the relics of St Tryphon are reposed; sculptures, paintings and other ecclesiastical bits and bobs complete a fairly extensive collection.

Trg Sv Tripuna's only other significant building of note is the **town hall** (Zgrada Skupštine). It's an imposing building which was the venue for a famous court case in 1918 involving four mutineering sailors (see p.64).

△ Boys playing cards, Kotor Old Town

Trg Bokeljske Mornarice and the Maritime Museum

From Trg Sv Tripuna another alley leads north under the **Drago Palace** (Palata Drago) – uninteresting save for its handsomely preserved Gothic windows featuring sculpted lions' heads – to **Trg Bokeljske Mornarice** (Square of the Boka Fleet), an animated little square that holds a cluster of lively cafés and bars. It also accommodates the refurbished seventeenth-century Gregorin Palace (Palata Gregorin), which since 1952 has been the home of the eminently enjoyable **Maritime Museum** (Pomorski muzej; May–Oct daily 8am–8pm; Nov–April Mon–Fri 9am–5pm, Sat 9am–noon; €2, including a very worthwhile audio guide). Doting on the region's illustrious seafaring heritage, the museum boasts excellent displays of coastal town plans and nautical maps, and all manner of weird and wonderful navigational aids. Best of all is an outstanding ensemble of model ships, including one of *Splendido*, captained by Ivo Visin from nearby Prčanj, who in 1859 became the first person from the future Yugoslavia (and the first Croatian) to circumnavigate the world. In the room devoted to Yugoslavia's exploits during World War II, there is part of the bow from the destroyer, *Zagreb*, sunk in the Gulf of Kotor in 1941 to prevent it from falling into enemy hands. Also displayed are several illuminating photos of the four Austro-Hungarian sailors (three Croatians and a Czech) suspected of organizing a local mutiny in the Gulf in November 1918 – although the revolt was unsuccessful, the four were found guilty and summarily executed in nearby Škaljari. Further displays include several mocked-up drawing rooms, including one belonging to the Austrian admiral, Marko Florio, whose salon contains sumptuous, late Baroque lemonwood furnishings – given Kotor's pre-eminence amongst Austria-Hungary's naval bases, sea captains of the nineteenth century could count on leading rather privileged lives.

Behind the museum, the tiny **Piazza Karampana** holds the city **fountain** of the same name. It's an awkward-looking contraption dating back to the end of the seventeenth century.

Trg Sv Luka and Trg od Drva

From the piazza it's a short walk to **Trg Sv Luka**, an elegant space enriched with more fine architecture. Standing in the centre is the diminutive twelfth-century Romanesque **Church of St Luke** (Crkva Sv Luka), with a Byzantine-style dome over the nave. The interior is almost bare, save for some fresco fragments on the south wall and an immaculately restored golden crucifix above the iconostasis. Across the square the hulking grey building is the early twentieth-century **Church of St Nicholas** (Crkva Sv Nikola).

Tucked away in the far corner of the Old Town, edging the north wall, the greenery-filled **Trg od Drva** (Wood Square) is overlooked by the **Church of St Maria** (Crkva Sv Marija), a handsome-looking pile constructed from alternate bands of cream and pink stone. The church is named in honour of the Blessed Ozana, a local nun credited with inspiring Kotor's residents into repelling the repeated advances of the Turkish admiral Barbarosa in the sixteenth century – scenes depicting Ozana's life are sculpted in bas-relief on the thick bronze door. Unfortunately, it's the one church that's usually closed. From the square, the **North Gate** (Sjeverna vrata) leads to a footbridge spanning the green River Škurda.

One of the few named streets in the Old Town, 29 Novembar (also known as Craftsmen's Street) stretches along the length of the eastern side of the Old Town all the way to the **South Gate** (Južna vrata), the third of the entrances. Sections of this street once held numerous craftsmen's shops, though all but one of these – a shoemaker's located near the Church of St Maria – have disappeared.

Eating

The Old Town has plenty of decent **restaurants** to pick from, and in addition there are lots of little places where you can find cheap snacks. There's also a colourful fruit and vegetable **market** (Mon–Sat) on the short promenade just outside the main Old Town entrance. All these restaurants open until around midnight.

Bastion Trg od Drva. The least touristy of the Old Town's eateries, this quiet, unassuming venue next to the North Gate offers a wide-ranging choice of fresh seafood. Moreover, it possesses a lovely flower-scented terrace looking across to the Church of St Maria.

Cesarica Stari Grad 375. Secreted away just behind the music school near Trg Sv Luka, this cosy little brick taverna possesses just a handful of simple wooden bench tables, around which hang lots of nautically themed paraphernalia. The food, meanwhile, features both fish dishes (including fish and chips) and grilled meats.

Galion Šuranj bb. Housed in a handsome stone villa on the water's edge around 200m from the Old Town, *Galion* is about as polished as it gets. You can dine in the light and airy interior – furnished with smart, white-clothed tables and elegant chairs – or on the wood-deck terrace suspended on stilts in the water. Upscale seafood dominates, with the likes of squid-ink risotto, seafood bouillabaisse and monkfish; afterwards take your pick from a selection of tempting desserts, like apple crumble or *panna cotta.*

La Pasteria Trg Sv Tripuna. With great views across to the cathedral from its large terrace, this lively restaurant offers an uncomplicated but varied choice of foods, namely pasta, pizza, salads (of sardines, cabbage and carrot or smoked ham and cheese) served with *lepinja*, hot sandwiches and sweet-and-sour pancakes. It's also the best place in town for breakfasts, served until noon.

Stari Grad Stari Grad 478. Located just off Trg od Mlijeka, this is the Old Town's most refined dining option. Housed within a lovely brick-vaulted cellar, it offers an impressive range of shellfish (mussels, oysters and lobster) and fresh fish (dentex and flounder), in addition to some good vegetarian options. Although the restaurant is air-conditioned, the pretty, vine-shaded terrace is a pleasant alternative.

Stari Mlin Located 7km north of Kotor just beyond the suburb of Dobrota, the "Old Mill" is one of the region's finest restaurants. The setting – a three-hundred-year-old mill at the source of the River Ljuta – is sublime, and complements superbly the first-rate food: freshwater fish, such as trout (kept in the large pond), and mixed fish stew are just some of the staples, while there are also traditional local dishes on the menu such as lamb baked in ash with potatoes. Fine wine, too.

Drinking and entertainment

The warren of alleys and squares within the Old Town contains any number of convivial **cafés and bars**, all rammed to the gills at the height of summer; most stay open until well into the early hours, often 2 or 3am. Ranged along the south side of Trg od Oružja, a trio of bright cafés vies for custom, though *Forza* just about edges it for both its coffee and service. The most popular evening venues are: *Pub Dock* on Trg od Kina, whose heavily-wooded interior is reminiscent of a British-style pub; *Portobello* on Trg Bokeljske Mornarice, where regular evening DJs draw large crowds; and *Citadella*, a vast open-air terrace positioned atop the bastion in the southwestern corner of the Old Town.

If you fancy a spot of **dancing**, then the place to head for is *Maximus*, next to the *Cattaro* hotel – a cavernous space, it comprises several Roman-themed dancefloors, each with its own music policy (house, pop, folk and so on). Top-name foreign DJs and concerts are a regular feature at the club during the summer months.

Prčanj

Heading north around the bay from Kotor, a narrow, winding road runs flat along the water's edge beneath Mount Vrmac to **PRČANJ**, some 10km distant, a quaint little resort spotted with fine Baroque houses. Like Perast (see p.55), it spawned numerous noteworthy sea captains, none more so than Ivo Visin, the first Yugoslav to circumnavigate the world (see p.64). The town is dominated by the oversized **Church of Our Lady's Temple**, an imposing edifice completed in 1909 after taking more than a century to build. The entrance is reached via a splendid double staircase and fronted by busts of local luminaries, including one of Visin, while the highlights of the interior are two gilded altars and a dazzling icon entitled the *Holy Virgin of Prčanj*.

Prčanj has some good **accommodation** possibilities. Named after Visin's ship, the *Hotel Spendido* (℡032/301 700, Ⓦwww.splendido-hotel.com; ➒) is an ultra-classy place whose rooms, with stone floor-tiling and wrought-iron furnishings, are supremely comfortable; they've got a fabulous waterside terrace and pool, too. Across the road, the family-run *Bokeljski Dvori* (℡032/336 113, Ⓦwww .hotelbokeljskidvori.com; ➏; closed Jan) has a mix of variously sized, clean and tidy rooms, some sea-facing, some hill-facing. The third option, just opposite the church, is the *Hotel Villa Prčanj* (℡069 395 109; ➏), a dazzling-white stone villa accommodating an equal number of bright and very modern rooms and apartments (€80–100), the latter with or without kitchen. Both the *Splendido* and the *Bokeljski Dvori* have excellent **restaurants**, the former offering freshly caught fish from the bay, the latter a homely and personable place serving similar dishes in addition to grilled-meat standards.

From Prčanj, the road continues to Lepetane on the other side of the peninsula (for ferries across to Kamenari, see p.54), beyond which, to the south, is Tivat.

Tivat and around

Buffered on one side by the sea and on the other by Mount Vrmac, **TIVAT** is the youngest town in the Boka region. For the most part, this laid-back resort is a rather unharmonious clump of late-socialist architecture, and while it possesses neither the vibrancy of Herceg Novi nor the history of Kotor, there's just about enough greenery to soften the edges, and a shiny horseshoe-shaped marina to add a modicum of glitz to proceedings – indeed, the potential is such that plans are afoot to transform the resort into Montenegro's premier marina. Moreover, there are some fine beaches within close proximity to town, in particular on the **Luštica peninsula**. The town's main annual event, shared with Kotor, is the Montenegrin Dance Festival, a major celebration of dance in all its myriad forms (see p.59).

Arrival, information and accommodation

Tivat's small **airport** (Ⓦwww.aptivat.com) is 3km south of town, and although there's no public transport into the centre, a **taxi** should cost no more than €5. There are several **car hire** companies based at the airport, including Avis (℡032/673 448), Europcar (℡032/671 894) and Kompas (℡069 423 800). The town's **bus station** (which is really just a roadside bus stop) is smack bang in the centre on Palih Boraca, from where it's a five-minute walk to the helpful and well-stocked **tourist office** at no. 9 (July & Aug daily 8am–9pm; Sept–June Mon–Sat 8am–3pm, Sun 8am–noon; ℡032/671 323, Ⓦwww.tivatonline.com). The **post office** (Mon–Sat 7am–8pm) is a few paces along from the bus station and there's **internet** access inside the pool hall just behind the *Mimoza* hotel.

Tivat has a liberal sprinkling of **hotels**, most of reasonable value, and many of them located within close proximity to the waterfront. The tourist office has a good catalogue listing local **private accommodation** (which costs €15–20), of which there is plenty in both Tivat and the neighbouring suburbs, but they cannot make bookings. The nearest **campsite** is at the *Lovćen* pension (see opposite) in Lepetane, though it's fairly rudimentary, with little in the way of amenities and only open for camping between June and August.

Hotels

Aurora Kalimanj bb ☎ 032/671 561, ✉ aurora@ t-com.me. Set in a pleasantly restful spot right beside the marina, and boasting a lush, flower-filled garden, this inauspicious building conceals decent enough rooms, though they're nothing beyond the ordinary. ❺

Lovćen Lepetane, 5km north of Tivat ☎ 032/686 006. Very simple motel-style place near the ferry dock in Lepetane, with rooms sleeping between two and four people; there's a small camping area here too (see opposite). Breakfast not available. ❷

Mimoza Moše Pijade bb ☎ 032/672 250, ✉ htpmi-moza@t-com.me. Somewhat past its sell-by date, this state-owned relic is just about the cheapest place in town. ❹

Montenegrino 21 Novembra 27 ☎ 032/674 900, ✉ montenegrino@t-com.me. Tivat's classiest option by some distance, this intimate residence possesses ten rooms of the highest order, fitted with elegant dark-wood furnishings and painted in deep-green and yellow tones. ❾

Palma 21 Novembra bb ☎ 032/672 288, ⊛ www .primorje.me. Occupying a cracking waterfront loca-tion, and housed in a characterful old building, this medium-sized hotel is popular with package tour-ists, though the rooms are a bit grey and careworn. Also has an excellent restaurant (see below). ❻

Pine Obala bb ☎ 032/671 225, ✉ htpmimozaad @t-com.me. Although it has rather dated, spar-tanly furnished rooms, this fairly priced place is in an appealing location set back slightly from the water. ❺

Villa Royal Kalimanj bb ☎ 032/675 310, ⊛ www .hotelvillaroyal.me. Just around the corner from the *Aurora*, this small, polished hotel has boldly coloured and immaculately furnished rooms and apartments, some of which have sea views. ❼

The Town

It won't take you long to negotiate Tivat's few sights, chief of which is the **Buća Museum and Gallery** (Muzej i Galerija Buća; Mon–Fri 9am–noon & 6–9pm, Sat 9am–noon; free), housed inside the seventeenth-century Buća summerhouse just off Nikole Đurkovića. Surrounded by a high wall, this modestly fortified structure was formerly the seasonal residence of the well-to-do Buća family, who hailed from Kotor (see p.62). Neatly arranged over four floors of the lofty stone tower, this modest museum holds two exhibitions: an ethnographic collection, with cos-tumes, weaponry and fishing paraphernalia; and a much more interesting assem-blage of archeological wares, with some terrific finds, including ceramic vessels, glass vases, ancient coins and amphorae dredged up from the Adriatic. Also worth a peek is the temporary gallery in one of the ground-floor rooms. The grounds also contain two **open-air theatres**, one larger and one smaller, which are regular venues for a busy summer programme of plays, concerts and other cultural events – check with the tourist office to see what's on.

North of the museum, and providing some respite from the heat, lies the town's **park**, an expansive area of fir, cedar and pine trees, as well as a range of exotic plants brought here by seafarers. Tivat lacks traditional sand or pebble **beaches** – instead they are of the concrete-platform variety, such as the one in front of the *Palma* hotel. There are, however, some lovely sandy beaches outside of town and on the Luštica peninsula (see p.69).

Eating and drinking

Tivat is hardly flush with places to eat, and many people choose to dine in the hotel **restaurants**. Adjoining the *Palma* hotel, and with lovely views out across to Luštica, *Marzamin* offers the best fresh fish dishes in town, along with some pretty good wine. In the centre of town, opposite the bus station on Palih Boraca, *Bacchus* is a fairly simple, vaguely nautically themed place, offering a decent selection of seafood, including crayfish, mussels and stuffed squid. Meanwhile, *Galija*, opposite the *Mimoza* hotel, is a frantic little pizzeria doling out variously sized, thick- and

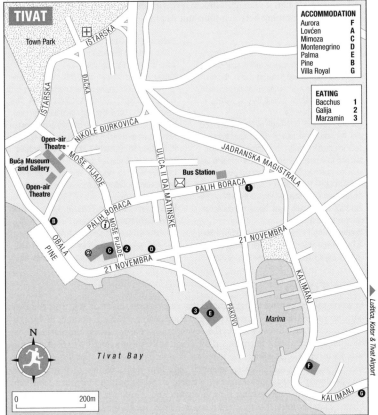

▲ Ⓐ, Lepetane, Gornja Lastva & Prčanj

TIVAT

Town Park

ISTARSKA

BAČKA

ISTARSKA

NIKOLE ĐURKOVIĆA

MOŠE PIJADE

Open-air
Theatre

Buća Museum
and Gallery

Open-air
Theatre

Ⓑ

OBALA

PINE

PALIH BORAČA

MOŠE PIJADE

@

21 NOVEMBRA

ⓒ ② ⓓ

ULICA II DALMATINSKE

Bus Station

PALIH BORAČA

JADRANSKA MAGISTRALA

①

21 NOVEMBRA

PAKOVO

③ Ⓔ

Marina

KALIMANJ

KALIMANJ

Ⓕ

Ⓖ

ACCOMMODATION

Aurora	F
Lovćen	A
Mimoza	C
Montenegrino	D
Palma	E
Pine	B
Villa Royal	G

EATING

Bacchus	1
Galija	2
Marzamin	3

N

Tivat Bay

0   200m

Luštica, Kotor & Tivat Airport

thin-crust pizzas. For **drinking**, Pine, the flower-scented waterside promenade, is where the majority of townsfolk congregate of an evening – here there are several convivial terrace cafés-cum-bars, none particularly distinguished, but all perfectly suited to supping and gazing.

Around Tivat

There are a smattering of sights around Tivat, some of which can be reached by bus. Looming over the town to the north are the lush **Vrmac hills**, which offer some good hiking. Across to the south, beyond the airport, is the evocatively named **Island of Flowers** with its church and monastery ruins, in addition to a couple of the areas's finest **beaches**, including one on the lovely Luštica peninsula.

North of Tivat

Just 3km north of Tivat, a narrow, twisting road ascends to **GORNJA LASTVA**, an idyllic hillside village with crooked, crumbling stone houses and a seventeenth-century church, from where there are superlative views of the bay and the Luštica peninsula directly ahead. From here it's possible to partake in a number of walks along the narrow ridge of the **Vrmac Massif**, the highest point of which is Sveti

Ilija at 785m. The most enjoyable of these is a seven-kilometre hike along the main ridge, via Pasiglav (where there are some unexplored archeological remains, including the battered ruins of St Nicholas's Church), Kuk, and Bogdašići to Utvrda Vrmac, sight of an Austro-Hungarian fortress; this should take no more than two hours. From Utvrda Vrmac, it's a steep 3km walk down to **Muo**, a small village just a couple of kilometres around the bay from Kotor. From Kotor you can return to Tivat by bus.

Back down on the main road, it's another couple of kilometres to **LEPETANE**, an attractive waterside settlement of bright stone villas, though it's more relevant as the port for **ferries** across to Kamenari (approx every 20min: June–Sept 24hr, Oct–May 5am–midnight; cars €4, bicycles €2, passengers free). The ten-minute crossing cuts considerably the time taken to reach Herceg Novi – the alternative is to follow the coast road via Kotor and Perast.

South of Tivat

There are a couple of interesting places to visit to the south of Tivat, including one of the area's best beaches. Just before the airport, a right turn brings you to the airport perimeter road, which loops round towards **Kalardovo**, a small but neat grey-gravelly beach whose shallow waters make it ideal for families with young children – the amenities are good (showers and toilets) and there's an appealing little **restaurant** here too, serving fish and grilled-meat snacks and meals. Back along the main road, and some 500m beyond the beach, is the **Island of Flowers** (Ostrvo cvijeće), a verdant, thickly wooded outcrop on top of which lie the scant remains of the ninth-century **St Michael's Monastery** (Manastir Sv Mihaela), demolished by the Venetians in 1452. A few steps away, and of more recent vintage, is the **Church of the Holy Trinity** (Crkva Sv Trojice), a pretty little stone edifice dating from 1833 – its frontage manifests a beautifully carved rosette and three window arches, while inside there's a wood-carved iconostasis. The island is joined to the mainland by an almost imperceptible bridge. Although difficult to imagine now, the island of **Sveti Marko** opposite was once, in the 1970s, a hugely popular *Club Med* resort, though today it lies overgrown and abandoned.

From the Island of Flowers, it's a short distance to the southern tip of the Luštica peninsula (see p.53), whose main settlement hereabouts is the village of **Radovići**. Some 5km south of here is the peninsula's star attraction, **Pržno beach**, a gorgeous, gently arcing belt of fine grey sand enclosed on two sides by shallow cliffs and backed by clusters of pine, olive groves and smooth grassy fields. As one of the coast's few designated Blue Flag beaches, it's extremely clean and there are excellent amenities here, including showers, changing booths and beach equipment for hire. It's also a lovely spot for a picnic – or if you haven't got your own provisions take advantage of the vast terraced **restaurant** backing onto the beach. Seven **buses** a day make the trip out to the beach from the bus station in Tivat; if you're coming by car, it'll cost €3 to enter the beach area.

Budva

The major resort in Montenegro, **BUDVA** is the coast's star turn. During the summer it's jam-packed with tourists, drawn to the town's fine array of **beaches** and associated watersports on offer, as well as its nightlife, which is the most pulsating anywhere along the coast. There is culture here, too, with churches and museums spread throughout the confines of the delightful **Old Town**, almost entirely rebuilt from the rubble of the 1979 earthquake (see box, p.85). Moreover, the town's plentiful supply of accommodation and excellent bus links make it a convenient base for exploring this stretch of the coast. Budva stages a couple of excellent summer **festivals** in June: the International Folklore Festival (Festival Folkolora), a four-day gathering of some of Europe's finest folk musicians at the beginning of the month; and, a few weeks later, the Mediterranean Song Contest (Pjesma Mediterana), which stars singers from across the Mediterranean, including several countries of the former Yugoslavia.

Some history

In legend Budva was founded by Cadmus, son-in-law of Aphrodite and sower of the famous warrior teeth; the town is said to have received its name from the ox cart in which Cadmus was exiled from Thebes. More certainly, records show that Budva was an important Greek settlement as early as 500 BC. Dented and damaged, razed and ransacked, the town struggled through from the collapse of the Roman Empire to the twelfth century when it became a prosperous, semi-autonomous city-state within the Serbian empire. In 1443 Budva collapsed into the arms of Venice to become its most southerly Adriatic possession, the subsequent four centuries of Venetian rule giving the town stability and a degree of protection from the Turkish raids harassing much of the rest of the coast – one of the Turks' chief aggravators was a fellow by the name of Sćepan the Small, a fearsome ruler whose rise to the throne was as intriguing as it was improbable (see box, below). Save for a brief period at the beginning of the nineteenth century when it came under the sway of the French, the town was occupied by the Austrians until the end of World War I, when, like the other coastal towns, it was incorporated into Montenegro. Following World War II, Budva emerged as one of Yugoslavia's main coastal resorts, particularly popular with foreign tourists. The wars of the 1990s put an abrupt end to that, and the town relied almost solely on domestic custom for more than a decade. Undoubtedly, though, Budva is back with a bang, with international tourists returning in greater numbers than at any point since the end of the 1980s.

Arrival, information and accommodation

Budva's large and well-run **bus station** is on Ivana Milutinovića, a five-minute walk from the beachfront and about fifteen minutes' walk from the Old Town. The small **tourist office**, located in the Old Town at Njegoševa 28 (June–Sept Mon–Sat 9am–9pm; Oct–May Mon–Fri 9am–4pm; ☎033/402 550, Ⓦwww.budva.travel), has some literature and a reasonably detailed free map of the Old Town.

Sćepan the Small

There can't have been many charlatans or impostors who managed to bluff their way to the throne with such an innocuous-sounding name as **Sćepan the Small** (Sćepan Mali). This diminutive character was selling herbs in Budva when a rumour went round that he was really a wandering Polish monk or, more grandly, the Russian Tsar Peter III, deposed in 1762 and presumed murdered. Whether the Montenegrins of the day were particularly gullible or Sćepan extremely personable isn't known, but we do know that he was installed as prince in 1766, declaring that although he was indeed Tsar Peter, for convenience's sake his subjects could carry on calling him Sćepan the Small. As it turned out he was a gifted ruler, uniting many of the Montenegrin tribes in concerted attacks on the Turks to the south. And this was to prove his undoing: in 1774 the Vizier of Skadar, fearful of Montenegrin solidarity, bribed Sćepan's barber to slit his throat, and Sćepan the Small went to an early (and presumably rather short) grave.

BUDVA

Tivat & Kotor

TAPLJSKI PUT

ZAOBILAZNICA

VANA MILUTINOVIĆ

Bus Station

TRG SUNCA

MAINSKI PUT

A

C B

JADRANSKI PUT

MEDITERANSKA

2

MEDITERANSKA

3

SLOVENSKA

ŠETALIŠTE

4 5

6 7

G

Necropolis

H

Cetinje

JADRANSKI PUT

F

D

ŠETALIŠTE

Slovenska Beach

Watersports Centre

SLOVENSKA

TRG SLOBODE

I

Bečići & Sveti Stefan

Marina

OLD TOWN

See Budva Old Town map

ADRIATIC SEA

0 — 400m

Sveti Nikola Island

ACCOMMODATION		EATING, DRINKING & NIGHTLIFE	
Aleksandar	I	BK Club	1
Autocamp Budva	D	Demižana	6
Blue Star	C	Garden Café	2
Grand Avala	H	Hacienda	3
Grbalj	A	Hemingway	4
Jaz Campsite	E	Jadran	7
Kangaroo	F	Old Fisherman's Pub	5
Mogren	G	Trocadero	3
Olympic	B		

As befits the coast's major beach resort, Budva is awash with **hotels**. They're reasonably well scattered, too, with a cluster sited close to the bus station and near the beachfront, and more in and around the Old Town, although those in this latter area are generally more expensive. Unfortunately, there's not a whole lot in the way of budget accommodation, though most of the town's hotels do drop their rates drastically outside the peak months of July and August. There's also a reasonable supply of **private accommodation**, particularly in the Old Town, which can be booked through the Ata Agency, just a few paces along from the tourist office at Njegoševa 16 (☎033/452 000, ⓦ www.budvatravelagency.com) – expect to pay €25–35 for a double room and €60–80 for a two-bed **apartment** at the height of summer. There are a couple of **campsites** (open June–Sept) in the vicinity of Budva, the most convenient of which is the small *Autocamp Budva* (☎033/458 923), a ten-minute walk from Slovenska beach on Velji Vinogradi. Some 2km north of town on the road out towards Tivat, there's the larger and more spacious *Jaz* campsite (☎033/451 699), located directly behind the beach of the same name.

Hotels

Aleksandar Trg Slobode ☎033/451 658, ⓦwww .budvanska-rivijera.me. This sprawling "village" complex at the southern entrance to town, located between the town's main beach (Slovenska plaža) and Jadranski put, is one of Budva's cheaper offer-

ings. The hostel-like rooms are minimally furnished but have a small stove and sink area. The complex incorporates a large number of more expensive apartments (€120). ⑥

 Astoria Njegoševa 4 ☎033/451 110, ⓦwww.hotelastoria.me. In a discreet location just inside the Old Town walls, this superb boutique hotel simply oozes class: the rooms, a mix of apartments and doubles, are supremely comfortable and beautifully designed, with funky furnishings, brilliant-white walls and ultra modern bathrooms. The rooftop terrace affords splendid sea views. ⑨

Blue Star Mainski put bb ☎033/451 612, Ⓦwww .montenegrostars.com. This self-styled business hotel, just down from the bus station, has good-sized and colourful (blue and gold star-patterned carpets) rooms, but they're nothing out of the ordinary. Guests can use the spa/pool facilities in the *Hotel Splendid* in Bečići free of charge (see p.77). ⑨

Grand Avala Mediteranska 2 ☎033/441 000, Ⓦwww.grandhotelavala.com. In a marvellous location on the beachfront just outside the Old Town walls, this gleaming glass edifice conceals large, handsome rooms with wood-panelled walls and an alluring chocolate-brown colour scheme. The hotel also has a vast complex of villas (not self-catering), accommodating between two and six people. In addition, there are three stunning pools, one of which juts out over the beach. ⑨

Grbalj Trg Sunca bb ☎033/452 300, Ⓦwww .hotelgrbalj.com. Just a short walk from the bus station, this small, quiet and unassuming hotel

is one of the most affordable places in town. The rooms are staid but clean, modern and reasonably well furnished. ⑤

Kangaroo Jadranski put bb ☎033/458 653, Ⓦwww.kangaroo.me. This neat little hotel (Australian owned in case you hadn't guessed), just off the main thoroughfare, possesses cool, airy rooms with lime-green walls and white-tile flooring, and spacious bathrooms. ⑦

Mogren Slovenska obala bb ☎033/451 102, Ⓔinfo@turizamcg.com. State-owned establishment that's a bit rough around the edges, but the rooms are adequate enough and it possesses a super location just outside the Old Town. ⑦

Olympic Mainski put 17 ☎033/455 106, Ⓦwww.hotelolympicbudva.com. Close to the bus station, this friendly place is the best budget option going. The rooms are basic but all have TV and a/c, and there are triples and quads available, too. ④

Vila Balkan Vuka Karadžića 2 ☎033/403 564, Ⓔvilabalkanbd@t-com.me. Along with the *Astoria*, this is the only place to stay in the Old Town. The *Vila* comprises five modern and reasonably-sized apartments, all with a small cooking area and good views over the harbour. Note that the rooms are actually above the *Hong Kong* restaurant, just around the corner from Vuka Karadžića. ⑦

The Old Town

If you're thirsting for a drop of culture, there's more than enough to keep you occupied within the confines of the **Old Town** (Stari Grad), perched on its own promontory to the west of the resort. Entirely Venetian in style and character, it's almost too spruce to be true – and in fact it is, having been almost entirely rebuilt following the 1979 earthquake. The huge **ramparts**, which enclose all but the sea-facing side of the Old Town, conceal a maze of cobbled streets and squares shined to a slippery buff, tightly packed ranks of houses tinted honey and red, and plenty of cafés, restaurants and boutique shops.

Trg Starogradski

The most obvious point of reference is **Trg Starogradski**, the largest of the Old Town's three squares, heavily scented with bougainvillea, palm and citrus fruit trees. It is home to no fewer than four ecclesiastical monuments, the biggest and most important of which is the sandy-coloured **St John's Church** (Crkva Sv Ivana). Rebuilt several times over (the last addition was the bell tower in 1867), its standout features are the mosaic altarpiece, depicting Christ being introduced to the people of Budva, and a twelfth-century icon entitled *Our Lady with Child* (known locally as "Our Lady of Budva"), housed in the Lady Chapel. Across the way, the early nineteenth-century **Church of the Holy Trinity** (Crkva Sv Trojice) has some well-preserved, though not particularly ancient, frescoes and a fine Baroque carved iconostasis. In front of the church is the grave of Budva's most famous writer, Mitrov Ljubiša (see p.74), while in between the two churches lie the scant remains of a Christian basilica, the date of which is unknown.

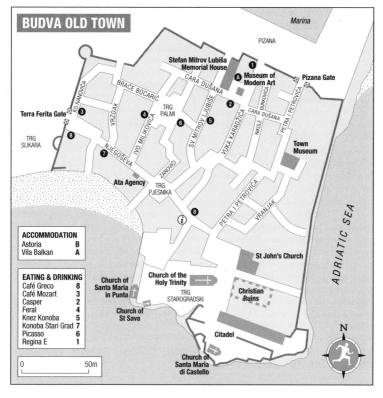

BUDVA OLD TOWN

Marina

PIZANA

Stefan Mitrov Lubiša
Memorial House

Museum of
Modern Art

Pizana Gate

BRAĆE BOCARIĆ

CARA DUŠANA

KO IVANOVIĆA

VRZDAK

Terra Ferita Gate

TRG
PALMI

IVO MILIKOVIĆA

SV MITROV LJUBIŠE

VUKA KARADŽIĆA

DUBROVNIK

CARA DUŠANA

NIKOLE

PETRA I PETROVIĆA

TRG
SLIKARA

NJEGOŠEVA

ZANOVIĆI

Ata Agency

Town
Museum

TRG
PJESNIKA

PETRA I PETROVIĆA

VRANJAK

ADRIATIC SEA

St John's Church

ACCOMMODATION	
Astoria	B
Vila Balkan	A

EATING & DRINKING	
Café Greco	8
Café Mozart	3
Casper	2
Feral	4
Knez Konoba	5
Konoba Stari Grad	7
Picasso	6
Regina E	1

Church of
Santa Maria
in Punta

Church of the
Holy Trinity

TRG
STAROGRADSKI

Christian
Ruins

Church of
St Sava

Citadel

Church of
Santa Maria
di Castello

0   50m

N

Over towards the far corner of the square stand two adjacent, and now derelict, chapels – the **Church of Santa Maria in Punta** and **Church of St Sava** (Crkva Sv Save), both of which were used by Napoleon as munitions stores following the French conquest of Dubrovnik in 1806. To the south of the square rises the substantial bulk of the **citadel** (Citedela; April–Oct 9am–7pm; €2, which includes access to the library), which dates from around the fifteenth century and offers splendid views from its raised terrace of the Adriatic and the collection of red and orange roofs of the town below. The citadel also houses a quite wonderful **library**, which holds an extensive collection of books – mostly nineteenth- and twentieth-century English editions – on the countries of the former Yugoslavia and the Balkans in general, including original versions of two early twentieth-century classics, Rebecca West's *Black Lamb and Grey Falcon* (see p.184) and Edith Durham's *Through the Land of the Serb*. There's also a copy of Petar Njegoš's *The Mountain Wreath*, arguably the most revered piece of literature to come out of the former Yugoslavia (see p.182).

(see p.184)

Along Njegoševa

Heading northwest from Trg Starogradski is **Njegoševa**, which is lined with numerous shops and a couple of cafés, and also houses the tourist office. About halfway along Njegoševa is **Trg Pjesnika** (Poet's Square), a quaint little space to the back of which a stone-arched gateway gives onto a shallow pebbly beach. Njegoševa winds up at the **Terra Ferita Gate**, one of the two original main entrances into the Old Town, the other being the Pizana Gate (see below). Exiting the Terra Ferita Gate, and over by the *Hotel Avala*, are the remains of an ancient Greek and Roman **necropolis** which, when the area was excavated in 1937, exposed a fantastically rich stash of grave goods (see below).

The town museum

Picking your way through a tangle of arched alleys will eventually bring you to the **town museum** (Grad muzej; Tues–Fri 8am–8pm, Sat & Sun 2–8pm; €2) at Petra I Petrovića 11, whose outstanding stockpile of archeological treasures was recovered from the town's Greek necropolis (see above) by the *Hotel Avala* following the 1979 earthquake. The museum's collection includes a superb array of ceramic vessels, plates and jugs, fibulae and military articles, the most important of which is an immaculately preserved Illyrian helmet. Trumping all this, however, is a dazzling hoard of gold jewellery, exquisite pieces of art ornamented with zoomorphic and floral motifs (a highly distinctive feature of Hellenic art), most impressively a brooch decorated with an eagle clutching a boy in its claws. Curiously, a Roman necropolis was uncovered on the same site, revealing some equally spectacular pieces – vessels and urns, terracotta figurines, and some extraordinarily well preserved glassware, the most eye-catching of which is a handful of variously coloured, miniature-sized amphorae. The remainder of the museum, essentially a modest ethnographic collection, is somewhat underwhelming, though its assemblage of nautical paraphernalia – instruments, costumes and the like – does a good job of portraying the town's illustrious maritime history.

Heading north of the town museum along Petra I Petrovića brings you to the town's northern entrance, the **Pizana Gate**, which faces the picturesque little marina.

The Museum of Modern Art and Stefan Mitrov Ljubiša Memorial House

Two streets away from the town museum, at Cara Dušana 19, the **Museum of Modern Art** (Moderna Galerija; Mon–Fri 8am–2pm & 4–8pm, Sat 4–8pm; free) is a bright space that mostly plays host to temporary exhibitions, featuring both local and national artists. A few paces away, at no. 15, stands the **Stefan Mitrov Ljubiša Memorial House** (Spomen Dom Stefan Mitrov Ljubiša; same times; free), which reflects upon the life and times of Budva's most prominent politician and writer, who was born here in 1822. A descendant of the indigenous Paštrovići clan (see p.79), Ljubiša championed long and hard for the rights of the local population in numerous treatises on various cultural and political issues – he later turned his hand to folksy short stories and poetry. He died, almost destitute, in 1878 in Vienna, before his remains were transferred to Budva several years later.

Beaches and activities

Budva's main **beach** (Slovenska plaža) curves round the bay from the Old Town to a headland that edges the resort of Bečići (see p.77). A long, fine, sandy stretch, with fairly shallow waters, it's absolutely crammed during the summer, which makes heading to one of the neighbouring beaches an appealing proposition. Facilities are reasonable, with lifeguards and showers dispersed at various intervals, while there are umbrellas (*suncobran*; €2) and loungers (*ležaljka*; €3) for hire all the way along. The beach also has a multitude of possibilities for activities on the water: the **Watersports Centre**, sited towards its southern end, offers jet skis (€60 for 30min), parasailing (€30 for one circuit of the bay), banana boats/rubber rings (€8 for 10min), as well as kayaks (€3 for 1hr) and pedaloes (€5 for 1hr).

The rocky coves around the cliffs just west of the Old Town make for a pleasant alternative to the bustle of Slovenska plaža. Accessed via a narrow concrete path which runs under the base of the cliff just beyond the *Grand Avala* hotel are two adjacent sandy beaches, **Mogren I and II**, which generally attract a slightly younger crowd. Lovely though these beaches are, best of all is the strand on the west (seaward) side of **Sveti Nikola Island** (known as Školj to the locals), which fronts the bay just offshore. Its heavily wooded cliffs shelter a long stretch of sand and pebble beach. During the summer, **water taxis** (€2.50) depart regularly from the marina by the Old Town, shuttling beach-goers back and forth.

Eating

The **restaurant** scene in Budva is pretty good, the majority of places not surprisingly accented towards freshly caught seafood. In addition to the places listed

△ Mogren Beach, Budva

below, there are also plenty of indistinguishable eateries – mainly pizzerias and fast-food joints – lining Slovenska and the streets behind. Most are open until midnight in the summer, and till 10pm the rest of the year. Expect to pay around €10 for a fish course with glass of wine for those restaurants listed here.

Demižana Slovenska obala 3. A beautifully shaded, palm-fronted terrace greets visitors at this upmarket fish restaurant which offers an appealing mix of the day's freshest fish (sea bass, bream, mullet) and shellfish (crab, lobster, oysters). Recommended.

Feral Trg Palmi. Appealing little fish restaurant with a lovely vine-covered terrace on an attractive Old Town square. The food is amongst the town's best, while the service is first class.

Jadran Slovenska obala 10. This eternally popular beachfront eatery has been doling out the town's finest fish and seafood (including crab and lobster), as well as some excellent Italian dishes, for years. The alternative to dining in the large, nautically themed interior is a table on the beach itself – lovely at sundown.

Knez Konoba Sv Mitrov Ljubiše bb. Tiny and homely bolthole in the heart of the Old Town, with just three tables inside and a couple out on the pavement. It's well regarded for its black risotto and mussels.

Konoba Stari Grad Njegoševa 14. Cosy, friendly and popular Old Town restaurant offering a superb selection of fish – squid, lobster and crayfish, to name just a few – while a good, filling meal for two is the mixed fish grill (€20 for two). Live guitar music most evenings, but best of all is the super little beach terrace out to the rear.

Picasso Trg Palmi. The food in this boisterous restaurant-cum-café is very simple (pizzas, sausages, omelettes, salads and the like), but its location, in a well-shaded, tree-filled courtyard is extremely pleasant.

Drinking and nightlife

Budva's **nightlife** is the liveliest and most diverse on the coast, and one of the reasons why it attracts such large numbers of partygoers. The more vigorous revelling tends to take place in various venues on Slovenska or just behind it on Mediteranska – along here during the summer, a string of open-air café-bars, complete with thumping music, strobe lighting and scantily clad dancing girls, vie for custom. Most cafés stay open until well into the early hours, typically 1 or 2am, and the clubbier places till 4 or 5am.

Cafés

Café Greco Njegoševa bb. Opposite the tourist office in the Old Town, this convivial bar has a fine stone terrace from which to sup a beer and kick back.

Café Mozart Njegoševa bb. Directly opposite the *Astoria* hotel, this is a café in two parts: a pleasant little hideaway tucked away just inside the Old Town walls and a vast terrace that spills out beyond in summer. Excellent cakes, ices, coffee and beer.

Casper Cara Dušana bb. Chilled hangout with a lovely tree-shaded garden and which, unusually for a café here, offers takeaway coffee.

Hemingway Mediteranska bb. Cool, large, glass conservatory-type building just across the road from the *Old Fisherman's Pub* that's slightly mellower than the other bars hereabouts.

Old Fisherman's Pub Slovenska obala bb. A few paces along from the *Jadran* restaurant, this heavily wooded, British-style venue (there's regular English football shown) offers good draught beer alongside pizza and other snack-type meals.

Regina E Vuka Karadžića bb. Positioned right next to the Pizana Gate, this smart place has good coffee and light snacks, and also possesses a large, bright, summery terrace just beyond the walls from where you can watch the shiny boats in the harbour.

Clubs

BK Club Popa Jola Zeca bb. Secreted away in the big building opposite the bus station, *BK* attracts a young (teens and early twenties) crowd but is tremendous fun and has live (rock and pop) music most nights.

Garden Café Mediteranska bb. The least pretentious of the bar/clubs also has the best and most diverse roster of live music – nightly during the summer, weekends out of season.

Hacienda Mediteranska bb. This hedonistic-sounding place is a fabulous good-time party venue, where you can also indulge in more sophisticated modes of dancing, like salsa.

Trocadero Mediteranska bb. Located on the opposite side of the building from *Hacienda*, it's another hugely popular dance venue, though not quite as much fun as the others.

Listings

Airlines JAT, Mediteranska 2 (☎033/451 662); Montenegro Airlines, Slovenska obala bb (☎033/451 735).

Banks There are numerous banks and ATMs along both Jadranska put and Mediteranska. Note that there's just one ATM in the Old Town, on Trg Pjesnika.

Car rental Europcar, 13 jula, Zgrada BSP (☎033/401 730); Gorbis, Slovenska obala bb (☎033/455 252, ⓦwww.gorbis.com); Kompas-Hertz, Mediteranska 7 (☎033/456 467); Meridian, Mediteranski sport centar (☎033/454 105, ⓦwww.meridian-rentacar.com).

Emergencies Ambulance (☎033/451 026); Fire (☎033/451 370).

Internet access During the summer, tented internet stalls are erected near the beach on Slovenska – otherwise, there's internet access available in the room below the *BK Club*, by the bus station (see opposite).

Left luggage There's a left-luggage office inside the bus station building (daily 6am–10pm; €2 for up to 24hr).

Pharmacies Stari Grad, Trg Pjesnika 5 (Old Town); Uniprom, Mediteranska 17.

Police Trg Sunca 5 (☎033/451 183).

Post office Just behind Slovenska at Mediteranska 8 (Mon–Sat 7am–8pm).

South to Bar

The strip of coast immediately south of Budva – often referred to as the **Budva Riviera** – has been intensively developed in recent years, and although the scenery is undoubtedly beautiful, you'll be hard pushed to escape the tourist hordes. Beyond the cramped resorts of **Bečići** and **Rafailovići** is delightful **Pržno**, from where it's a short hop to the coast's signature site, the island hotel of **Sveti Stefan**, at long last being restored to its former glory. Leaving Sveti Stefan, the scenery becomes even more alluring, and the resorts more strung out; chief amongst these is **Petrovac**, easily the prettiest and most relaxing hangout between Budva and Bar.

Bečići and Rafailovići

The first resort after Budva is **BEČIĆI**, whose long, sandy beach is backed by a dense concentration of fairly expensive **hotels**. Dominating all is the five-star *Hotel Splendid* (☎033/773 777, ⓦwww.montenegrostars.com; ⑨), whose grandiose, glittering lobby marks this out as the coast's most opulent establishment. Its understatedly elegant rooms are immaculately furnished and feature super-cool glass partitions between the bedrooms and bathrooms; superior facilities include a couple of gorgeous swimming pools and spa centre. Not far off in the glamour stakes is the *Queen of Montenegro* (☎033/662 662, ⓦwww.queenofmontenegro.com; ⑨), a short walk away on Narodnog fronta; another sprawling complex, this also has impeccably appointed rooms as well as a 24-hour casino.

Bečići blends imperceptibly into the smaller resort of **RAFAILOVIĆI**, whose fine sandy beach is extremely popular with families with young children. There's pretty cheap **accommodation** here in the form of the rather rudimentary but clean and generally efficient *Šumadija* hotel (☎033/471 003; ④), some 200m up from the beach. A particularly good **restaurant** along this stretch of coast is *Tri Ribara*, on the promenade above the beach; on its attractive, well-covered stone terrace, you can indulge in a wide variety of fish (mullet, sea bass, black bream) in addition to lighter fare such as cuttlefish salad and seafood risotto.

Pržno

Situated in its own sunny little cove just a couple of kilometres on from Rafailovići is **PRŽNO**, the most appealing of the resorts along this stretch of coast. Despite the presence of a major resort hotel, this erstwhile fishing village has managed to retain an easygoing, low-key atmosphere, with lots of white stone villas clustered around a small, very pleasant beach, lapped by clear, shallow waters. The roofless stone structure on the oversized rock just a short way out from shore – and which is allegedly some five hundred years old – once functioned as a refuge for local villagers who would flee here when under attack by raiders from the mainland.

Buses stop on the main road just above Pržno, from where it's a two-minute walk down to the *Maestral Resort* (☎033/410 109, ⓦwww.maestral.info; ⊙), a cumbersome orange brick building at the entrance to the village. It's actually an upmarket place with smart facilities, including its own tract of beach, a beautifully designed outdoor pool and a casino (open 24hr in the summer). There's further, albeit fairly expensive **accommodation** at the *Kažanegra Apartments* (☎033/468 429, ⓦwww .kazanegra.com; €90–140), Obala 12, which has variously sized, but all exceptionally comfortable, apartments in an old stone house perched on a cliff over the sea.

There are three extremely good **restaurants** in Pržno. Just across from the *Kažanegra Apartments* is *Blanche*, a cool, modern establishment with an appealing, bright white-stone terrace overlooking the sea; although its food is of an international bent, it has a strong Italian theme. For fish you should walk a few paces along to *Zago*, a small, family-run place whose brick interior, decorated with old photographs and pictures, gives it a distinctive local feel. Finally, in an old fisherman's house on the beach itself, there's *Konoba More*, a welcoming little tavern serving pasta, grilled meats, and freshly caught crab.

Miločer, Sveti Stefan and around

Pressed around a tiny red-coloured cove a short way south of Pržno, **MILOČER** gained its prestige thanks to the presence here of the former Yugoslav royal

△ Pržno

family's **summer palace**. Framed by cypress-fringed hills, the Palladian-style palace sits low and flat behind the fine shingle **King's Beach**, and surrounded by perfectly manicured lawns. It will eventually function as the *Hotel Miločer*, another first-class establishment.

Just around the headland from the palace is the coast's star turn – the fantastically picturesque village of **SVETI STEFAN**, images of which adorn much of the country's tourist literature. The island is perched on an outcrop of rock and joined to the mainland by a narrow isthmus which arcs out into two perfectly formed sandy beaches. Between the two world wars all its inhabitants left to seek work further up the coast, and their small, red-tiled stone houses – built in the fifteenth and sixteenth centuries – became derelict and uninhabitable. In the early 1950s it was decided to save the buildings, if not the town, by converting each of them into self-contained tourist suites. During Tito's reign, the resort played host to leading Communist apparatchiks, subsequently becoming a favoured holiday hideaway for monarchs and movie stars, such as Elizabeth Taylor and Richard Burton. Its decline in the 1990s mirrored the fortunes of the country in general, but it is soon due to reopen as a five-star *Aman* resort. Unless you are staying here, you'll have to pay a small fee for the privilege of wandering around the narrow cobblestone alleyways, sculpted gardens and tiny Greek Orthodox chapel – in any case, the island looks far more alluring from high above the shore. The **beach** to the left of the causeway is free, the one to the right is for the use of hotel guests only.

On a rise overlooking Sveti Stefan is **Praskvica Monastery** (Manastir Praskvica), consisting of the larger Church of St Nicholas, a neo-Gothic edifice built in 1847, and the neighbouring Church of the Holy Trinity, with seventeenth-century frescoes. It was within this complex that the children from the Paštrovići, a once semi-autonomous clan hailing from the nearby hills of the same name, were schooled.

Practicalities

Buses stop on the main road just above the village, from where it's a short, winding walk downhill to the beaches. There is plenty of **accommodation** here, though none of it in the budget range. About halfway down the hill leading to Sveti Stefan, at Vukice Mitrović 2, is the ☆ *Hotel Villa Montenegro* (☎033/468 802, ⓦwww.villa-montenegro.com; ◉), an impeccable (and very expensive) twelve-room villa. Most rooms, all of which are wi-fi enabled, have sea-view terraces (the views out to the Adriatic and of Sveti Stefan itself are unparalleled) and some have a kitchenette, while additional facilities include a smart outdoor pool, gym, jacuzzi and Turkish bath. Airport transfer (from either Podgorica or Tivat) is free if required. Directly opposite is the somewhat more affordable *Vila Drago* (☎033/468 477, ⓦwww.viladrago.com; ◉), a family-run venture which has half a dozen smart, airy and spacious rooms with balconies. Another very accomplished place is *Hotel Romanov* (☎033/468 452, ⓦwww.hotelromanov.com; ◉), further up the hill, which has beautifully designed rooms painted in either orange, lime-green or sky-blue tones. The one **campsite** hereabouts is the *Crvena Glavica Autocamp* (☎033/468 070; June–Sept), about 1km beyond Sveti Stefan; it's pretty basic, but the setting – a secluded, sloping olive-grove – does compensate somewhat.

Rijeka Reževića

A further 5km on from Praskvica is the pretty little village of **RIJEKA REŽEVIĆA**, capped by a diminutive stone church, from where a path through a forest leads down to a secluded sand and stone beach. On the opposite side of the road, under the bridge, is the *Izvor* **restaurant** (noon–midnight; closed Dec–Feb), a welcoming, family-run place well worth a visit for its diverse fish menu (fish pâté, clams, cuttlefish, squid and the catch of the day, which could be anything) and home-produced wine.

A kilometre further south and just a couple of kilometres shy of Petrovac, is the roadside **Reževići Monastery** (Manastir Reževići), whose main church, the Holy Trinity, was consecrated in the late eighteenth century. In contrast to the bright exterior, which features an elegant stone tower adorned with four arched windows on each side and a beautiful stone-carved rosette just above the entrance, the interior is rather sombre, painted with dark blue and burgundy frescoes. Adjacent is the smaller and older (it was originally thirteenth-century) Church of the Dormition, which has retained many of its frescoes and icons, notably a *Christ's Passion*. The monks here cultivate their own oil and honey, which you can buy from the little souvenir shop by the entrance.

Petrovac and around

Backing onto a magnificent crescent-shaped bay some 8km south of Sveti Stefan, **PETROVAC** is one of the coast's more laid-back and stylish resorts. Unblemished by unsightly hotels or other high-rises, it retains a tranquil air absent from many of the other resorts along this stretch of coast. A good time to be here is for the **Petrovac Jazz Festival** (ⓦ petrovacjazzfestival.tripod.com) at the end of August, a terrific three-day gathering featuring international-class acts playing on stages on the beach and by the fortress. Within striking distance of Petrovac is the lovely **Gradište Monastery**, which looks out over the expansive **Buljarica** beach, also an important birding habitat.

Arrival, information and accommodation

From the **bus station** at the top edge of town, it's a ten-minute walk down to the beachfront and the hub of all activity. **Internet** access is available at the nameless café next to *Molly's* Irish pub. There are several **hotels** in Petrovac, most of which are located just a stone's throw away from the beach. As in many places along this stretch of the coast, prices are hiked up considerably in July and August, in some cases almost doubled. By far the classiest place, though incredibly expensive, is the *Monte Casa* (ⓣ 033/426 900, ⓦ www.montecasa.com; ⓪), a sparkling new spa hotel located a few paces up from the western end of the promenade at the edge of a pine wood; the rooms are immaculate, with lots of smooth wood and cream-coloured furnishings, while the facilities (indoor and outdoor pools, saunas, whirlpool and gym) are first rate. At the opposite end of town, tucked away just behind the beach in its own bit of parkland, is the *Rivijera* (ⓣ 033/422 100, ⓦ www.riviera-petrovac.com; ⓪), which accommodates smart, colourful and well-equipped rooms; its impressive facilities include an outdoor pool with jacuzzi and tennis courts. Two slightly more affordable places (at least outside the peak summer months) are the rather down-at-heel *Castellastva* (ⓣ 033/461 321, ⓔ castellastva@t-com.me; ⓪; May–Sept), whose rooms are a little colourless and tired, but it suffices; and, across the road from the *Castellastva*, the *Palas* (ⓣ 033/421 100, ⓔ palassales@t-com.me; ⓪; April–Sept), another stern-looking building but which conceals bright, tidy rooms, some of which have sea-facing views.

The Town

The town's **beach**, formed of a reddish, gravelly sand, is backed by a tidy tree-lined promenade (Obala), framed with bleached white-stone buildings that house numerous restaurants and bars. Over to the north of the bay, the remains of a sixteenth-century Venetian **fortress** (Kastel Lastva) shelter the tiniest of harbours,

Coastal life

There are few stretches of coastline anywhere in Europe that can match the beauty and diversity of the Montenegrin littoral. Lively, fun-filled resorts, long strips of clean, sandy beach and a plethora of water-borne activities cater to those looking for good times, whilst Venetian-inspired towns, historic ruins and ancient monasteries will satisfy those thirsting for a drop of culture. Throw in a mouth-watering array of seafood and some terrific festivals, and the enchanting Montenegrin coast has got something for everyone.

Petrovac Beach ▲

Zorbing at Budva ▼

Old Town, Budva ▼

Life's a beach

If you're simply looking for a sandy beach on which to flop, then make a beeline for the resorts of **Petrovac**, **Buljarica** or **Pržno** (on Luštica), or for the **Velika Plaža** ("Great Beach"), near Ulcinj, which all boast long, fine stretches of strand perfect for chilling out. The more actively inclined, however, make straight for **Herceg Novi** or **Budva**, both of which offer an exciting complement of sea-borne pursuits: there's sea-kayaking around the picturesque Kotor Bay from Herceg Novi, while at Budva, Montenegro's major resort, there are great facilities for jet-skiing and waterskiing, as well as more unusual activities like banana boating and zorbing. With its open-air beach bars, Budva also boasts the coast's most buzzing nightlife. If you have young children in tow, meanwhile, the clear, shallow beaches at Pržno, **Kalardovo**, near Tivat, and **Bečići** are ideal, all offering safe swimming and lifeguard supervision.

A fine legacy

Having been occupied by, amongst others, Greeks, Romans, Ottomans, Venetians and Hapsburgs, it's little surprise that Montenegro's coast has been endowed with a wide range of architectural and artistic styles. The **Venetian** influence is perhaps strongest, and most clearly defined along the central and northernmost stretches, a territory they controlled for the best part of three centuries. Although substantially rebuilt following the 1979 earthquake, **Budva**'s fabulous Old Town retains vestiges of Venetian patronage; it pales in comparison with **Kotor**, however, whose streets and squares are stuffed with handsome Baroque and Renaissance palaces, stately buildings and elegant little churches. Similarly, **Perast** embraces an abundance

Seafood

One of the greatest coastal pleasures is sampling the fantastic seafood dishes available in the resorts' many fish restaurants. The Adriatic offers up an endless variety of fresh catch, with fish, shellfish and octopus forming the mainstay of most menus. One staple you'll find almost everywhere is squid (*lignje*), either fried or grilled; make sure you try **črni rižoto**, or black risotto, made with large chunks of squid soaked in its own black ink. Also emphatically not to be missed is **fish stew**, which combines sprats or anchovies with white wine, seasoned with celery, garlic and parsley.

▲ Fish restaurant, Perast

▼ Miločer

of sumptuous architecture, manifest in the crumbling palaces and mansions that once belonged to the town's sea captains. The Austrians' most enduring legacy, meanwhile, is the erstwhile island fort of **Mamula**, just offshore from Herceg Novi.

Although their influence was less pronounced along the coast than it was inland, the **Ottomans** still managed to build huge fortresses, such as the one at Herceg Novi, and construct numerous mosques, particularly in **Ulcinj** where there are now more than twenty – the town was also heavily influenced by Algerian corsairs who patrolled this part of the coast in the sixteenth century. The original wall fortifications of Ulcinj's Old Town meanwhile date from the time of the **Greeks**, who also held sway in Budva, as evidenced by a relatively recently discovered necropolis. The **Romans'** presence is felt most keenly in its former stronghold of **Risan**, where the one remaining villa holds some first-rate mosaics, while they also had a substantial hand in the development of **Stari Bar**. Finally, **Byzantine** influence can be experienced in much of the coast's ecclesiastical heritage, notably Orthodox

Velika Plaža ▲

Pržno beach, Luštica ▼

monasteries like **Gradište**, near Petrovac, and **Savina**, in Herceg Novi, both of which also contain some superb iconography.

Montenegro's top 10 beaches

▶ **Velika Plaža** The daddy of them all, the fine grey sands of the "Great Beach" stretch for some 12km from Ulcinj down towards the Albanian border. See p.90.

▶ **Pržno** This superb beach on the Luštica peninsula is deservedly one of the most popular along the entire coast, with gorgeous yellow sands, clean waters and excellent facilities. See p.69.

▶ **King's Beach, Miločer** Pristine shingle strand located just below the former Yugoslav royal family's residence. See p.79.

▶ **Sveti Stefan** Two shallow, arcing banks of sand either side of the narrow isthmus linking the mainland to this beautiful island. See p.79.

▶ **Pržno** Not to be confused with its namesake on Luštica, this sunny little bay embraces a delightful beach lapped by clear warm waters. See p.78.

▶ **Kalardovo** An idyllic little spot, just a short hop from Tivat, distinguished by its diminutive grey-gravel beach and calm, shallow waters. See p.69.

▶ **Sveti Nikola** Secluded island retreat featuring a tidy stretch of sand and pebble; the ideal place to enjoy a bit of peace and quiet. See p.75.

▶ **Petrovac** This characterful, gently arcing beach is known for its distinctive, reddish gravelly sand, and is extremely popular with families. See p.80.

▶ **Buljarica** Wide and exposed, this sweeping sand and pebble affair is backed by a large expanse of wetland, a haven for migrating birds. See p.81.

▶ **Valdanos** Beautifully sited in a horseshoe-shaped bay below a vast olive grove, this predominantly stone beach is ideal for a bit of seclusion. See p.89.

and a bronze relief records the names of those who perished in the two world wars. Just offshore stand two rocky outcrops, namely **Katič** and **Sveta Nedelja**, each adorned with a chapel, while around the headland at the southern end of the bay, there's another lovely, and far more secluded, beach by the cove at **Lučice**.

There's little in the way of cultural excitement here, but there is one curiosity to the north of town in the form of a well-preserved **mosaic**, thought to date from the time when Petrovac was an important route on the Roman road through the Adriatic. Although signposted (Kasnoantički Mosaik) from the centre, it's a little tricky to find, located as it is in someone's back yard; as a marker, use **St Toma's Church** (Crkva Sv Tome), which sadly now lies derelict and in a parlous state. From here, walk diagonally through the large tree-lined garden for about 100m and you'll see the dusty glass pavilion in which the mosaic is preserved. There are also a few other relics knocking about in the partially excavated yard.

Eating and drinking

There are some good **restaurants** lining Obala. The upmarket *Ambassador*, about 200m from the harbour, specializes in Russian cuisine – such as *borsch* (red-beet soup), *pelmeni* (meat-filled dumplings) with sour cream and *blini* (filled pancakes) – but it is the seafood that is truly outstanding: try sea bass, or dorada and shrimps coated in Tabasco and garlic. Another place worth trying, both for its seafood and its pasta, is *Fortuna*, positioned roughly halfway along Obala. **Drinking** mostly takes place along here, too, not least at *Molly's* Irish pub near *Fortuna*, with all the predictable trappings of a faux-Irish gaff; alternatively try *Kastello*, inside the fortress, which turns into a bit of a disco haunt at weekends.

Buljarica and Gradište Monastery

Barely 1km south of Petrovac begins the sweeping pebble and sand beach of **BUL-JARICA**, the longest between Budva and Bar at nearly 2.5km. The vast wetland adjoining the beach is interspersed with canals and reed beds, which makes it an important site for migrating birds such as the rare pygmy cormorant. There's fabulous **accommodation** and food at the *Montebay Villa* (☏033/401 656, ⓦwww.montebayvilla.com; ❸), just 100m from the beach; this striking stone-built villa possesses four beautifully styled rooms as well as two suites, while the very classy restaurant serves predominantly French cuisine. There's **camping** here, too, at the year-round *Maslina* campsite (☏033/402 648), just 200m from the beach.

Attractively perched on an outcrop at the foot of the Pelištice mountain, and commanding lovely views over Buljarica, **Gradište Monastery** (Manastir Gradište) comprises three churches atmospherically set amidst bright green lawns swept with olive and citrus fruit trees. The monastery's traumatic history has seen it plundered by the Turks in 1785, partially destroyed during both world wars, then substantially damaged during the 1979 earthquake (see box, p.85). The largest of the three churches – and the only one open for viewing – is **St Nicholas** (Crkva Sv Nikole), this incarnation erected at the end of the sixteenth century on the ruins of an older church. Many sumptuous frescoes, dating from around 1620, adorn the interior, the most significant of which are those of St Sava and St Simeon from the Serbian Nemanjić dynasty on the south wall (to the right as you enter); also of particular note are the throne icons representing St Nicholas and Christ – here, one particularly amusing painting stands out, that of the fifth saint in the bottom panel of the throne icon representing Christ, who has a donkey's head (the so-called "Holy Donkey"). A few paces away is the striking **Church of St Sava** (Crkva Sv Save), with its alternate bands of red- and white- trimmed stone, while completing the trilogy is the diminutive **Dormition of the Mother of God Church** (Crkva Uspenja Bogorodice), located up the steps behind St Nicholas. A distinctive feature of each church is its little bell tower with an open windowpane. If you're coming by car take the turn-off from the main road (it's signposted) and park at the small car park, from where it's a fairly stiff ten-minute walk up; if travelling by bus ask the driver to drop you off on the main road at the turning up to the monastery.

Sutomore and around

Continuing south from Buljarica, the road runs below ranges of sharp-summited mountains, green and blue under thin vegetation. A couple of kilometres to the south of **Čanj**, a low-key resort with a wide, open beach popular with families, the remains of two Turkish castles sit grafted onto the grey rocks high above the road. Known as Haj ("Fear") and Nehaj ("No Fear") – collectively **Haj-Nehaj** – they were built by the Turks as protection against Montenegrin raids on their trading caravans. Unfortunately, though not surprisingly, their prominent and rather improbable location means that they are inaccessible.

Immediately south of Haj-Nehaj is **SUTOMORE**, a small, rather down-at-heel resort strung out along a long sand and pebble beach. It is at its quietest, least congested and most agreeable at the southern end. Sutomore is also where the **Sozina road and rail tunnels** emerge; the former, some 4189m long, was completed in 2005, and has cut the journey from Virpazar on Lake Skadar to the coast by some 45 minutes – the other route passes over the mountains and emerges at Petrovac; the toll is currently €3.

Sutomore's **train station** sits just above the main road (which itself is just above the beach); here you'll find a small **tourist office** (daily 9am–5pm) and the **bus stop**. Sutomore has some **accommodation** possibilities, open between April and September only, and while the hotels are mostly old and uninspiring, they're much cheaper than anything else going in the neighbouring resorts. The overly conspicuous white block at the beginning of the main promenade, Obala Iva Novakovića, is the hotel *Nikšić* (℡030/373 422, @htl-niksic@t-com.me; ❺); its rooms are old-fashioned, but all have TV, a/c and balcony. Two hundred metres further along Obala is the *Motel Puki* (℡030/307 084; €20 per person), a very basic but clean hostel-style place with tiny rooms (and shared shower facilities) sleeping between two and five people. At the southern end of the resort, just below the road and rail lines, is the *Zlatna Obala* (℡030/313 780, @zlatnaobala@t-com.me; ❹), a sprawling hillside complex housing small, dark rooms. The town also has a good stock of **private accommodation** (❷–❸), on which the main tourist office can advise (there's a good booklet available) but cannot make any bookings. There's nowhere of any note to **eat**, so just take your pick from the range of pizzerias and snack-type joints along the promenade.

Bar and Stari Bar

As Montenegro's only port and the coast's main transport hub – road, rail and ferries all converge here – **BAR**'s importance as a transit point far outweighs anything the town has to offer from a tourist perspective. It is possessed, however, of one heavyweight attraction in the shape of the ancient ruins of **Stari Bar**, which lie just 5km away. Through the centuries, Bar has been variously ruled by Byzantines, Venetians and Ottomans, though there's next to nothing to show for this. Its current layout is a result of the 1979 earthquake (see box, p.85), after which it was renewed and revamped, its importance consolidated around the same time upon completion of the rail route to Belgrade. In a major development that will further strengthen Bar's transport links, the town is scheduled to be the southernmost point of the proposed highway linking the coast to Belgrade.

Arrival and information

The **train station** is some 1.5km southeast of town, and the **bus station** 200m further along the road – it's a dull thirty-minute trudge into town, so a **taxi** (€2–3) is a more appealing option. Alternatively you could wait for the bus that loops between town and Stari Bar (see p.84), though there are no set times. From the **ferry terminal**, it's just a 200-metre walk straight ahead through the palm-tree-filled park to the **tourist office** on Obala 13 jula (May–Sept daily 8am–9pm; Oct–April Mon–Sat 8am–8pm; ☎030/312 912, ⓦwww.visitbar.org), which has a good range of maps and brochures; there's also a small, rather limited tourist office inside the train station but it keeps rather peculiar hours (daily 7–11am & 7–10pm). The **post office** is at Jovana Tomaševića 44 (Mon–Sat 7am–8pm), and there's **internet** access at Multiprint on Vladimira Rolovića; tricky to find, it's opposite the Robna Kuča store (itself just 200m east of the shops and super-markets) and above the *Samba* sign. **Car rental** is available from Kompas, Jovana Tomaševića 24 (☎030/602 680, ⓦwww.kompas-car.com), and Meridian, Jovana Tomaševića 30 (☎030/314 000, ⓦwww.meridian-rentacar.com).

Accommodation

Bar town possesses several **hotels**, by far the best (and most expensive) of which is the *Princess*, Jovana Tomaševića 59 (☎030/311 013, ⓔinfo.princess@azalea-hotels.com; ⑨). This classy waterfront establishment has plush rooms with ultra-modern fittings, including large, wall-mounted plasma screens, while its

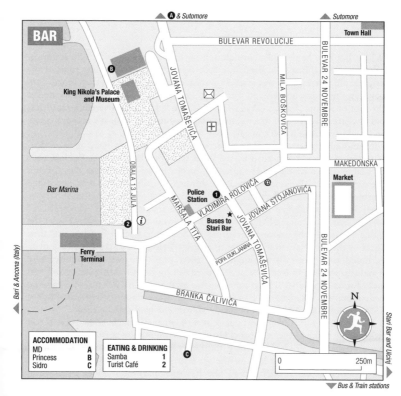

BAR

▲ **A** & Sutomore ▲ Sutomore

Town Hall

BULEVAR REVOLUCIJE

JOVANA TOMAŠEVIĆA

MILA BOŠKOVIĆA

BULEVAR 24 NOVEMBRE

B

King Nikola's Palace and Museum

OBALA 13 JULA

MAKEDONSKA

Market

Bar Marina

Police Station **❶**

VLADIMIRA ROLOVIĆA @

JOVANA STOJANOVIĆA

MARŠALA TITA

❷ ⓘ ★ Buses to Stari Bar

JOVANA TOMAŠEVIĆA

Ferry Terminal

POPA DUKLJANINA

BULEVAR 24 NOVEMBRE

◀ Bari & Ancona (Italy)

BRANKA ĆALIVIĆA

N

Stari Bar and Ulcinj ▶

ACCOMMODATION	
MD	A
Princess	B
Sidro	C

EATING & DRINKING	
Samba	1
Turist Café	2

C

0 — 250m

▼ Bus & Train stations

myriad facilities include indoor and outdoor pools, plus fitness and massage studios. Somewhat more down-at-heel is the *Sidro* (☎030/312 200, ✉sidro@lukabar. t-com.me; ❸–❹), in a barren location on Obala (no number) some 300m south of the ferry terminal; although basic, the rooms are clean, tidy and air-conditioned. Finally, about 1.5km west of town, just off the road towards Sutomore, the *MD* hotel (☎030/305 124, ✉malisic.d@t-com.me; ❺) is a decent if unspectacular place with bright, minimally furnished rooms; they've also got some triples and quads.

The Town

Backed by a precipitous coastal range, the town is largely an unengaging mishmash of modern building and oily docks. The one site of note is **King Nikola's Palace** (Palata Kralja Nikole), located on the waterfront about 200m north of the tourist office in the area known as Topolica. Modelled on the Blue Palace in Cetinje (see p.118), this rather unassuming building was constructed in 1885 as a residence for Nikola, then later given to his daughter, Zorka, and her husband, Petar Karađorđević, as a present. Recently renovated, it now houses the town's **Historical and Archeological Museum** (daily May–Sept 9am–2pm & 6–8pm; Oct–April 9am–2pm; €2). It's a small but rich collection, holding fragments (mosaics, pillars and stones) from Stari Bar, Venetian ceramics from the fifteenth and sixteenth centuries, and numerous amphorae dredged up from the Adriatic. Upstairs, the rooms have been reconstructed as per the time of King Nikola, complete with late nineteenth-century furnishings and costumes, and display an impressive array of Turkish battalion flags.

Stari Bar

Whilst Bar may be devoid of antiquities, it's just a short bus ride 5km southeast of town to **Stari Bar** (Old Bar; daily 8am–8pm; €1), the crumbling ruins of the original old town which was severely damaged during a nineteenth-century scrap between the Montenegrins and Turks. Access to the site, spectacularly located at the foot of Mount Rumija (1594m) and surrounded by hills covered in centuries-old olive trees, is free, but it is worth buying the brochure available at the entrance (€1), which will help you navigate your way around.

It is thought there was a settlement here as early as 800 BC, which (more certainly it's known) was demolished by the Romans in the third century BC in favour of a larger urban centre closer to the sea, on the site of present-day Bar. Around the sixth century, Emperor Justinian established a fortified tower here, and in the tenth century it assumed the name Antinbaris (as in, opposite the Italian city of Bari). In time it emerged as one of the Adriatic's key political and economic centres, its citizens earning a living from crafts, olive oil and the salt trade. Under the Balšić dynasty in the fourteenth century the town was further fortified, and then again by the Venetians in the sixteenth century, before the Turks assumed power. Although the majority of the buildings – there were once over two hundred here – and surrounding bulwarks were destroyed during fierce fighting between Turks and Montenegrins in 1878, and the massive earthquake in 1979 put paid to what little there was left, a number of key buildings were rebuilt or renovated in the 1980s. Funds soon dried up, however, and little else has been done since.

The first point of interest you come to is the open-air stage, a few paces across from which is the former **Customs House**, now among the most complete buildings. It holds a photographic display illustrating just how much damage was caused by the earthquake, particularly to the western part of the town; at the heart of this area once stood **St Nicholas's Church**, a small portion of which remains and

The 1979 earthquake

Whilst the Balkans, and in particular the eastern Adriatic seaboard, are no stranger to **earthquakes**, none in modern times has had as devastating an impact as the one that hit Montenegro on **April 15, 1979**. Registering 7.1 on the Richter scale, the epicentre occurred somewhere between Bar and Ulcinj. The centres of both these towns were ravaged – including the total collapse of a couple of large hotels in Ulcinj – as were the ancient ruins of Stari Bar close by, which were already in a rather parlous state. The historic old-town cores of both Kotor and Budva also suffered heavy damage, while the impact of the quake was felt as far up the coast as Herceg Novi, where parts of the old town walls collapsed into the sea. Nor was the interior spared, though damage to buildings and properties in Podgorica, Cetinje and Nikšić was relatively light in comparison. Just over one hundred people lost their lives in Montenegro – in addition to another thirty-five across the border in Albania – with an estimated one hundred thousand left temporarily homeless. Although reconstruction began apace, it was fully ten years before the Budva and Kotor old-town areas were restored to something like their former selves.

displays some remarkable Byzantine-era frescoes. From here it's a short climb up to the **Old Citadel**, from where there are lovely views of the valley dropping sheer below – across the way stands the almost completely rebuilt seventeenth-century **aqueduct**, a pretty seventeen-arch structure with a channel and pipes along its upper surface. To the east is a cluster of neatly restored buildings, including **St John's Church**, the **main palace** (now an art studio) and, behind this, **St Venerande's Church**, traces of whose fourteenth-century original were discovered during reconstruction. Just below here, at the heart of the complex, are the splendidly restored **Turkish baths** (*amam*) and the completely rebuilt **clocktower**.

Buses depart for Stari Bar (every 15min in summer, hourly during the rest of the year; €1) from the bus stop on Jovana Tomaševića in the modern town.

Eating and drinking

Bar town is pretty much devoid of anywhere decent to **eat**. The only worthwhile place is the *Samba* restaurant, on the corner of Jovana Tomašiveća and Vladimira Rolovića (daily 7am–midnight), with standard fish and grill dishes; otherwise there is a smattering of samey pizzerias along Vladimira Rolovića. The best place for a **drink** is the *Turist Café*, a large glass-fronted pavilion in the small park right opposite the tourist office.

In **Stari Bar**, along the cobbled street sloping down from the entrance to the ruins is the delightful and colourful little *Kaldrma* restaurant (daily 10am–10pm). Its timber-framed ceilings, low wooden seats, cushions and rugs make you feel as if you've just stepped into someone's living room, and the food, all organically cultivated, is exceptional, and includes olive bread, sheep's cheese and *japrak*.

Ulcinj and around

The most southerly town on the Montenegrin coast, **ULCINJ** (Ulqin in Albanian) is immediately different from anywhere to the north. The Venetian influence that is dominant from the northernmost reaches of the coast down to Bar is absent here, and Ulcinj, just 18km shy of the Albanian border, has a marked oriental flavour. This is little surprise given that more than eighty percent of the population is

Albanian – Turkish-style houses huddle around the bay in the cramped Old Town and up in the surrounding hills, and there are no fewer than 26 mosques in town. Beyond the Old Town and beachfront, the centre is a pleasantly incoherent maze of traffic-clogged streets lined with a ragbag assortment of shops and cafés. Whilst Ulcinj is not exactly flush with sights, its distinct Muslim character and excellent nearby beaches make it well worth a day or two of your time.

Some history

A settlement was founded here some time around the fifth century BC by Greek colonists from the erstwhile Georgian state of Colchis, as evidenced in the enormous "Cyclopean Walls" – immense blocks of stone – that still form part of the Old Town fortifications. Captured by the Romans from the Illyrian Olchiniata tribe in the second century, it was recast as Olcinium, later evolving into a key maritime centre, initially under the domain of the medieval Serbian state of Raška, then the Balšić dynasty in the mid-fourteenth century. The Venetians came to Ulcinj in 1405, ruling until 1571 when the town was taken over by a party of Algerian **corsairs** – survivors of the great naval battle of Lepanto – led by Bey of Algiers, Uluz Azi. For the next three centuries it was home to a mixed bag of pirates, thieves and merchants – Algerian, Moroccan and Turkish buccaneers who plundered shipping in the Adriatic and Mediterranean, burnt towns and generally did as they pleased. In particular, famous pirates such as Ali Hodža and Lika Ceni earned notoriety for their daring raids on merchant ships belonging to Venetian and Dalmatian towns. Gradually these corsairs adopted Albanian-style customs and formed a wholly Muslim town, which it has largely remained to this day. A flourishing black **slave trade** emerged, too, the main port of export being Tripoli in North Africa, from where children as young as three or four were purchased; there are still a handful of families of African descent in Ulcinj today.

Although liberated from the Turks in 1878, when the town was virtually reduced to rubble, Ulcinj didn't actually accede to Montenegro until two years later, following numerous drawn-out squabbles over territories in the region. Until World War I, the town maintained a healthy fleet of ships, with many of its inhabitants employed in the shipyards that once stood beneath the Old Town. The 1979 earthquake (see box, p.85) destroyed much of the rebuilt town again while, more recently, in 1999, Ulcinj provided refuge for thousands of Kosovars who had fled Kosovo following NATO's intervention in the province. The town's population doubled in a matter of days and there were few households in Ulcinj that did not take someone in; whilst most returned following the end of the conflict, some remained.

Arrival, information and accommodation

The **bus station** is on Bulevar Vellazerit, a five-minute walk east of the main drag, Bulevar Skenderbeu. There is, as yet, no tourist office in town. There are numerous options for checking the **internet** along Bulevar Skenderbeu, including places above the *Avanti* and *Zeppelin* cafés, and another next to the *Grand* restaurant (see p.88). The **post office** is on Majka Tereza (Mon–Sat 7am–8pm).

The town is reasonably well served with **hotels**, the best of which is the *Mediteran Resort*, a ten-minute walk up from the beach on Hafiz Ali Ulqinaku (T030/403 124, W www.hotel-mediteran.com; ⑥–⑧) – renovated and with a completely new wing, it has accommodation in various categories, though all rooms are clean, smart and well presented. Over in the Old Town, housed in neatly trimmed white-stone buildings, are the *Dvori Balšića*, and its twin, the *Palata Venezia* (both T030/421 457, E realestate@t-com.me; suites only ⑨). From both the sea views are terrific, though the suites (with dining area and kitchenette) are a little grey and gloomy, and fairly pricey for what is on offer. A more modern alternative is the very pleasant *Dolcino*, Hafiz Ali Ulqinaku bb (☎030/422 288, ⑩www.hoteldolcino.com; ⑥), whose big, colourful and smartly furnished rooms provide excellent value for money. About 1km east of town, in a pine wood above a couple of small cove beaches (including a naturist one), the *Albatros* (☎030/423 266, ⑩www.albatros-hotels.com; ⑥) is a large, rather dated establishment with pretty average rooms, but it's one of the cheapest options in town. For **camping**, you'll have to head to Valdanos (see p.89), Velika Plaža (see p.89) or Ada Bojana (see p.89).

The Town

Ulcinj today has precious little to show for its ancient history, although the **Old Town**, sited high up on some cliffs to the southwest of town, retains vestiges of its colourful past. Largely destroyed during the earthquake in 1979, the citadel, embraced within its thick reinforced walls, is for the most part a dilapidated ruin, though there are now a couple of hotels and a clutch of restaurants here. There is also the **town museum** (Grad muzej; May–Sept daily 8am–noon & 5–9pm; Oct–April Mon–Fri 8am–2pm; €1), a small complex of three buildings clustered around the old slave market, often referred to as the Square of Slaves. The first of them, the fourteenth-century **church-mosque**, whose minaret was unceremoniously chopped off leaving an enlarged stub, keeps numerous archeological

---

Street names

Street names in Ulcinj can be somewhat confusing: many have dual names (in Serbian and Albanian), and some are still referred to by their old Serbian names; this is particularly the case on what few maps of the town exist. Some of the key ones are: Bulevar Maršala Tita, now Bulevar Skenderbeu; Ulica Milutinovića, now Ulica Hafiz Ali Ulqinaku; Ulica Nikole Đakovica, now Ulica 28 Decembar; Bulevar Bratstva Jedinstva, now Bulevar Vellazerit; and Đura Đakovića, now Ulica Mehmet Gjyli.

curiousities– Illyrian earthenware, Greek and Roman pottery, cathedral pillars and Turkish tombstones. Across the way is the **Balšić Tower**, a chunky stone edifice which, save for the odd art exhibition, usually stands empty; the tower is notable, however, for the two altars on its top floor, where the seventeenth-century Jewish dissident and passionate advocate of Talmudic reform, Sabetha Sebi (Sabbatai Cevi), used to come and pray in secret. Housed in the third building is the **ethnographic collection**, featuring the standard hunting and fishing exhibits and local folk costumes. More interesting are the amphorae and several Turkish displays, notably the mock-up Muslim living room with a *sofra*, a low circular table around which people would kneel and eat. It's also worth asking to have a look inside the ground floor of the museum's office building (near the entrance), where a maquette illustrates how the citadel looked prior to the earthquake. More curiously, etched into the walls are drawings of boats – the etching just inside the entrance is thought to be some four hundred years old – which would indicate that this was once a dwelling place for pirates.

The **Cathedral of St Nicholas** (Catedrala Sv Nikola), a rare concession to the Christian faith hereabouts, stands just to the west of the citadel, its lawns carpeted with rows of lovely olive trees – interestingly, the church was rebuilt as such in 1890, having previously functioned as a mosque. Arcing below the citadel is the gunmetal-grey town **beach** (Mala Plaža, or "Small Beach"), which is very pleasant but gets extremely crowded in the summer – for that reason alone you're better off heading to the vast expanse of the Great Beach (Velika Plaža), south of town (see p.90).

It's a short walk down from the citadel to the **Pasha Mosque** (Pažina Džamija), designed by Ali Pasha I in 1719 and the only mosque in the country with a working *amam*. The minarets are conspicuously shorter here than elsewhere, the result of reconstruction following damage from the earthquake. Heading further towards the heart of town, the next mosque you come to is the **Namazdjah Mosque** (Namazdjah Džamija), built in 1828 and complete with a fine-looking clocktower. Beyond here, the **Bregut Mosque** (Bregut Džamija), built by the sea captain Ahmed Djuli in 1783, is the largest of the lot. On Tuesdays and Fridays, the indoor food **market** opposite the Bregut Mosque is well worth a browse for its vast and colourful selection of fruit, vegetables, nuts and honey, while vendors along the parallel street, 28 Decembar, hawk clothes and various other bits of junk.

Eating, drinking and nightlife

Ulcinj has a small but decent selection of **restaurants**. The finest, both for its setting and food, is the sophisticated *Grand*, on Bulevar Skenderbeu, which has some imaginative fish dishes such as black ravioli pasta with squid, and shrimps with cognac and tomato, in addition to a particularly fine steak menu; the nightly pianist adds to the overall classiness of the place. Some 300m down the same road, *Manhattan* is a cosy little upstairs trattoria with big bay windows, serving good fish grills and steaming plates of pasta; just across the road, the slightly more polished *Sidro* serves similar dishes. Close to the *Mediteran Resort* on Hafiz Ali Ulqinaku, *Aragosta* is a welcoming little local with heavy wooden tables and benches, and fishing nets strung along the walls – the fish here, too, is top notch, in particular the seafood spaghetti. There are few places to eat in the Old Town beyond a couple of pizzerias.

There is no shortage of places to **drink** in town, the most popular venues in the summer being the beach bars hidden among the trees on the headland to the south of Mala Plaža, mostly frequented by bronzed young bloods. Take your pick from exotically named venues such as *Ibiza*, *Solara di Mar* and *Tropicana* – they're all similarly riotous. The glass-fronted cafés behind Mala Plaža do brisk trade in the

△ Velika Plaža

summer, too. There are also several places to dance down by the beach, notably the open-air *Mediteran* **club**, on a platform underneath the Old Town. Outside the summer months, most drinking occurs in the bustling little cafés along Skenderbeu.

Around Ulcinj

There are several appealing excursions to be had in the outlying vicinity of Ulcinj, though you will need your own transport to reach them. To the north, the lovely **Valdanos** bay offers restful seclusion, while to the south, stretching all the way towards the Albanian border, is the vast expanse of the **Velika Plaža** ("Great Beach"), at the end of which sits the predominantly naturist island resort of **Ada Bojana**, worth visiting for its superb fish restaurants alone. Heading inland, nature asserts itself in the shape of **Lake Saško**, a wild, isolated spot popular with fishermen and ornithologists.

Valdanos

Six kilometres north of Ulcinj, a side road descends through the coast's largest sanctuary of olive groves to **Valdanos**, a delightfully secluded horseshoe-shaped bay with a stony beach backed by neat rows of slender pine trees. It's not the best place for swimming, but is a lovely spot for a picnic and does possess a small **campsite** (☎030/402 402; May–Sept) with basic amenities, including hot showers.

Milena Canal and Ada Bojana

Four kilometres south of Ulcinj is the **Milena Canal** (Porto Milena), dug in 1885 on the orders of Prince Nikola, and named after his wife, Princess Milena. Crossing the bridge, you'll see clusters of wooden huts on stilts in the water, from which large nets are lowered into the shallow lakes, an age-old technique called *kalimera*.

Just beyond the canal begins the immense expanse of **Velika Plaža** (Great Beach), whose fine grey sands – which are mildly radioactive (though perfectly safe), and thus apparently attractive to arthritis sufferers – run right down to the Albanian border, some 12km away. Although one long unbroken stretch, Velika Plaža is actually divided up into several individual beaches, each with exotic names such as Copacabana, Tropicana, Neptun and Safari; signposts along the main road clearly indicate the turn-off for each one. Velika Plaža is backed by rows of maquis and pine trees, while the tract of land between here and the main road, known as **štoj**, is spread with fields of melon-beds. Beyond here, on the other side of the road, lie the **saltpans** (Ulcinjska solana), where a limited amount of salt extraction still takes place today; it's also an important sanctuary for migrating birds, including cormorant, Dalmatian pelican and occasionally flamingo. For camping round here, there is the large, open *Neptun* **campsite** (☎030/412 941; May–Sept), situated by the beach of that name.

Connected to the mainland by a bridge, the tiny, triangular-shaped islet of **Ada Bojana** sits at the mouth of the **River Bojana** (Buna in Albanian) on the Albanian border. Much of this flat and sandy accretion, bordered on two sides by the Bojana and the Adriatic on the other, is given over to a nudist colony and (non-naturist) campsite (☎030/411 351), but it does offer relaxing walks amongst the greenery that fronts the beach. In summer, **water taxis** offer one-hour trips (€5) around the island and up the coast to Ulcinj. There are also several excellent fish **restaurants** here, mostly serving identical dishes. The best and most characterful of these is ⁂ *Kod Miška* (☎069 022 868; reservations advisable; daily 10am–11pm), whose dishes are amongst the finest on the coast – they offer superb fish soup, an exquisite fish appetizer (a mix of black risotto, octopus, prawns and fish paste) and any number of grilled or oven-baked fish mains such as mullet, sea bream or sea bass. Partly positioned on a pontoon, the restaurant's warm and smartly decorated interior also features a rather cool, upturned hull of a boat.

Vladimir and Lake Šasko

By the petrol station at the southern entrance to Ulcinj, signposts point the way to **VLADIMIR**, some 18km distant, where three roads branch off in different directions: one heads north over the mountains to Lake Skadar, another to Sukobin and the border with Albania, and a third down to **Lake Šasko** (Šasko jezero). Connected to the Bojana River, this small and wild freshwater lake has abundant fish stocks, and is also home to numerous species of bird, such as stork, heron and cormorant. There's a well-regarded (unnamed) **restaurant** (daily 8am–midnight) just a couple of hundred metres from the lake, easily identifiable by its sturdy stone-built stilts, so designed to prevent it from sinking into the marsh. Close by lie the scant ruins of the sixth-century medieval city of **Svač**, originally a fortified Illyrian settlement but finally laid to waste by the Ottomans in the sixteenth century.

Travel details

Trains

Bar to: Bijelo Polje (4 daily; 3hr 30min); Kolašin (4 daily; 2hr 30min); Mojkovac (4 daily; 3hr); Podgorica (7 daily; 1hr); Sutomore (7 daily; 10min); Virpazar (10 daily; 25min); Vranjina (10 daily; 35min).

Buses

Bar to: Budva (every 1hr–1hr 15min; 1hr 15min); Herceg Novi (10 daily; 2hr 30min); Kotor (8 daily; 1hr 45min); Nikšič (1 daily; 2hr 30min); Petrovac (every 1hr–1hr 15min; 40min); Podgorica (7–8 daily; 1hr 45min); Pržno (every 1hr–1hr 15min; 1hr); Sveti Stefan (every 1hr–1hr 15min; 55min); Tivat (9 daily; 1hr 30min); Ulcinj (7 daily; 30min).

Budva to: Bar (every 1hr–1hr 15min; 1hr 15min); Cetinje (every 30min; 1hr); Herceg Novi (every 30min–45min; 1hr 15min); Kotor (every 30–45min; 30min); Nikšič (12 daily; 1hr 45min); Petrovac (every 1hr–1hr 15min; 25min); Podgorica (every 30min; 1hr); Pržno (every 1hr–1hr 15min; 10min); Sveti Stefan (every 1hr–1hr 15min; 15min); Tivat (every 30–45min; 30min); Ulcinj (3 daily; 1hr 30min).

Herceg Novi to: Bar (6 daily; 2hr 30min); Budva (every 30min–1hr; 1hr 15min); Cetinje (every 45min–1hr 15min; 1hr 15min); Kotor (every 30min–1hr; 45min); Nikšič (8 daily; 2hr 15min); Perast (every 30min–1hr; 30min); Podgorica (every 45min–1hr 15min; 2hr); Risan (every 30min–1hr; 25min); Tivat (every 1hr–1hr 30min; 1hr).

Kotor to: Bar (6 daily; 1hr 45min); Budva (every 30min–1hr; 30min); Cetinje (every 45min–1hr 15min; 1hr); Herceg Novi (every 30min–1hr; 45min); Nikšič (8 daily; 2hr 15min); Perast (every 30min–1hr; 15min); Podgorica (every 30min–1hr; 1hr 30min); Risan (every 30min–1hr; 20min); Tivat (7 daily; 20min); Ulcinj (2 daily; 2hr).

Petrovac to: Bar (every 1hr–1hr 15min; 40min); Budva (every 1hr–1hr 15min; 25min).

Pržno to: Bar (every 1hr–1hr 15min; 1hr); Budva (every 1hr–1hr 15min; 10min).

Sveti Stefan to: Bar (every 1hr–1hr 15min; 55min); Budva (every 1hr–1hr 15min; 15min).

Tivat to: Bar (4 daily; 1hr 30min); Budva (every 45min–1hr; 30min); Cetinje (every 45min–1hr 15min; 1hr 15min); Herceg Novi (7 daily; 1hr–1hr 30min); Kotor (6 daily; 20min); Lepetane (Mon–Sat hourly, Sun every 2hr; 15min); Nikšič (3 daily; 2hr 15min); Podgorica (every 45min–1hr 15min; 1hr 30min); Radoviči (Mon–Sat 7 daily, Sun 3; 45min); Ulcinj (1 daily; 1hr 45min).

Ulcinj to: Bar (6 daily; 30min); Budva (3 daily; 1hr 30min); Herceg Novi (3 daily; 2hr 45min); Kotor (3 daily; 2hr); Podgorica (6 daily; 2hr); Tivat (3 daily; 1hr 45min).

International trains

Bar to: Belgrade (3 daily; 9–11hr).

International buses

Bar to: Belgrade (1 daily; 3hr 30 mins); Dubrovnik (1 daily; 10hr).

Budva to: Belgrade (8 daily; 8hr); Dubrovnik (2 daily; 2hr 15min); Sarajevo (2 daily; 6hr); Split (3 weekly; 5hr 30min).

Herceg Novi to: Dubrovnik (2 daily; 1hr); Split (3 weekly; 4hr 30min).

Kotor to: Belgrade (8 daily; 8hr); Dubrovnik (3 daily; 1hr 45min); Sarajevo (1 Friday; 6hr); Split (2 weekly; 5hr 20min).

Tivat to: Belgrade (8 daily; 8hr); Dubrovnik (3 weekly; 1hr 30min); Sarajevo (2 weekly; 6hr); Split (3 weekly; 5hr).

Podgorica, Cetinje and around

CHAPTER 2 # Highlights

* **Café life, Podgorica** Kick back and enjoy a beverage or two in one of the capital's many convivial outdoor cafés and bars. See p.104

* **Birdwatching on Lake Skadar** There are some outstanding birdwatching opportunities on the Balkans' largest lake, including the magnificent and rarely seen Dalmatian pelican. See p.109

* **Wine** Looming over Lake Skadar's western shore, the Crmnica hills are where Montenegro's finest wines are harvested, most notably the ubiquitous Vranac – try some in the village of Godinje. See p.111

* **Cetinje** Check out the fascinating museums and admire the fine architecture of Montenegro's laid-back and unassuming former royal capital. See p.112

* **Lovćen National Park** Hike through the rocky slopes of Lovćen, visit Njegoš's grand mausoleum, and admire the glorious views down to the Bay of Kotor. See p.120

* **Rijeka Crnojevića** A wonderfully relaxing spot, this quaint little fishing village is renowned for its delightful stone-arched bridge and the excellent fish sourced from the river that flows through its heart. See p.119

▲Triple-arched bridge, Rijeka Crnojevića

2

Podgorica, Cetinje and around

As the country's commercial, cultural and political heart, pretty much everything converges in **Podgorica**, yet with a population of just under 150,000 – which comfortably makes it one of Europe's smallest capital cities – it retains a distinctly languorous and provincial air. After its almost total destruction during World War II and the rash of unsightly postwar redevelopment that followed, there's little in the way of genuinely exciting sights – hence it's not really a place to linger, and most people don't. However, its location close to both the coast and mountains, and standing as the country's main transport hub, means that you're quite likely to touch base with the city at some point. From Podgorica it's a short journey south to lovely **Lake Skadar**, the largest body of water in the Balkans; as one of the most important birding sanctuaries in southeastern Europe, it's a haven for ornithologists. There's plenty of culture to take in here, too, with island monasteries and the ruins of a couple of ancient fortresses.

In stark contrast to Podgorica, **Cetinje**, 30km to the west, has been endowed with a rich cultural and historical legacy – largely thanks to its one-time status as the country's capital until Podgorica took over the reins in 1948. An almost timeless air pervades this somnolent little town, and its clutch of stately buildings and first-rate museums make it an obvious and enjoyable day-trip, either from the capital itself or from the coast. Moreover, you don't have to venture far from town to sample some of Montenegro's marvellous natural heritage: rugged limestone **Lovćen National Park**, just a stone's throw away, affords ample if not particularly strenuous walking opportunities, though for most people its chief draw is the mausoleum of poet-prince Petar II Petrović Njegoš, which sits atop Jezerski vrh, one of the park's two highest peaks. Njegoš's birthplace is just outside the park in the idyllic village of **Njeguši**, which lies on the Cetinje–Kotor road, as spectacular a route as any in the country.

If you've got wheels, a worthwhile detour just off the road between Podgorica and Cetinje – and easily reachable from either – is the picturesque little fishing village of **Rijeka Crnojevića**, known for its pretty stone-arched bridge.

There are regular **buses** from Podgorica to both Cetinje and Lake Skadar and a **train** service between Podgorica and Lake Skadar, but to reach the other places covered in this chapter you'll have to rely on your own transport.

Podgorica and around

Situated in the centre of the fertile Zeta Plain and encircled by barren-crested karst mountains, **PODGORICA** (meaning "Under the Hill"), is a thoroughly modern city, having been almost completely rebuilt after World War II. In her 1940s masterpiece, *Black Lamb and Grey Falcon*, Rebecca West described Podgorica as a city "built without eloquence", and it's a fair bet that West would have been no more impressed by its current incarnation. The hasty redevelopment that followed in the aftermath of World War II left a characterless agglomeration of high-rise flats, distinguishable only by their flat pastel colours, and this drabness is evident almost everywhere you go in the city. That said, the cramped little **Old Town** quarter does retain vestiges of the city's Ottoman past and is worth an afternoon's stroll.

There is further respite from the concrete uniformity in the form of the **Morača River**, which slices its way through the heart of the city, as well as in the odd splash of greenery. A more concerted gloss has been applied in recent years, with glass-and-steel office blocks sprouting up alongside spruced-up public spaces and small shopping precincts. And despite the obvious lack of tourist infrastructure – expensive, business-oriented hotels predominate – the city wears its sociability well, manifest in a tight concentration of choice restaurants and a vibrant drinking scene. Moreover, its relatively central location means that nothing is really that far away – both Lake Skadar, to the south, and the magnificent mountain interior to the north, are less than 45 minutes away, while you can be cooling off down by the coast within an hour. During the summer, Podgorica is one of the hottest cities in the Balkans, with temperatures often touching forty degrees – another reason to make a beeline for the more obvious attractions just a short dash away.

Some history

A settlement of sorts has existed around here since the first century BC, during which time it is known that two Illyrian tribes, the Docleates and Labeates, inhabited the valley of the Zeta River around 3km north of the city, and proceeded to engineer the city of **Doklea**, which grew under the Romans to become an important trading post; extensive remains of the city can still be seen today. Following the decline of the Roman Empire and repeated sackings by Goths and Slavs in the fourth and fifth centuries, Doklea was well and truly put to the sword by a catastrophic earthquake around 518, and attention turned to the nearby smaller settlement of **Birziminium**, which had been built by the Romans as a stop on the caravan route. Birziminium, on the site of the present-day city, assumed the name **Ribnica** in the tenth century under its new Slav settlers, after the river on which it was established.

The name **Podgorica** first appeared in documents in 1326, and the town developed into a key trading post along the route between Ragusa (present-day Dubrovnik) and the state of Nemanjići, in Serbia. The Ottomans eventually reached Podgorica in 1474, precipitating four centuries of **Turkish rule** during which time the city was heavily fortified (only a few grubby remains are left of the fortress) and established itself as an important military centre. Yet despite the ensuing Islamization of the city, there's relatively little left to show for it, save for a couple of mosques, a clocktower and a bath house.

With the decline of the Ottoman Empire, in 1878 the city was annexed into Montenegro proper. This paved the way for a period of economic and cultural advancement, with the establishment of banks and the first commercial company (a tobacco plant) and the foundation of hospitals, schools, libraries and media institutions. At the end of **World War I**, during which time the city was occupied by Austro-Hungarian forces, Montenegro was incorporated into the **Kingdom of**

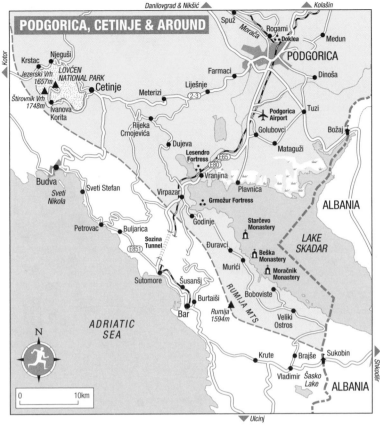

Serbs, Croats and Slovenes – recast as the **Kingdom of Yugoslavia** in 1929. But with political power firmly centred in Belgrade, the de facto capital of Yugoslavia, Podgorica was unable to realize any tangible measure of autonomy.

Bombed to oblivion during **World War II** by the Allies – the Italians and Germans had established a command here – Podgorica underwent a rapid rebuilding programme that was a gesture of the new nation's pride as much as anything else. The city was also declared the administrative capital of the Socialist Republic of Montenegro on July 13, 1948 – thus relieving the old royal capital, Cetinje, of the honour – and renamed **Titograd**, in honour of Josip Broz Tito, chief commander of the Partisan resistance movement and, subsequently, president of the Yugoslav Federation.

In 1992, just as Yugoslavia was about spectacularly to implode, the city's name reverted to **Podgorica** (some twelve years after Tito's death). Although the city suffered few of the traumas that befell its neighbouring capitals – in particular Belgrade, Sarajevo and Zagreb – during the Bosnian wars it wasn't immune to the severe economic hardship that devastated the region following the imposition of sanctions. And despite its generally healthy relationship with Belgrade, Podgorica still resented the degree to which it remained in tow to the Serbian capital. All that changed on June 3, 2006, when thousands converged on Trg Republike to celebrate the country's official declaration of **independence**. Several years on, the city is gradually transforming itself into a modern, self-sustaining European capital.

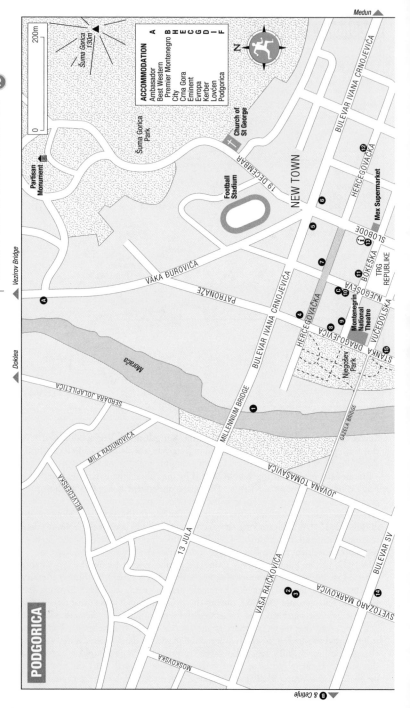

PODGORICA

ACCOMMODATION

Ambasador	A
Best Western	B
Premier Montenegro	H
City	E
Crna Gora	C
Eminent	G
Evropa	G
Kerber	D
Lovćen	I
Podgorica	F

Šuma Gorica 130m

200m

0

Šuma Gorica Park

Partisan Monument

Medun

Church of St George

Football Stadium

NEW TOWN

19 DECEMBAR

VAKA ĐUROVIĆA

PATRONAŽE

BULEVAR IVANA CRNOJEVIĆA

BULEVAR IVANA CRNOJEVIĆA

HERCEGOVAČKA

HERCEGOVAČKA

Mex Supermarket

SLOBODE

BOKEŠKA

NJEGOŠEVA

TRG REPUBLIKE

DRAGOJEVIĆA

VUČEDOLSKA

STANKA

Montenegrin National Theatre

Njegošev Park

Morača

Veziriv Bridge

Doklea

MILLENNIUM BRIDGE

GAZELA BRIDGE

SERDARA JOLAPIJELIĆA

MILA RADUNOVIĆA

BELVEDERSKA

13 JULA

JOVANA TOMAŠEVIĆA

VASA RAIČKOVIĆA

SVETOZARA MARKOVIĆA

MOSKOVSKA

BULEVAR SV

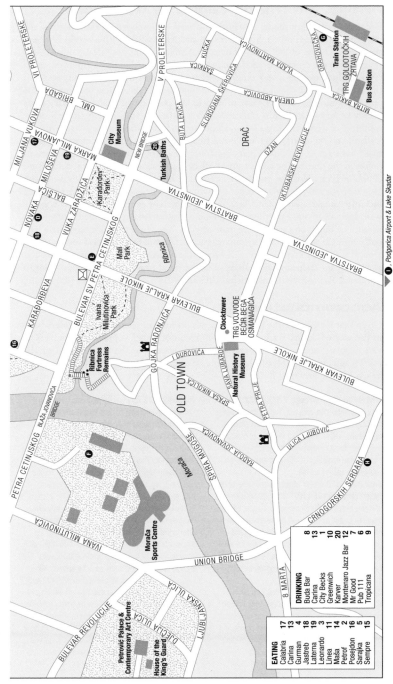

Podgorica Airport & Lake Skadar

Train Station

TRG GOLOOTOČKIH ŽRTAVA

Bus Station

ORAHOVAČKA ⓖ

VLADA MARTINOVIĆA

OMERA ABDOVIĆA

MITRA BAKIĆA

VI PROLETERSKE

V PROLETERSKE

KUČKA

ŠARKIĆA

SLOBODANA SKEROVIĆA

BUTA LEKIĆA

City Museum

MILJANA VUKOVA

MARKA MILJANOVA ⑰

OML. BRIGADA

I BRIGADA

NOVAKA

BALŠIĆA

MILOŠEVA ⑲

DRAČ

DŽAN

OKTOBARSKE REVOLUCIJE

NEW BRIDGE

Turkish Baths ⑳

Karadordev Park

VUKA ZARADŽIĆA

ⓓ ⑱

Ribnica

BRATSTVA JEDINSTVA

BRATSTVA JEDINSTVA

Mali Park

ⓔ

KARAĐORĐEVA

BULEVAR SV PETRA CETINJSKOG

Ivana Milutinovića Park

⊠

BULEVAR KRALJE NIKOLE

GOJKA RADONJIĆA

Clocktower

TRG VOJVODE BEĆIR BEGA OSMANAGIĆA

Ribnica Fortress Remains

ⓕ

I ĐUROVIĆA

SAVA LUBARDE

Natural History Museum

SPAŠA NIKOLICA

OLD TOWN

PETRA PRLJE

BULEVAR KRALJE NIKOLE

PETRA CETINJSKOG

BLAŽA JOVANOVIĆA

BRIDGE

Morača

RADOJA JOVANOVIĆA

SPIRA MUGOŠE

ULICA LJUBOVIĆ

CRNOGORSKIH SERDARA

ⓗ

IVANA MILUTINOVIĆA

Morača Sports Centre

UNION BRIDGE

8 MARTA

BULEVAR REVOLUCIJE

Petrović Palace & Contemporary Art Centre

House of the King's Guard

DEČIJA ULICA

LJUBLJANSKA ULICA

EATING
Calabria	17
Carina	13
Gurman	4
Jastreb	18
Laterna	19
Leonardo	3
Linea	11
Maša	14
Petrof	2
Posejdon	16
Sarajka	5
Sempre	15

DRINKING
Buda Bar	8
Carina	13
City Becks	1
Greenwich	10
Karver	20
Montenaro Jazz Bar	12
Mr Good	7
Pub 111	6
Tropicana	9

Arrival, information and city transport

Podgorica's small but modern **airport** is located in Golubovici, 11km south of the city. Amenities are limited, but the major car hire companies have booths here and there are a couple of ATMs. Montenegro Airlines' flights are met by minibus for transfer into the centre – even if you're travelling with a different airline you could try your luck getting a seat on one. Otherwise, there's no public transport from the airport into the city, and so your only option is a taxi – these wait outside the terminal building, with a set fare of €15 to any point in the centre. The city's **bus** (*autobuska stanica*) and **train** (*željeznička stanica*) stations are adjacent to each other southeast of town on Trg Golootočkih žrtava, from where it's a twenty-minute walk along Okotobarske revolucije and Bratstva jedinstva into the centre – alternatively, minibus #6 (€0.50) departs from opposite the bus station, stopping at various points in the centre. The city's **tourist office** is at Slobode 47 (Mon–Fri 8am–8pm; ☏020/667 535, ⊛www.podgorica.travel). The helpful staff here can advise on any aspect of the city, as well as other attractions in the region, and there's plenty of literature to take away, including a free city map. The centre of Podgorica is easily walkable and in any case the city's public transport system is limited, with just a handful of **bus** routes serving the main arteries. The few attractions there are in the outlying areas are not served by public transport. If you require a **taxi** expect to pay around €0.50 per kilometre, or €3–4 for a ride across the centre. Taxis can be found at ranks by the train and bus stations and outside the *Crna Gora* hotel, but it's best to call ahead. Reliable companies include PG Taxi (☏9704) and City Taxi (☏9711).

Accommodation

Given that it's well off the tourist track, it's no surprise that Podgorica offers little in the way of decent accommodation in terms of either volume or variety. The vast majority of the city's **hotels** are aimed squarely at the business end of the market and only a couple of places could be termed mid-range. All the places listed below include breakfast in the price.

Ambasador Vaka Đurovića 5 ☏020/272 233, Ⓔvb-ambasador@t-com.me. This squat, concrete building perched just above the Morača River, a ten-minute walk north of Trg Republike, contains just three double rooms and six suites – they're comfortable enough, if a little cramped, and it's somewhat overpriced. ❼

Best Western Premier Montenegro Bulevar Sv Petra Cetinjskog 145 ☏020/406 500, ⊛www.bestwestern-ce.com/montenegro. Located around 1km out to the west of town in the new business area, this is by far the most comfortable (and expensive) hotel going – warm, open rooms complete with big beds, large plasma TV screens and oak bureaux. There's wi-fi in the lobby but surprisingly few other facilities. ❾

City Crnogorskih serdara 5 ☏020/441 500, Ⓔrecepcija@cityhotel-montenegro.com. A short way south of the centre, this spanking new hotel has well-sized, appealingly presented cream and beige rooms, with plentiful furnishings including armchairs, big plasma TVs and wi-fi. ❻

Crna Gora Bulevar Sv Petra Cetinjskog 2 ☏020/634 271, ⊛www.hotelcg.com. This large, Communist-era hotel holds a clutch of modern, comfortable rooms alongside its older grey, uninviting ones, all at a range of prices. ❼–❽

Eminent Njegoševa 25 ☏020/664 545, ⊛www.eminent.me. This small and very pleasant central hotel comprises six smart, modern double rooms and seven apartments, all colourfully furnished; they're fairly priced, too. ❻

Evropa Orahovačka 16 ☏020/623 444, ⊛www.hotelevropa.me. This rather overpriced place offers neat if somewhat boxy rooms, but has the advantage of being just a few paces from the train station. Some of the rooms overlook the tracks, though relatively few trains pass by anyway. ❼

Kerber Novaka Miloševa 6 ☏020/405 405, ⊛www.hotelkerber.me. This is comfortably the most pleasant of the city-centre hotels (despite its inauspicious location at the end of a small shopping arcade): warm, modern rooms with sunny yellow and green decor, cool, low-slung beds and jacuzzi showers. They've also got laptops and DVD players for hire. ❽

Lovćen Petrovački put bb ☎020/625 219, ⓦwww.hotellovcen.me. Dour, old-fashioned place on the main road in from the airport, about 3km shy of town. It's convenient if arriving late or leaving early, however, and also the cheapest option going. ⑤

Podgorica Bulevar Sv Petra Cetinjskog 1 ☎020/402 501, ⓔrecepcija@hotelpodgorica@t-com.me. Sited on the banks of the River Morača, this unsightly concrete and stone structure actually conceals fresh, good-looking rooms – they're spacious, bright and designer-furnished, with big bathrooms. ⑦

②

The City

Podgorica's sights can be more or less divided up into two areas either side of Bulevar Sv Petra Cetinjskog, the city's busy east–west thoroughfare. To the north of here is the **New Town**, which is essentially the main commercial district, while to the south is the **Old Town** quarter, containing vestiges of the city's Ottoman past.

The New Town

The hub of the **New Town** (Nova Varoš) area, and the geographical and social heart of the city, is Trg Republike, a busy and energetic if not particularly charming square. Laid out around and beyond Trg Republike in an orderly grid-like system are the city's main shopping and commercial streets, principally Slobode – which becomes something of a *korzo* after 5pm when it's closed to traffic – Hercegovačka, the main pedestrianized shopping avenue, and Njegoševa, bursting with pavement cafés and bars.

The City Museum

A short walk east of Trg Republike at Marka Miljanova 4 is the **City Museum** (Grad muzej; Tues–Fri noon–8pm, Sat & Sun 9am–2pm; €2). The museum posseses the standard collection of archeological finds (bronze and copper pots, jewellery and glass fragments) and medieval weaponry – much of which was retrieved from Doklea (see p.106) – but the most stimulating part of the exhibition is the **ethnographic section**, in particular a lovely display of eighteenth- and nineteenth-century national folk costumes. Invariably richly coloured and embroidered, the most luxurious of these garments was the *jelek*, a short, sleeveless, unbuttoned leather jacket, underneath which a *džamadan*, a lavishly decorated red vest with silk braids, would normally be worn. Weapons – typically a pistol, rifle or *yataghan* (Turkish dagger) – were deemed requisite to any Montenegrin costume; though ostensibly carried for reasons of self-defence, in reality they were worn for ornamental purposes. *Opanak*, distinctively shaped leather slippers usually with a horn-shaped ending, were the most common form of peasant footwear in the region, and are still worn in some rural areas today. Look out, too, for some beautifully woven rugs patterned with colourful motifs, as well as the collection of nineteenth-century icons and some finely crafted ecclesiastical embroidery.

The city bridges

A short walk west of Trg Republike along Bulevar Ivana Crnojevića, is the striking **Millennium Bridge** (Most Milenijum), linking the centre to the expanding residential district to the west. Although a recent addition to the city's architectural landscape – it was only built in 2005 – the bridge, a 140-metre-long, cable-stayed structure, immediately assumed the mantle of city symbol, albeit for lack of anything else. During the summer, townsfolk flock to the shallow shores and cool waters of the Morača below to seek much-needed respite from the sweltering heat. Around 1.5km further up the river is the **Vezirov Bridge** (Most Vezirov), this one

△ Millennium Bridge, Podgorica

having replaced the original which was blown up by retreating Germans during World War II. These days the bridge is the setting for the spectacular Morača River Dives competition each July (see p.105).

The Church of St George and Šuma Gorica

Back on Bulevar Ivana Crnojevića, a short walk north up along 19 Decembar and past the football stadium, is the diminutive **Church of St George** (Crkva Sv Đorđe), the only church of any historical note in Podgorica. A simple, sixteenth-century structure adorned with nineteenth-century icons, the church sits at the foot of **Šuma Gorica**, a fir-tree covered hill popular with walkers and runners. En route to the top, you'll pass a monument to Partisan soldiers, a cumbersome white block sheltering a black marble tomb; the inscription, in Cyrillic, simply says "Partisan Soldiers".

The Old Town

Bounded on two sides by the Morača and Ribnica rivers, and on the other by the traffic-choked thoroughfare of Bulevar Kralja Nikole, is the **Old Town** (Stara Varoš) area, formerly the city's Muslim quarter. From the Blaža Jovanovića Bridge, steps lead down to the water's edge and the confluence of the two rivers. Spanning the Ribnica is a small sixteenth-century **stone-arched bridge**, on the other side of which lie the messy and ovegrown remains of the old **Ribnica Fortress**; it's difficult to believe now but an enormous castle, erected by invading Turks in 1474, once stood on this site. Beyond here you can pick your way through a tangle of narrow cobbled streets lined with stone-walled houses into the Muslim quarter where a couple of small **mosques**, Glavatovici and Osmanagiči, remain.

Emerging on to the small Trg Vojvode Bećir bega Osmanagića, you are confronted with the eighteenth-century **clocktower** (Sahat Kula). Standing some thirty metres high, it is the city's most complete remnant from the Ottoman period, and despite being totally at odds with the chaotic modern surroundings, the tower (which doesn't actually have a clock) stands its ground quite admirably. On the west side of the square, the **Natural History Museum** (Prirodnjački muzej; Mon–Fri 9am–noon; free) doesn't contain very much at all, but if you've got fifteen minutes to spare, then take a peek inside at the stuffed birds and amphibians from Lake Skadar. The clocktower aside, the most significant Ottoman landmark is the old **Turkish Baths** (Amam), secreted away under the New Bridge (Novi most) in the Ribnica River gorge a ten-minute walk east of the Old Town – a set of steps next to the bridge leads down to them. In order to accommodate the bridge, the city planners decided to lop the roof off, but it's survived to become a thriving little cultural centre, incorporating a bookshop, gallery and café (see p.105).

West of the Morača River

Across the Morača River from the Old Town – you can either cross at the Union Bridge (Most Union) or walk down Ivana Milutinovića from Bulevar Sv Petra Cetinjskog – is Podgorica's most inviting building, the **Petrović Palace** (Dvorac Petrović). Located in one of the city's few leafy areas, this unassuming and slightly weathered peach-coloured building was the one-time residence of Duke Mirko Petrović Njegoš, father of King Nikola I Petrović (see box, p.114). It now houses the **Contemporary Art Centre** (Mon–Fri 9am–2pm & 4–9pm, Sat 10am–2pm; €3), comprising a modest selection of twentieth-century Montenegrin art, a smattering of African and Asian works and – usually most worthwhile – a series of rotating exhibitions. The adjacent **House of the King's Guard** (Perjanički dom) also stages various temporary shows.

Eating

Podgorica has a pretty good range of **restaurants**, plenty of which serve decent local and national cuisine. Top-notch seafood is particularly popular, while another regular staple is the delicious *Njeguški pršut* (air-dried ham). Expect to pay around €8–10 for a two-course meal with a glass of wine. Most restaurants are air-conditioned, which is a blessing given that smoking is permitted just about everywhere (some establishments do have no-smoking sections) and the heat can be stultifying during the summer. The majority of the city's restaurants are fairly well dispersed around the New Town area, though the choicest ones are located a short walk west of the Morača River.

The best choice for quick-fix **snacks** is the handful of kiosks along the south side of Trg Republike, selling *burek*, *pljeskavica*, hotdogs and the like; there's also great cheese- and meat-stuffed *burek* at *Sarajka*, Ivana Crnojevića 133. For post-drinking munchies, try *Gurman*, on the corner of Hercegovačka and Stanka Dragojevića (open till 5am). Another good option for light snacks are the many bakeries (*pekara*) scattered about town, serving freshly prepared bread, sweet and savoury pastries and strudels; one of the best is *Jastreb* at Slobode 32 (Mon–Sat 6am–11pm, Sun 6am–2pm). There are several well-stocked **supermarkets** around town, the best of which are the one in the basement of *Carina* (Mon–Sat 7am–10pm, Sun 7am–1pm; see p.104), and Mex, just across the road on the corner of Slobode and Vukova (Mon–Sat 6.30am–11pm, Sun 6.30am–1pm).

Restaurants

Calabria Marko Miljanova 61. Modelled on a traditional *konobar*, this agreeable and welcoming piz-

zeria has a barn-like, medieval-style interior with stone-flagged flooring, chunky wooden bench seating and lanterns. The thin-crust pizzas are the best in town and there's a decent choice of grilled meat plates, too. There's no signage, so it's tricky to find: look out for the two lanterns hanging outside. Mon–Sat 8am–midnight, Sun 1pm–midnight.

Carina Slobode 43. Part of a hugely popular conglomeration also comprising a café (see below), pizzeria and bakery, the modern restaurant (located upstairs to the rear of the complex) offers fresh fish, local meats (the Njeguški steak is terrific) and Italian dishes. It can, though, get a little noisy given its proximity to the neighbouring café section. Daily 10am–11pm.

Laterna Marko Miljanova 41. Located just 100m down from *Calabria*, and not dissimilar in appearance, with heavy stone flooring, wooden beams and lamps. In addition to the standard pizzas and pastas, the comprehensive menu (in English) offers an impressive variety of local dishes including flat-bread sandwiches, mixed and stuffed kebabs, grilled trout and some fabulous local cheeses. Not as smoky as *Calabria*. Mon–Sat 9am–midnight.

Leonardo Svetozara Markovića bb. Ignoring the bizarre location amidst a jumble of apartment blocks, this place comes highly recommended. Located just off Vasa Raičkovića, it's worth the walk not only for its accomplished international menu – grilled salmon, roast lamb, paella, blue cheese and walnut gnocchi, aubergine and prawns, to name just a few dishes – but also for the warm, homely interior (colourful walls adorned with pottery) and personable service. Daily 8am–midnight.

Linea Trg Republike 22. Cool, contemporary restaurant which, though styled as a pizzeria, offers much more, including cold soups, salads and chicken and pork dishes. The upstairs section is a more casual and café-like, while downstairs in the cellar the smartly laid tables and white-cloth-backed chairs lend an air of formality to proceedings. There's outdoor seating, too. Daily 8am–midnight.

Maša Bulevar Sv Petra Cetinjskog 31, a ten-minute walk west of the centre. If seafood is your thing, then this smart yet informal place is the business – it offers the full gamut of top-end fish possibilities (perch, sole, red mullet, scorpion fish), though for those on a more modest budget, there's plenty else to choose from, including pasta, risotto and schnitzels. Afterwards, you can pop downstairs for coffee and cake in the cavernous glass-covered café. Daily 7am–midnight.

Petrof Svetozara Markovića bb. Next door to *Leonardo*, and similarly classy, the food here is weighted more towards seafood (seafood salad, risotto with octopus). The small but pleasant interior is softly lit and stylishly furnished, and there's a cool, shaded terrace to dine out on. Daily 8am–midnight.

Posejdon Stanka Dragojevića 8. Although it advertises itself as a fish restaurant – the shellfish lamps and nets strung over the walls are a bit of a giveaway – there's more to the menu than eel, squid and bass, such as the gut-busting Karađorđje steak (rolled pork steak stuffed with cheese). Daily 11am–11pm.

Sempre Stanka Dragojevića 14. Just a few paces down from *Posejdon*, this small, welcoming and most enjoyable restaurant is deservedly popular with visiting foreigners. Homemade pasta is the speciality of the house, in particular ravioli, gnocchi and black spaghetti. Mon–Sat noon–11pm.

Drinking

Podgorica's young folk are enthusiastic, sociable drinkers, and staying out late is very much the civilized thing to do. The city's **cafés** are fairly boisterous affairs, many doubling up as evening bars. The most popular ones are concentrated within a small area embracing Hercegovačka, Njegoševa and Stanka Dragojevića and, with a few exceptions (noted below), the majority stay open until around 2 or 3am. **Live music** is generally confined to the odd bar, with flyers indicating what's on.

Cafés and bars

Buda Bar Stanka Dragojevića 26. Largest, loudest and hippest of the city's bars, this swanky venue, with tall wooden tables and stools, and low-slung red velvet chairs, draws a good-looking crowd. Regular DJ nights liven things up even further.

Carina Slobode 43. The café section of this large complex (see above), popular with both young and old, incorporates a loungey upstairs seating area and a sprawling pavement terrace. The deliciously creamy cakes from the downstairs parlour are worth sampling. Mon–Sat noon–11pm.

City Becks Stanka Dragojevića. This atmospheric summertime-only bar down by the river (accessed via steps through Njegošev Park) is little more than a wooden deck, with lounge seating and a stage for concerts, but it's a rocking good place for an evening out.

Greenwich Njegoševa 27. The most characterful of several hugely popular bars lining this street; hence it's usually rammed. *Greenwich* is also one of the better places to catch live music (typically jazz, blues and Latino) and there are regular party nights here, too.

Karver Obala Ribnice bb. This mellow, quirky little hangout, housed inside the city's old Turkish bath house by the Ribnica River, is equally enjoyable for a daytime coffee or evening beer. There's occasional live music (usually jazz) and readings, as well as a good bookshop (see below). Daily 9am–11.30pm.

Montenaro Jazz Bar Hercegovačka 85. One of the few places in the city to catch quality live music, though the schedule is erratic. If there's no gig on, it's a relaxing place to kick back for a quiet, contemplative drink.

Mr Good Hercegovačka 33. Pleasant if slightly anaemic-looking bar, which is always busy and has a good selection of beers on tap, including Nikšičko. Mon–Sat noon–11pm.

Pub 111 Bulevar Ivana Crnojevića 99. The central feature of this funky two-floored pub-cum-bar is a row of saloon-style train compartments, each one with its own TV screen. The good-time atmosphere is further cranked up with nightly DJs.

Tropicana Bokeška 16. Just across from the National Theatre, this simple place draws a mix of arty types and business people, and is ideal for a spot of contemplative drinking.

Entertainment

The **Montenegrin National Theatre** (Crnogorsko Narodno Pozorište), adjacent to the City Hall at Stanka Dragojevića 18 (☎020/664 085), is the country's premier cultural institute. It stages a reasonable diet of theatrical shows and classical music concerts, including the city's premier music festival, **A Tempo**, a series of piano-oriented classical concerts featuring both domestic and international musicians that takes place over ten days in April. The only city-centre **cinema**, Kultura, at Marko Miljanova 64, is a small affair; films are usually shown in their original language and subtitled. Aside from A Tempo, the city's most enjoyable event is the **Morača River Dives** (Skokovi sa Vezirovog mosta) competition each July, where divers of world-class repute compete in dramatic plunges from the Vezirov Bridge, north of town.

Shopping

There are few **shopping** areas of note in the centre itself, although a wander up and down Hercegovačka, Njegoševa and Slobode might yield the odd find; these are, however, mostly boutique-type shops, selling a classier brand of shoes and clothing. There are a handful of good **bookshops**, the most interesting of which is Karver (daily 9am–10pm), housed inside the old Turkish bath house (see p.103). In the centre of town, LPS, Njegoševa 28 (daily 9am–9pm), has the best stock of English-language books, especially novels and children's books, and magazines, while Gradska Knižara, Trg Republike 40 (daily 8am–10pm), stocks a good range of guidebooks and maps, as well as novels by ex-Yugoslav authors translated into English. Currently awaiting completion, Podgorica will soon be home to Montenegro's largest **shopping mall**, Delta City, which is likely to accommodate a smattering of international names.

Listings

Airlines Montenegro Airlines, Slobode 23 (Mon–Fri 8am–8pm, Sat 8am–2pm; ☎020/664 433); JAT (Yugoslav Airlines), Njegoševa 25 (Mon–Fri 9am–6pm, Sat 9am–1pm; ☎020/664 730); Malev, Marko Miljanova 32 (Mon–Fri 9am–6pm, Sat 9am–noon; ☎020/625 242).

Airport information Podgorica Airport ☎020/872 016.

Car rental Adut, Obala Ribnice 9 (☎020/230 809, ⓦwww.adutrentacar.com); Delta, Gojka Radonjića

31 (☎020/625 114, ⓦwww.rentacar-delta.com); Kompas Hertz, Trg Božane Vučinić bb (☎020/602 680, ⓦwww.kompas-car.com) and at the airport (☎020/244 117); Meridian, Bulevar Džordža Vašingtona 85 (☎020/234 944, ⓦwww.meridian-rentacar.com) and airport (☎069 316 666); Perfect, Cetinjski put bb (☎020/206 065, ⓦwww.perfectgroup.me).

Embassies and consulates UK, Bulevar Sv Petra Cetinjskog 149 ☎020/205 460, ⓦukinmontenegro.fco.gov.uk; US, Ljubljanska bb ☎081/225 417, ⓦpodgorica.usembassy.gov.

Emergencies Ambulance (☎94); police (☎92); fire (☎93).

Hospitals Podgorica Hospital, Ljubljanska 1 (☎020/225 125 or 243 726).

Internet access There are very few places in town where it's possible to log on, but they include Karver cafe/bookshop (daily 9am–10pm; see p.105) and www.klub, Bokeška 4 (daily 8am–2pm).

Left luggage Inside the bus station building (daily 6am–10pm; €2 for up to 24hr).

Pharmacies There are quite a few pharmacies around the centre, most of which have long opening hours: Maxima, Slobode 11 (daily 9am–9pm); Montefarm, Slobode 32 (24hr); Sveti Vrači, Slobode 68 (Mon–Sat 8am–10pm, Sun noon–9pm).

Police ☎020/202 851.

Post office The main post office is at Slobode 1 (Mon–Fri 7am–8pm).

Sports The city's sports society, Budućnost Podgorica, incorporates several (fairly successful) sporting clubs, including FK Budućnost, the main football team, who play at the main stadium, Stadion Pod Goricom, and basketball, handball and volleyball clubs, whose matches take place at the Morača Sports Centre near the *Hotel Podgorica*. Podgorica's second club, Zeta, plays in the suburb of Golubovici, some 11km south of the city. The most reliable place to find out about match schedules is the tourist office. With the exception of the football matches, entry is usually free.

Travel agents Kings Lake Tours, Ivana Vujoševića 20 (☎020/624 625, ℮laketours@t-com.me), offers boat tours on Lake Skadar. Montenegro Express, Moskovska 21 (☎020/234 787, ⓦwww.montenegro-express.com), in addition to trips to Lake Skadar, offers tours of Ostrog Monastery and Biogradska and Durmitor national parks.

Around Podgorica

If you've absorbed Podgorica's few sights and still find yourself with a few hours to spare, then there are one or two attractions beyond the city worth venturing to, though you will need either a taxi or your own wheels in order to reach them.

Doklea

Sited 4km north of the city are the ancient ruins of **Doklea** (open access; free), once the largest city in the state of Duklja (present-day Montenegro), but which today constitute the country's foremost archeological site. Sited on a plateau by the confluence of the Morača and Zeta rivers, the city was founded in 1AD and settled by Illyrian tribes. Doklea's greatest period of advancement came during the third century AD, when it was nominated capital of the Roman province of Prevalis, before consecutive sackings by Goths and Slavs, not to mention a few earthquakes, precipitated rapid decline. Periodic excavation of the site, which began in the late nineteenth century and continued during the 1950s and 1960s, uncovered further evidence of a once sizeable settlement (possibly inhabited by as many as forty thousand people) that incorporated a basilica, necropolis and thermal pools. What remains amongst the soft, weed-choked turf is fairly extensive, and includes large segments of wall (one portion stretching for some 200m), randomly scattered pillars and partially inscribed stones.

Getting here is a little tricky given the almost total lack of signage: heading west across the Millennium Bridge, take the first right and continue for about 2km until you arrive at the small settlement of Rogami; here, cross the bridge and once on the other side, take the (lower) road which veers to the right – continue for another kilometre or so, cross the rail tracks and the site is in front of you. A taxi should cost no more than €10–12 return.

Medun

Twelve kilometres northeast of Podgorica is the village of **MEDUN**, once the seat of the Illyrian Labeatae tribe. It was established in the fourth century BC but sacked by the Romans in 167 AD. All that's left of the ancient town (then known as Meteon) is a small necropolis perched along a narrow ridge looming high over the village. Medun's other claim to fame is as the birthplace of renowned local

△ The ruins at Doklea

warrior and scribe, **Marko Miljanov** (1833–1901), whose most famous work was *The Examples of Humanity and Bravery*, a lengthy treatise on Montenegro's struggle for independence in the nineteenth century. Born of a Serbian father and Albanian mother, Miljanov initially served under Prince-Bishop Danilo in Cetinje, successfully fighting in a number of battles against the Turks before becoming head of the Kuči clan, made up of Montenegrins, Serbs and Albanians and so named after the surrounding geographical region.

Housed in Miljanov's former home is an eponymously titled **museum** (Muzej Marko Miljanov; Tues–Sat 9am–5pm; €1), a surprisingly enlightening affair comprising many of Miljanov's manuscripts and other personal effects (a jacket, sword, pipe and various timepieces), alongside a fine assemblage of beautifully embroidered costumes, weaponry and musical instruments, such as the *gusle*, a single-stringed, guitar-shaped fiddle played widely throughout the Balkans. Just above the museum, crowning the remains of the necropolis, is a small chapel, in front of which is Miljanov's solitary **grave**. From here there are fantastic views of the surrounding hills, with the hazy shimmer of Lake Skadar in the distance.

Getting here is slightly tricky as there are no signs whatsoever. Take the E65/E80 road (signposted Belgrade) north out of the city, and at the fork by the traffic lights turn right. Keep going along this road, which slowly winds upwards through the stony hills for some 10km – if you're cycling, it's a pretty exacting ride.

Lake Skadar

Consuming the greater part of Lake Skadar National Park, the second largest of the country's four designated parks, **Lake Skadar** (Skadarsko jezero), some 25km south of Podgorica, is the most substantial body of water in the Balkan peninsula.

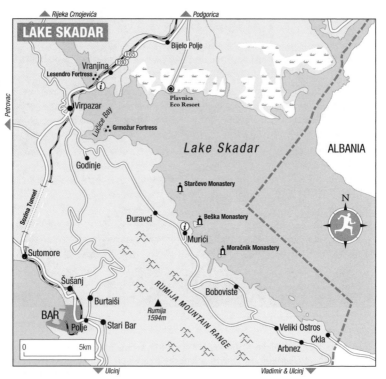

Bordered to the east by Albania (to which a third of the lake belongs), and enclosed on three sides by bare-topped karst mountains, Lake Skadar maintains an eerie, almost magical presence; timeworn villages and monasteries dot the lakeshore, and the lake's shallow blue waters, reflecting the myriad colours of vegetation, shimmer through the thin summer heat-haze.

Some 44km at its longest point, 14km wide and with an average depth of around 6m, the lake is fed by water from the Morača River and drains into the Adriatic via the Bojana, which flows along the Albanian border. It's also supplied with fresh water from numerous springs in the karst floor; known as *oko* (eyes), these are a result of the fact that part of the lake lies below sea level. The northern and eastern shores, where the lake is shallower than elsewhere, are characterized by large swathes of marshland which during springtime burst forth with vegetation of white and yellow water lilies, reed groves and dense clusters of willow. Here, too, are the lake's two settlements of note, namely **Vranjina**, home to an impressive visitor centre, and **Virpazar**, a small fishing village with some good accommodation and eating possibilities. In contrast, the **western shore** is more remote. Studded with rocky islets and sharply indented bays, it's also home to the lake's foremost cultural monuments in the shape of several island-bound monasteries.

Lake Skadar National Park is one of the most important **birding sanctuaries** in the Balkans (see box, opposite). The lake also contains more than forty species of **fish**, including abundant stocks of carp, chub, eel and mullet, and its shores are home to a huge variety of other fauna – otters and polecats, to name but two. Vegetation on the lake is plentiful, not least in the form of a rather peculiar local deli-

Birdwatching and other activities on Lake Skadar

There are few places in the Balkans, let alone Montenegro, that can match Lake Skadar for the sheer variety of its **birdlife**. Drawn to the lake by its plentiful food stocks and favourable Mediterranean climate, over 280 types of bird have been recorded here, a large number migratory or wintering but many also breeders. Amongst them are some rare and unusual species, such as the whiskered tern, great white egret, great and pygmy cormorant, glossy ibis and grey heron; eagles and bustards are present here in large numbers, too. There are five ornithological reserves around the lake, one of which, **Pančeva Oka**, halfway along the eastern shore, is the main nesting site for Dalmatian pelicans, the lake's star turn and one of the most rarely seen birds hereabouts. There is also a birdwatching tower here, as there are in other spots around the lake, such as **Raduš**, near Grmožur on the western shore, and **Manastirska Tapija**, in between Plavnica and Vranjina – useful if you're not visiting as part of an organized tour. Agents providing **tours** of the lake, which usually includes bus transfer from Podgorica and lunch, include Montenegro Express and Kings Lake Tours (see p.106) – expect to pay around €40 for a half-day trip.

The lake also provides plentiful opportunities for **fishing**, the season running from June to mid-March. Permits (€5 per day) can be obtained from the main visitor centre in Vranjina (see below). Between May and September, when light winds drift over the lake, it's also possible to try your hand at **windsurfing**; the best port of call is the Pelikan Windsurfing Club based in Vranjina (℡069 077 869, ⊛www.pelikansurf.me), which can supply rental equipment (€7 per hour).

cacy called *kasaronja*, a sort of water chestnut that steadfastly refuses to bear fruit in times of drought, despite the unlimited supplies of water in the lake itself.

The lake is easily accessed from Podgorica by bus or train, both of which stop off at Vranjina and Virpazar.

Vranjina and around

Travelling south from Podgorica, the low and featureless plain soon gives way to reed-filled swamps and low green hills. The first lake settlement of any kind is **VRANJINA**, a small fishing village of well-proportioned stone houses huddled under the hill of the same name; there is also a **train station** (single-platform) here, about five hundred metres beyond the village, and **buses** stop at the entrance to the village. From the station it's around 1km to the lake's main **visitor centre** (May–Sept daily 8am–6pm; Oct–April Mon–Fri 8am–4pm; ℡020/879 103; €3), which stands at the head of a long causeway bisecting the northwestern corner of the lake, along which both the road and the rail line pass. In addition to an enlightening fifteen-minute multimedia presentation (in English) on Lake Skadar, there are informative exhibits pertaining to all four of the country's national parks, as well as a small ethnographic collection. Useful maps and leaflets can also be picked up here, and staff can book accommodation on the lake's western shore (see p.111).

Jutting out into the lake roughly midway along the causeway are the substantial ruins of **Lesendro Fortress**, a nineteenth-century stronghold built during the rule of Petar II Petrović Njegoš as a military defence against the Turks – following Montenegrin independence in 1878, the fortress continued to function as an arms depot until the end of World War I. It is possible to access the ruins on foot (park by the visitor centre if you're in a car), but you will have to walk alongside the rail tracks (in fact far less hazardous than the road – just watch your back).

Below the visitor centre and overlooking the lake, the accomplished *Jezero* **restaurant** has lake and sea fish prepared in the manner of your choice – with its conservatory-style interior and summery terrace, it's a terrific place to eat in warmer weather; there is also a large **wine shop** here (daily 10am–6pm), offering some of the region's finest wines, such as Vranac and Krštac. In the car park next to the visitor centre there are several booths with companies offering **boat trips** on the lake (€50 for three people with guide; 1hr 30min) or rowing boats for hire (€25 for 1hr, accommodating up to five people).

Plavnica

Over on the north shore of the lake, and just 20km south of Podgorica, is the **Plavnica Eco Resort** (T 020/443 700, W www.plavnica.info), a flash new tourist complex set around a marina in lush, landscaped surroundings, comprising some classy places to eat, a swimming pool and other amenities. At the time of writing, the resort had just a handful of plush and very expensive suites available (€200), though there are plans to turn it into a fully fledged hotel, while the fancy restaurant offers excellent freshwater and sea fish. There's another restaurant on the large *Plavnica* boat, which itself offers four-hour **lake cruises** (two or three times a week; €10) in the summer, taking in a stop at the beach at Murići on the western shore; refreshments are available on the boat but at extra cost. The resort also offers pedaloes (€5 per hour for four to five people), kayaks (€3 per hour for one or two people) and motorboats (€50; with guide only) for hire.

Virpazar

A compact little village with a small harbour, **VIRPAZAR** is the lake's main settlement and possesses the best range of places to eat and sleep. About 800m east of the village (in the direction of Podgorica) is the **train station**, but as there is no footpath from the station, it's actually safer to walk along the side of the tracks than along the road. **Buses** stop by the entrance to the village. **Hotels** include: the *Pelikan* (T 020/711 107, W www.pelikanzec.com; ⑤), a private little guesthouse

△ Beška Monastery, Lake Skadar

at the entrance to the village, with seven very simple but clean rooms; and the *13 July* (☎020/711 120; ●; closed in winter), a short walk across the bridge on the opposite side of the village – it's a bit dowdy but the rooms are perfectly adequate. The last alternative is the small guesthouse directly opposite the *Pelikan*, which has three decent and well-furnished rooms (reception is in the bar downstairs; ☎020/711 160; ●). The *Pelikan*'s popular and characterful **restaurant**, adorned with nautical ephemera and old photographs, offers fish from the lake, such as eel and carp. There's similar fare at the *Badanj*, a small, taverna-like place with stone walls and a thick timber-beam ceiling, sited right next to the bridge. Both these places also have **boats** for hire (€20 for two people for 1hr).

The western shore

Travelling south through Virpazar brings you to Skadar's remote and rocky **western shore** which, from a visitor's perspective, constitutes the most absorbing section of the lake. You will, though, really need your own transport if you wish to explore this little-frequented stretch. Just beyond Virpazar, the road forks (take the left), whereupon it climbs steadily upwards, along the park boundary and through woods of hornbeam, oak and wild chestnut.

Godinje

Around 4km distant, and overlooking Lučice Bay, is the hillside village of **GODINJE**, distinguished by its unique chain system of conjoined houses, complete with passages and tunnels in between them – allegedly they were built this way so that the villagers could escape detection by the Ottomans. Just by the roadside house (which sells refreshments) in the centre of the village, the road rises steeply to the oldest part of the settlement – **Stari Selo** – where there are some fine examples of these cramped, and now mostly ramshackle, old dwellings with their stone-paved terraces. One of the houses (there are no numbers here, so you'll have to ask) is occupied by Miodrag Leković (☎069 476 591), who cultivates a variety of the local Vranac **wine**, and is available for tasting sessions – expect to pay around €3–4 for three tasting samples and some ham and cheese. For a nominal fee he'll also row you over to **Grmožur**; sited some 500m out from shore, this small island-fortress was built in 1834, functioning as a prison during the rule of Njegoš, hence the somewhat fanciful tourist brochure comparisons with Alcatraz.

Murići and around

Beyond Godinje, the road crawls higher and tighter, cutting inland so that the lake is out of sight. Several kilometres on, near Đuravci, the lake reveals itself once again, the shore below studded with innumerable picturesque islets and rocky coves. Just beyond the sign for Đuravci, a narrow road tapers down to **MURIĆI**, site of a lovely pebbly lakeside beach. Here, too is the lake's second **visitor centre** (May–Sept daily 9am–5pm), which, in addition to tourist brochures, has displays on local folk art and the region's economic activities, the most important of which is olive growing. There's also some **accommodation** in the form of several wooden bungalows (€25 per day for the bungalow; contact the visitor centre in Vranjina – see p.109) and a small camping area, and a large but basic **restaurant** offering simple grill and fish dishes.

Lying just off this strip of the western shore are three monasteries, one of which, the late fourteenth-century **Beška Monastery**, sits directly opposite the beach in Murići. On an island to the north of Beška is **Starčevo Monastery**, founded in 1377 and once an important literary outpost; why this little spot should have been chosen is unclear, but what is known is that numerous books were written, bound and decorated here. To the south is **Moračnik Monastery**, built during the fifteenth century and distinguished by a large quadrangular-shaped tower (*pirg*), which functioned as a defensive unit against the Turks. To visit any of the monasteries, enquire at the visitor centre or, alternatively, contact Selko Paljevič in Murići (☎069 360 938), who will happily organize visits. Boats cost €10 and can accommodate up to three people.

South of Murići

From Murići the road turns inland, through countryside of stone walls and large grey boulders, before an uphill stretch and a brief last glimpse of the lake and the jagged spine of the magnificent **Prokletije Mountains** ("The Accursed Mountains") away in the distance. Thereafter, the road continues to within touching distance of Albania, before turning sharply and descending to Ulcinj, via Vladimir (see p.90).

Cetinje

Nestled in a shallow bowl surrounded by clipped woods and frozen limestone peaks, **CETINJE**, 30km west of Podgorica, is the spiritual heart of the country. Once the royal capital of Montenegro, it also withstood repeated Turkish assaults over the centuries – thus the town exerts a peculiarly romantic hold over many Montenegrins.

Travelling in the 1930s, Canadian journalist Lovatt Edwards described Cetinje as "sleepy and undistinguished, a city of pensioners" – and whilst this simple mountain town of around twenty thousand inhabitants retains a languid, almost timeless air, it certainly offers a pleasing antidote to Podgorica's faceless modernity. The town's wide, tree-lined boulevards might now be somewhat shabby in places, and the pastel-coloured tenements a little flaky, but Cetinje's once illustrious past is still very much in evidence, thanks to some grand, if timeworn, public buildings and a raft of *fin-de-siècle* mansions that once housed diplomatic missions. Indeed, and as unlikely as it may seem, Cetinje still has political relevance today: a number of government offices have been relocated here from Podgorica and the town is the official seat of the country's president.

What Podgorica palpably lacks in terms of cultural interest, Cetinje more than makes up for, with a cluster of eminently enjoyable attractions scattered around town. The one downside here is the lack of any real tourist infrastructure, with just a couple of places to stay and few places of note to eat or drink. But Cetinje remains a good base from which to step out into the surrounding mountains, most obviously **Lovćen National Park**, at the heart of which is Mount Lovćen, home to the mausoleum of the revered poet-prince, Petar II Petrović Njegoš. Cetinje is easily done as a day-trip destination, from either Podgorica or the coastal towns, Budva (see p.69) and Kotor (see p.58) – the serpentine route up from the latter is nothing short of spectacular.

Some history

The seeds of Cetinje were sown by the Zeta ruler **Ivan Crnojević**, who erected a castle and monastery on the plain below Mount Lovćen around 1482. As the secular and spiritual centre of the state, Cetinje represented a major prize for the Turks but, try as they did on numerous occasions, they never contrived to conquer the town. Under Prince-Bishop **Petar II Petrović Njegoš** (see box, p.121), Cetinje prospered, and by the time of his death, the town, although essentially still a small

CETINJE

N

◄ Lovćen National Park

◄ Orlov Krš

◄ 2, 3, Russian Embassy, Podgorica & Budva

Gradski Stadium

BOŽA

BAJA PIVLJANINA

NIKCA OD ROVINA

Bank of Montenegro Building

Former French Embassy

JOVANA TOMAŠEVIĆA

President of Montenegro's Residence

TRG GOLOOTOČKIH ŽRTAVA

Bus Station

GRAHOVSKA

TRG SLOBODE

13 NOVEMBRA

NJEGOŠEVA

BALŠIĆA

IVANBEGOVA

VUKA MIĆUNOVIĆA

BRIGADE

NOVICE CEROVIĆA

DEČANSKA

PAZAR

❶

Government House (National Museum)

V CRNOG

BAJA PIVLJANINA

Zetski Dom Theatre

MARTINOVIĆA

ZMAJEVA

TRG REVOLUCIJE

TRG DVORSKI

❹

Turkish Embassy

V BATRIĆA

Tablja

Ethnographic Museum

❺

Biljarda

Cetinje Monastery

Palace of King Nikola

Old Pharmacy

❻

NJEGOŠEVA

TRG UMJETNOSTI

P

ⓘ

P LUBARDE

Former British Embassy

ALEKSE ŠANTIĆA

Church of the Virgin Mary's Birth at Ćipur

NOVICE CEROVIĆA

Vladičina Bašta

Blue Palace

Ⓑ

ACCOMMODATION

Grand	B
Motel Zicer	A

EATING & DRINKING

Belveder	2
Gradska Kafana	5
Hogar	1
Konak	3
Mala Kuzina	4
Yellow Moon Café	6

0   100m

and rather squalid village at the heart of a backward and impoverished region, had been augmented by a handful of state residences and residential areas.

Following the **1878 Treaty of Berlin** – whereby Montenegrin independence was formally recognized – Cetinje assumed a political influence that far outweighed its economic and territorial significance. It suddenly found itself a capital of some strategic importance, and all the major European countries vied with each other in courting the favour of the king of Montenegro from their brand-new diplomatic missions. This period, under the reign of **Prince Nikola**, was also a time of significant economic and cultural advancement for the town; rapid urban expansion went hand in hand with the construction of numerous important public and private buildings, such as the Blue Palace and Government House, as well as the establishment of a hospital, schools, libraries and Montenegro's first theatre. The glory days weren't to last much longer, however, and following occupation by the Austro-Hungarians in 1916, and Montenegro's assimilation into the Kingdom of Serbs, Croats and Slovenes in 1918 (subsequently the Kingdom of Yugoslavia), Cetinje's star began to wane. Its status was further diminished after World War II, when Titograd (now Podgorica) was nominated the capital of the new republic.

Arrival, information and accommodation

The **bus station**, such as it is, is located five minutes' walk north of the centre on Trg Goolootočkih žrtava. The **tourist office** (Mon–Sat 8am–8pm, Sun 9am–5pm), housed in a newly built lime-green concrete hut, is on the edge of the large car park just a few paces from Trg Dvorski, the main square; it has a reasonable amount of literature on the town but as yet no maps to hand out. You won't fail to notice the **tourist train**

King Nikola I

Born into the Petrović-Njegoš dynasty in 1841, **Nikola** bore some striking similarities to Petar II, the country's greatest-ever ruler. A man of fine physique, Nikola was a successful **military leader** and no mean **poet** either, his most celebrated work being *Onamo, 'namo* ("There, over there"), a popular Montenegrin anthem. Following the assassination of his uncle, Danilo II, in 1860, he inherited the title of prince, the same year marrying Milena, daughter of the vojvoda, Petar Vukotič. During his 58-year reign Nikola brought most of the clans to heel, but his greatest single achievement came in 1878 when his army occupied the strip of coast from Budva to Ulcinj, thus extending his territories to the Adriatic seaboard. "Follow me Montenegrins – on to Bar, on to our Serb Bar, on to our Serb Sea!", he exhorted his men before leading them into battle against the hitherto Turkish-occupied Adriatic port.

After the collapse of the Ottoman Empire, Europe's major countries were keen to curry favour with King Nikola, and they did so by establishing an embassy or legation in the then capital, Cetinje – a situation Nikola skilfully exploited, extracting as much money from them as he could. At the same time he oversaw a series of military, administrative and educational reforms begun by Petar II, in addition to giving Montenegro its first constitution in 1905 and introducing Western-style press freedom and criminal law codes.

Nikola also earned the sobriquet the "father-in-law of Europe": of his nine daughters (he also sired three sons), five were married off into royal European households, one of whom, Ana, married Prince Franz Joseph of Battenburg, kin of the Mountbatten family. Having assumed the title of **king** in 1910, his reign ended in 1916 when, amid accusations of treachery from Serbia, he allowed the Montenegrin army to be captured by the Austrians. He fled to France where he died in exile in 1921. His remains (along with those of Queen Milena) were only returned for burial in Cetinje in 1989.

sitting outside the tourist office, which offers thirty-minute jollies around town taking in all the major sights (daily 9am–5pm, on the hour; €1.50). The **post office** is at Njegoševa 28 (Mon–Fri 7am–8pm), while there are a few smoky dives along this street offering **internet access** – however, these do come and go.

Put simply, accommodation in Cetinje boils down to three choices. The town's main **hotel** is the *Grand* (T041/235 047, Whotel-grand.tripod.com; ⑨), something of a misnomer for this brutish-looking concrete building located at the southern end of the main park – the rooms are dowdy and rather careworn with little in the way of furnishings. More appealing is the *Motel Zicer* (T041/231 177; ②–④), housed inside the long stone building next to the bus station; this welcoming place has bright, pine-furnished en-suite rooms (single, double and multis) with comfortable beds and TVs. The last possibility is a **private room**, bookable through the tourist office – these are limited, however, so it's best to call ahead.

The Town

Most of Cetinje's key sights are located along Njegoševa, the town's long main north–south axis, and around Trg Dvorski. Running parallel to Njegoševa is Baja Pivljanina, at the bottom end of which is a cluster of fine buildings, including several former embassies. Note that if you plan on visiting the three main museums (they are collectively entitled the National Museum of Montenegro) then the all-in-one ticket (€7 and available from any of the museums) is excellent value.

King Nikola's Palace and Ethnographic Museum

Taking centre stage on Trg Dvorski is the **Palace of King Nikola** (Palata Kralj Nikole; daily 9am–5pm; €5), a long brown-plastered building that looks more like a lesser nineteenth-century mansion than the home of Montenegro's only monarch – the only slight concession to grandeur is an extended porch atop which is a ceremonial balcony. Unfortunately, there's precious little remaining of Nikola's original possessions (just a chair and a desk), as most of it was pillaged during World War II. Instead, the interior is an approximation of how it would have appeared during his reign (see box, opposite), with austerely decorated rooms stuffed with ornately carved furnishings from Vienna, Persian carpets, Ming vases and portraits of governing rulers. Downstairs is a collection of weaponry and bullet-riddled flags taken from the Turks at the Battle of Vučji Do in 1876. Note that you can only visit the palace with a guide, so you may have to wait for a handful of people to gather before being shown around.

More diverting is the rather splendid **Ethnographic Museum** (Etnografski muzej; daily May–Sept 9am–5pm, Oct–April 8am–4pm; €2), housed in the neatly restored former Serbian embassy diagonally across the square from the palace. The greater part of the museum collection comprises a sumptuous assortment of Montenegrin costumes dating from the nineteenth century; men would typically be attired in a *jerkin*, a tight-fitting, finely embroidered waistcoat, while women's traditional costume consisted of a *košulja*, a frilly cream-coloured blouse, over which a *koreta*, a long, light-green sleeveless jacket, would usually be worn. Look out, too for several examples of shepherds' *kabanica*, thick woollen garments in which they would carry food and other goods. Although now a dying art, lace-making has been popular in the region for centuries, the most renowned centre being the coastal village of Dobrota near Kotor, where it's still practised by a handful of women. There are some fine examples of this exquisite craft on display here, as well as intricately woven cloths featuring peasant or folk motifs, many of which are technically superb. Traditionally, most lace and embroidery products were sold to the church, as evidenced by the extensive array of church vestments.

The Biljarda

On the western side of Trg Dvorski, the **Biljarda**, also known as Njegoš's Museum (Njegoš muzej; daily 9am–5pm; €3), takes its name from the billiard table that was dragged up here from Kotor at great effort and expense upon the orders of **Petar II Petrović Njegoš** (see box, p.121). A squat, two-storeyed structure built in 1838, it originally functioned as Njegoš's residence, thereafter housing a printing press, various state and educational institutions and military offices.

Overall, the collection – mainly incidental bric-a-brac from his life and administration including pictures and portraits – is a bit hit and miss, but there are one or two worthwhile exhibits, notably the **billiard table** itself; made in Vienna in 1807, it's in remarkably good nick. It's interesting to note how much lower the table is compared to today's editions: Njegoš was six feet eight inches tall, so negotiating his way around it would, one would imagine, have been no easy task. Elsewhere there's a selection of his reading material, held in a beautiful carved wooden cabinet, and an original manuscript of *Gorskog Vijenca* ("The Mountain Wreath"), written by Njegoš in 1847 and considered the greatest of all Yugoslav epic poems. Another of the more interesting items is a handwritten passport he made for himself when he went to St Petersburg for his investiture as an Orthodox bishop.

In a large glass pavilion attached to the side of the Biljarda, the huge **relief map** of Montenegro was constructed by officers of the occupying Austrian army in 1917. Part of an intelligence-gathering exercise, the map illustrates just how mountainous Montenegro really is, and as you walk around, it's easy to see why no foreign power ever managed to garrison the country effectively.

The National Museum

A short walk north of the Biljarda stands the **Government House** (Vladin Dom), a grandiose edifice completed in 1910 which today accommodates the sprawling **National Museum of Montenegro** (daily 9am–5pm; €3). The ground floor is devoted to **Montenegrin history**, with a voluminous collection of artefacts spanning the centuries, but predominantly centred on the country's military affairs. Admirable though this arsenal of trophies is, it's a trifle repetitive and not helped by the absence of English captioning; the display of Turkish battle standards seized at Grahovac (1858) and Vučji Do (1869) – the Turks were comprehensively routed at both – is impressive, however.

More satisfying is the **art collection** on the first floor, which offers a thoroughgoing assessment of nineteenth- and twentieth-century work by artists from countries of the former Yugoslavia. Pre-eminent amongst these was the Croatian sculptor Ivan Meštrović, though the pieces on display here are far from representative of his best work – you're better off making the trip up to Mount Lovćen to view his immense sculpture of Njegoš's mausoleum (see p.122). Also on display is work by the distinguished group of Slovene impressionists, Rihard Jakopič, Matija Jama and Ivan Grohar, arguably the most influential of all artists to come out of the former Yugoslavia. Two of Montenegro's most prominent artists were natives of Cetinje, namely Milo Milunović, who veered between Impressionism and Cubism, and Petar Lubarda, considered to be the most important of the postwar Yugoslav painters and best known for his dramatic landscape and battle canvases, two fine examples here being *Montenegrin Hills* and *The Battle of Kosovo Polje*.

The fabulous **Collection of Icons** holds the museum's showpiece item, namely the **Icon of Our Lady of Philermos**, exhibited separately in the so-called Blue Chapel (Plava kapela). Believed to date from the thirteenth century, it is spectacularly ornamented, the robe decorated with diamonds and sapphires and the horseshoe-shaped halo, made by goldsmiths in St Petersburg and Moscow in the eighteenth century, encrusted with diamonds and rubies.

△ Cetinje Monastery

Cetinje Monastery, Ćipur Church and Orlov Krš

Pressed up into the hillside just behind the Biljarda, the formidable, chalk-coloured **Cetinje Monastery** (Manastir Cetinje; daily 8am–8pm) was completed by the founder of the Njegoš dynasty, Prince-Bishop Danilo, in 1701. Part church, part fortress and part munitions store, the monastery buildings housed a rudimentary administration under the aegis of Danilo and his successors, who fused together the functions of prince and bishop to forge a dynasty of theocratic rulers. A tiny cruciform **chapel**, carved from neatly hewn stone, contains the tombs of Prince Danilo and Petar I, the uncle of the celebrated poet king. Its most celebrated, if somewhat macabre, relic is the **right hand of St John the Baptist**: having endured a rather circuitous route via Constantinople, Malta, Russia and Estonia, the wizened hand (minus two fingers) ended up in the possession of the Communists in Serbia after World War II, before being transferred to Cetinje in 1978. It's held within a glass coffin, and you can ask one of the monks to see it. Also interesting is the **treasury**, holding a fine display of fifteenth- and sixteenth-century icons and religious books. The most important of these is **Oktoih** ("The First Voice"), a gospel dating from 1493 – it's one of the oldest printed books in existence and certainly amongst the first ever printed in a Slavonic language.

On a small hill behind the monastery are the scant remains of the **Tablja**, a small stone tower built by Petar II in 1835, which was used for impaling Turkish heads on. On the adjacent plateau stands a four-pillar belltower, while, standing on the foundations of Cetinje's first monastery church (1484), just across from the Biljarda, is the diminutive **Church of the Virgin Mary's Birth at Ćipur**, a simple, single-aisled structure. Inside lie the gleaming marble tombs of King Nikola I and Queen Milena, whose remains were transferred here from the Russian Church in San Remo in 1989. If the church is closed, ask at the tourist office.

About 200m south of the monastery, a path leads up to a prominent rise known as **Orlov Krš** (Eagle's Crag), at the top of which is the **mausoleum of Bishop Danilo**. Although it's little more than a canopied stone block, it's worth making the stiff twenty-minute climb up here for the tremendous views of the town and the surrounding hills, thickly cloaked in beech and fir.

Trg Umjetnosti and around

Dividing up the northern and southern halves of Njegoševa is **Trg Umjetnosti**, a modest little square in and around which are a number of historically interesting buildings, including several former embassies. A few paces back towards Trg Dvorski at Njegoševa 45 is the **old pharmacy**, purportedly the second oldest apothecary in the Balkans (the oldest is in Dubrovnik). Still functioning after more than one hundred and fifty years, the dark wooden fittings have been beautifully preserved, as has the collection of prescriptions, jars and implements.

Heading south from here, a few steps beyond the *Yellow Moon Café*, is the former **British embassy**, the last of the embassies to be built in Cetinje (1912). It's a simple, two-storeyed building, much less distinguished than many of the other embassies, and now virtually drained of any colour; today it houses the town's music academy. One hundred metres further down, on the edge of the main town park, stands the stately **Blue Palace** (Plavac Dvorni; daily 10am–2pm & 4–8pm), built in 1895 for Crown Prince Danilo and so named on account of its colour, though it's actually more mottle-grey in appearance. Immaculately restored, the palace now functions as an art gallery, with rotating exhibitions.

East of Trg Umjetnosti, just beyond the former Turkish embassy on Baja Pivljanina, is the smoothly symmetrical, bright cream-coloured **Zetski Dom Royal Theatre**. Constructed piecemeal between 1884 and 1892, it was Montenegro's first purpose-built theatre, staging the country's first play, *The Balkan Empress* by King Nikola I Petrović, in 1888. Reconstructed in 1931 following a battering by the Austro-Hungarians, it took on its present incarnation in the wake of the 1979 earthquake. Just around the corner from here on Batrića is the **Russian embassy**, the largest and most flamboyant of all the missions, its facade fancifully ornamented with rosettes and garlands.

North of the centre

At the northern end of Njegoševa lie several buildings of architectural and historical importance. Just beyond the intersection of Njegoševa and Jovana Tomaševića is the **President of Montenegro's residence**, an unflattering stone block building whose entrance is flanked by two rather superfluous statues, behind which two smartly attired but very bored-looking guardsmen stand to attention. Directly opposite is the former **French embassy**, a fine Secessionist-style building completed in 1910 and covered in a patchwork of variously coloured ceramic tiles;

today it accommodates the Central National Library. On the same side a little further up the street stands the **Bank of Montenegro building** – Montenegro's banking institution was founded in 1906, when it simultaneously introduced its first legal tender, the perper.

Eating and drinking

Cetinje has very few options when it comes to eating and drinking, and you'll have to head a short way out of town to sample the best food. In town, there's nothing beyond a handful of **pizzeria/snack-type places**, such as *Hogar*, halfway down Njegoševa, which serves pizzas, grilled meats and salads, and *Mala Kuzina*, next to the post office, which doles out hamburgers and sausages.

The best **restaurant** hereabouts is the *Belveder* (daily 10am–11pm), located 2km back out on the road to Podgorica. This distinctive-looking building, with a raised stone terrace affording marvellous views, has a lovely interior with lots of rustic trappings and a roaring log fire; amongst the many varied (albeit predominantly meat) options are roast lamb, Njeguški steak and smoked carp from Lake Skadar. To get here, take a right off the Podgorica road – it's a further 800m along a narrow track. Heading in the opposite direction, 4km beyond Cetinje on the Budva road, the *Konak* restaurant (daily 8am–11pm) has a similarly rustic feel, though while the food is decent enough, it's not nearly as enjoyable as the *Belveder*.

During warmer weather, most townsfolk congregate in the pavement **cafés** spilling out onto Njegoševa and Trg Dvorski – just take your pick. At the far end of Njegoševa, the *Yellow Moon Café* is a colourful, cheery place frequented by arty types, and it occasionally hosts live music. *Gradska Kafana*, occupying the former Bulgarian embassy on Trg Dvorski, is also worth visiting, if only to mull over the once grand salon-style interior.

Around Cetinje

Surrounding Cetinje are a sprinkling of eminently worthwhile destinations, though to reach them you will require your own vehicle. The most prominent is **Lovćen National Park**, an impressive limestone range offering good, but not overly strenuous, hiking, and which is also the site of Petar Njegoš's suitably imposing mausoleum. Two villages worth making the effort to get to, not least for the culinary possibilities on offer, are **Njeguši**, renowned for its ham and cheese, and **Rijeka Crnojevića**, a delightful rustic idyll located just off the main road between Cetinje and Podgorica.

Rijeka Crnojevića

Around 8km east of Cetinje, a road breaks off from the main highway towards **RIJEKA CRNOJEVIĆA**, some 10km distant. Flanked by precipitously slanting hills, this wonderfully picturesque fishing village is located at the source of the Crnojevića – the river, a glittering emerald-green colour, flows for about 5km before dumping into Lake Skadar.

The village's most celebrated feature is a romantic-looking triple-arched **stone bridge**, built in 1853. Neatly trimmed grass banks slope down from the promenade to the water's edge, where dozens of fishing boats gently bob. Midway along the promenade is the *Stari Most* **restaurant** (daily 1–10pm), a handsome-looking establishment offering some of the most select fish and seafood in the region – in particular smoked carp and grilled eel from Skadar – as well as some fine locally grown wines; the views out onto the river and across to the bridge are quite lovely on a warm summer's day.

There is no **accommodation** in the village itself, but about 5km east of Rijeka Crnojevića, back in the direction of Podgorica, is the *Gazivoda Hotel* (☎020/712 037; ●). Though it is actually just a basic guesthouse, with six very simple double rooms (available April–Oct only), the price is almost worth paying for the views alone, with a superlative panorama overlooking the head of Lake Skadar.

Lovćen National Park

Encompassing the central and highest part of the Lovćen Massif, which rises precipitously from the coast, **Lovćen National Park** – proclaimed as such in 1952 – is the third largest of Montenegro's four national parks. It's predominantly an area

△ Lovćen National Park

If you commit just one figure from Montenegrin history to memory, make it **Petar II Petrović Njegoš**, for it was he who laid the foundation for the modern Montenegrin state. Born in 1813 in the village of Njeguši, in the foothills of Mount Lovćen, Njegoš was quite a remarkable man, as interesting as he is unknown outside Montenegro and the former Yugoslavia: six foot eight inches tall and stunningly good-looking, he was not only a successful secular ruler but a bishop, diplomat and notorious hounder of the Turks, poet of distinction and a crack shot to boot. The story always told of him, quite possibly because it was witnessed by the English nobleman, Sir Gardiner Wilkinson, is that he would frequently call for a lemon to be thrown into the air and shoot through it before it hit the ground – "a singular accomplishment for a bishop", mused Sir Gardiner. Just for good measure he also spoke French, German, Russian and Latin, reading their literature, philosophy and jurisprudence in the original.

Njegoš was born Radivoje "Rade" Tomov Petrović into the Petrović-Njegoš family, a dynasty that had served as the prince-bishops (or *Vladikas*) in Montenegro for well over a century. Growing up amongst illiterate peasants, Njegoš left home at the age of 11 to attend Cetinje Monastery, at that time the only place of learning in Montenegro. Upon his uncle's (Petar I) death in 1830, Njegoš, then aged just 17, inherited the title of bishop of Cetinje, hence becoming the unofficial supreme ecclesiastical **ruler** of Montenegro. As ruler and reformer his greatest achievement was to persuade the feuding clan chiefs to introduce fair taxation as well as a codified set of laws based upon common right into their primitive mountain communities. Njegoš was also, by some distance, the most culturally enlightened of the Petrović prince-bishops, founding schools and libraries, as well as importing a printing press, which functioned inside the Biljarda, the residence Njegoš had built for himself in 1838.

But it is for his achievements as a **poet** that Njegoš is truly venerated. Tutored by the pre-eminent Serb poet Simo Milutinović, Njegoš's work was greatly influenced by the French Romantics. Although he was incredibly prolific, by far his most important work was *Gorshi Vijenac* ("The Mountain Wreath"), an epic hymn to liberty that is widely acknowledged to be unequalled in the poetry of the former Yugoslavia. Following his death in 1851 he was buried in a small chapel atop Mount Lovćen, which was subsequently destroyed by the Austrians during World War I. Having been transferred to Cetinje Monastery his remains were returned to the rebuilt chapel in 1925, before this was, somewhat controversially, replaced by Meštrović's mausoleum in 1974.

of rocky limestone slopes, distinguished by huge crevices, fissures and depressions. Dominating the heart of the park are the twin peaks of **Štirovnik vrh** (1748m), crowned by a telecommunications tower, and **Jezerski vrh** (Lake Crest; 1657m), final resting place of Petar II Petrović Njegoš (see box above) and the reason why most people visit the park.

From Cetinje, a well-surfaced road (the start of which is well signposted from the centre of town) skirts the southern boundary of the park before entering it properly just before the hamlet of **IVANOVA KORITA**, some 12km distant – a kiosk marks the official entry point, where a small fee is payable (€2 per person). The drive up from Cetinje is lovely, as the road wends its way through countryside thick with beech, oak and linden tree, and small roadside huts appear from nowhere selling *Njeguški sir* and *pršut* – see p.122. In Ivanova Korita, there is a **visitor centre** (summer daily 9am–5pm; ☎069 328 858), where you can pick up walking maps of the area and view an exhibition on the local flora and fauna. Just across from the visitor centre there is **accommodation** in the form of several wooden bungalows, each fitted with a sleeping area (four beds), kitchen and small dining room space (€40 per day for the bungalow; same phone number as visitor centre, ⓔjpnpcg@t-com.me); it's also possible to **camp** here (€5 per tent).

Beyond Ivanova Korita, the road climbs steadily, ending at Jezerski vrh, whose summit bears the **mausoleum of Petar II Petrović Njegoš** (daily 8am–6pm; €3). Arriving at the small car park, it's a stiff walk up 461 chunky concrete steps lining a tunnel that runs through the mountain. Designed by Croatia's most famous sculptor, Ivan Meštrović, the mausoleum was only completed in 1974 when the component parts were lugged up from Budva. It's a magnificent piece of work – a massive Petar, with open book resting on crossed legs, and an eagle watching over, carved out of a single block of black granite. Just behind the sculpture is the chapel (fronted by two enormous caryatids), its ceiling smothered in gold mosaic, while Njegoš is buried in a simple white tomb in the darkened crypt to the rear of the chapel.

From the crypt a narrow stone path leads to a rotunda, from where there are sensational views of the stark, grey mountains, and the shimmering Bay of Kotor way down below – it's as glorious as anything Montenegro has to offer. Back down beside the car park is a **restaurant**, and though the menu isn't particularly extensive, the food (roast and grilled meats) is good; you can also grab a drink and simple snack here.

Whilst Lovćen doesn't present the kind of **walking** opportunities as in, say, Durmitor or the Prokletije, there are several hiking trails within the park and certainly a couple of walks that, if you have the time, are well worth completing. The best of these is the waymarked trail from **Bukovica**, near the village of Njeguši on the Cetinje–Kotor road (see below), up to **Jezerski vrh** – an easy to moderate walk of around four hours. From Jezerski vrh, it's also possible to walk down to Kotor via the village of **Krstac** – itself several kilometres further on from Njeguši on the Cetinje–Kotor road.

Across the Lovćen Pass to Njeguši

One of the most dramatic trips in Montenegro, if not all Europe, is the road from Cetinje to Kotor, some 20km distant. Skirting the eastern fringe of Lovćen National Park, the road snakes upwards, cutting deep into the barren karst slopes, a lunar landscape of crags and boulders that swallows rain and melting snow, repaying the land with thin, patchy vegetation. As the air thins and cools, the road eventually reaches the **Lovćen Pass** (around 1000m), at which point the Gulf of Kotor reveals itself in glorious picture-book clarity. The sinuous descent through dozens of hairpins is truly spectacular, each bend more heart-stopping than the last. The road descends slowly to reach **NJEGUŠI**, a tidy little village of pretty stone cottages that gave birth to the Petrović-Njegoš clan. The village is just as well known for its excellent culinary specialities, *Njeguški sir* (cheese) and *Njeguški pršut* (ham). Delicious with *lepinja*, a delightfully doughy flat bread, and a drop of the local red Vranac wine, these centuries-old delicacies feature on almost all local menus; it's alleged that, upon completing his design of Njegoš's mausoleum, Meštrović demanded nothing more than "a wheel of cheese and a smoked ham".

Note that there is no public transport along this route.

Travel details

Trains

Podgorica to: Bar (10 daily; 1hr); Bijelo Polje (5 daily; 2hr 45min); Kolašin (5 daily; 1hr 45min); Mojkovac (5 daily; 2hr 15min); Virpazar (10 daily; 35min); Vranjina (10 daily; 25min).
Virpazar to: Bar (10 daily; 25min); Podgorica (10 daily; 35min); Vranjina (10 daily; 10min).
Vranjina to: Bar (10 daily; 35min); Podgorica (10 daily; 25min); Virpazar (10 daily; 10min).

Buses

Cetinje to: Budva (every 30min; 1hr); Herceg Novi (every 1hr–1hr 15min; 1hr 45min); Kotor (every 1hr–1hr 15min; 1hr 15min); Podgorica (every 30min; 45min); Tivat (every 1hr–1hr 15min; 1hr 15min).

Podgorica to: Bar (9–10 daily; 1hr 45min); Bijelo Polje (every 45min–1hr; 2hr); Budva (every 30–45min; 1hr); Cetinje (every 30–45min; 45min); Herceg Novi (every 30–45min; 2hr); Kolašin (every 45min–1hr; 1hr 20min); Kotor (every 30–45min; 1hr 30min); Nikšić (every 30–45min; 1hr); Pljevlja (2 daily; 3hr 30min); Tivat (every 30–45min; 1hr 30min); Virpazar (9–10 daily; 50min); Vranjina (9–10 daily; 40min); Žabljak (2 daily; 3hr).

International trains

Podgorica to: Belgrade (3 daily; 8–11hr).

International buses

Podgorica to: Belgrade (8 daily; 7–8hr); Dubrovnik (1 daily; 3hr 30min); Sarajevo (4 daily; 6–7hr).

The mountains

CHAPTER 3 # Highlights

* **Ostrog Monastery** Improbably yet thrillingly sited high up in a cliff face, the seventeenth-century Ostrog Monastery is Montenegro's most important pilgrimage site. See p.129

* **Piva Canyon** Shadowed by vertiginous mountains and cut through by the rushing eponymous river, the Piva Canyon is nature at its dramatic best. See p.135

* **Hiking in Durmitor** Hike to your heart's content amidst some of the country's most exalted peaks, such as Bobotov kuk and Međed. See p.142

* **Tara River Canyon** Montenegro's most spectacular natural feature combines a thrashing river – affording superb white water rafting – and the Tara Bridge, one of Europe's most extraordinary feats of engineering. See p.141

* **Biogradska National Park** Mountains, lakes and ancient virgin forest constitute this beautiful and green landscape, which also offers some lovely walking opportunities. See p.149

* **Plav** Absorb some intriguing Islamic architecture, take a dip in the crystal blue lake, or go and explore the awesome Prokletije mountain range bordering nearby Albania. See p.157

▲ Durmitor National Park

The mountains

Almost entirely mountainous, the magnificent Montenegrin **interior** packs in some of the most stunning scenery anywhere in the Balkans. Vast ranges rise harsh and rugged while below the occasional road or track snakes its way through barely accessible terrain, into cavernous canyons or past snow-topped peaks, glacial lakes and deep forests. It can be an inhospitable land in places: there are few large settlements, and many of the smaller towns and alpine-style villages are cut off during the winter by the often brutal snows.

The attractions are plentiful but the interior's biggest draw is the **Durmitor National Park**, the largest of the country's four designated parks, packed with jagged peaks, theatrical canyons – most obviously the stunning **Tara River Canyon** with its wild, thrashing river – and deep mountain lakes. The tangle of well-worn paths furrowed across the Durmitor Massif is popular with hikers in the summer months though the crowds are rarely oppressive here. Hiking aside, the park presents a stack of possibilities for adrenaline-fuelled activities such as rafting, canoeing and skiing, alongside more traditional sporting pursuits like horseriding, cycling, fishing and swimming. The centre for most of these pursuits is **Žabljak**, the country's premier ski and adventure resort. To the east of Durmitor, the much smaller **Biogradska Gora National Park** is an invigorating mix of virgin forest, green mountain pasture and glacial lake, offering further opportunities for hiking, as does the **Bjelasica** mountain range which surrounds it. Here, too, is the country's second ski resort, which lies close to the mountain resort of **Kolašin**.

The interior is palpably short on major urban conurbations, the only settlement of any real size being the industrial though not unattractive town of **Nikšić**. Whilst many inland towns have struggled to cope with the collapse of the socialist economy, Nikšić, with its steelworks, bauxite mine and brewery, remains an exception. Otherwise, the towns of the interior, such as **Pljevlja**, **Bijelo Polje** and **Berane** are small, low-key affairs, most of them left impoverished following the Balkan wars and years of decaying industry and under-investment – hence tourist facilities are almost negligible in many of these places. That said, the legacy of the area's Ottoman rule, most obvious in the many mosques, is interesting to explore in places like Pljevlja and Bijelo Polje, while most appealing of the lot is the little town of **Plav**, tucked away in the easternmost corner of the country. The town has some particularly distinctive Islamic architecture as well as a pristine lake, while its proximity to the wonderful **Prokletije Mountains** bordering Albania makes it even more worthy of a detour.

There is plenty more cultural heritage on offer in the form of numerous **monasteries** scattered around the countryside, several of which really are worth making the effort to get to. **Ostrog**, near Nikšić, is the site of Montenegro's

127

THE MOUNTAINS

Pristina ▲

SERBIA

KOSOVO (SERBIA)

BOSNIA-HERZEGOVINA

CROATIA

Belgrade ◀
Sarajevo ◀
Podgorica ▶
Kotor & Tivat ▶
Herceg Novi ▶

N

0   20km

Nova Varoš
Duga Poljana
Sjenica
Tutin
Bač
Lučanski Stanovi
Radovac
Pejë/Peć
Junik
Dečani Monastery
Decan/Dečani
Deravica 2656m
Maja Kolata 2528m
PROKLETIJE MTS
KOMOVI MTS
Plav Lake
Plav
Gusinje
Vusanje
Rožaje
Ibarac
Kaludra
Berane
Andrejevica
E80
E65
Crni Vrh
Nedakusi
Ravna Rijeka
Bijelo Polje
Mojkovac
Polja
Kolašin
BJELASICA MTS
BIOGRADSKA GORA NATIONAL PARK
Lim
Tara
Taševo
Prijepolje
Uvac
Lim
E763
21
Pljevlja/Rance
Komine
Pljevlja
Gradac
Kovren
TARA CANYON
Tara
Tara Bridge
Gornja Bukovica
Monastery of St George
SINJAJEVINA MOUNTAINS
Redice
Morača Monastery
E80
E65
MAGANIK MOUNTAINS
Gorica
Spuž
Nikšić
Ostrog Monastery
E762
Danilovgrad
Žabljak
Bobotov kuk 2523m
DURMITOR NATIONAL PARK
DURMITOR MTS
Trsa
Plužine
Šavnik
VOJNIK MTS
Jasenovo Polje
Rastovac
Bogatići
Lake Slansko
Grahovo
Šćepan Polje
Mrtanje
Soko Fortress
TARA CANYON
Drina
PIVA CANYON
Veliki Vitao 2397m
Plivsko Lake
Goransko
Piva Monastery
Piva
GOLIJA MOUNTAINS
Vilusi
Klobuk
Lake Bilecko
Risan
Foča
E762
Gacko
Belića
Nevesinje
Stolac
Brsecine
Trebinje
Gruda
Debeli Brijeg
Dubrovnik
E65
20

most important pilgrimage church, while both **Morača**, located in the valley of the same name, and **Piva**, across to the west near the Bosnian border, hold some outstanding frescoes. If you've got your own transport a most worthwhile side-trip is to the marvellous **Dečani Monastery**, just across the border in **Kosovo**.

While having your own wheels clearly enables you to explore this largely remote region more freely, there is a reasonable **bus** network linking the towns of the interior. The country's single **rail** line, meanwhile, runs north–south from Bijelo Polje to Mojkovac and Kolašin before continuing to Podgorica and the coast.

Danilovgrad and Ostrog Monastery

From Podgorica, buses trundle the short distance northwest along the main E762 road to the restful town of **Danilovgrad**, beyond which lies the Bjelopavlići Plain, a wonderfully picturesque, baize-like valley floor patchworked with green- and straw-coloured fields. A little further on lies **Ostrog Monastery**, Montenegro's holiest shrine, theatrically sited high up in the cliff face.

Danilovgrad

Unlikely as it may seem, **Danilovgrad**, located 16km northwest of Podgorica, was originally conceived by Prince-Bishop Danilo (after whom it was named) in the late nineteenth century as Montenegro's first capital city. While Prince Nikola furthered these plans, they never came to fruition, and it has remained a quiet little market town ever since.

Tourist facilities are almost nonexistent but if you do decide to stop off, there is a moderately interesting **town museum** (Muzej grad; Mon–Fri 8am–3pm; free), located next to the high school on Vaka Đurovića, where fragments of Roman pillars and columns, Illyrian weapons and an unusual collection of stone chains, which hark back to the time when the town was renowned for its stone-making enterprises, are on display. The main street, Baja Sekulića, leads down to a bridge crossing the Zeta River, next to which is a small gallery and, outside, some curious bits of sculpture. This is the work of the so-called **Danilovgrad Art Colony**, which each year organizes a symposium for international sculptors who create artworks using the white stone common to the region.

Practicalities

From the main **bus station** it's a five-minute walk to Baja Sekulića – note that the minibuses that shuttle back and forth between Nikšić and Podgorica use the secondary road which runs parallel to the fast main road (E762), though all buses arrive and depart from the bus station. If you do need to stay, contact the local **tourist office** at Sava Burića 2 (☎020/816 016, ✆tod@t-com.me), who should be able to arrange some **private accommodation**. Down by the riverbank next to the bridge is the *Obala* **restaurant/café**, good for light snacks and daytime coffee or an evening beer – it's a fun little party place in summer when everybody spills out onto the banks.

Ostrog Monastery

Several kilometres north out of Danilovgrad, it's just about possible to detect a white speck grafted into the grey, vertiginous rock face on the opposite side of the valley. In a setting that is as unforgettable as it is improbable, this is **Ostrog**

Monastery (Manastir Ostrog; daily May–Sept 6am–5pm; Oct–April 5am–4pm), Montenegro's most important place of pilgrimage.

Although it's possible that the monastery's initial foundations might have been laid by hermits some time earlier, Ostrog was officially founded in the mid-seventeenth century by Vasilije Jovanović, more commonly known as **St Basil of Ostrog** (see box, below). Ostrog actually comprises two complexes, the first of which, the larger **lower monastery**, is centred around the Church of the Holy Trinity, built in 1824, and is also the location of the majority of the monastic residences, including the modern *konak*. The white, rock-hewn **upper monastery**, a tough little three-kilometre walk uphill (but also accessible by car), holds two diminutive cave-churches, one of which, the Holy Cross, features some splendid rock-painted frescoes by the great seventeenth-century Serbian artist Radul, depicting revered saints (including St Sava and one of St Basil), scenes from the life of Christ, and religious holidays. Nearby, the Church of the Presentation keeps the relics of St Basil. In truth, there's not an awful lot to see here, but the tight corridors and passageways of the monastery, lined with icons and mosaics, are certainly atmospheric, and on a clear day the views from the small terrace fronting the upper monastery entrance are fabulous.

Ostrog is actually reached via a road that turns off at the village of **BOGATIĆI**, itself some 20km along the main road from Danilovgrad. From here it's around 8km to the monastery up a narrow and often precipitous asphalt road, which can be tricky to negotiate in parts, especially when confronted with one of the many coaches that somehow crawl to the top. If you don't have your own wheels (and don't fancy the extremely strenuous walk), then pick up one of the **taxis** that wait down by the main road to take you up to the monastery (about €15 return). If travelling on the Podgorica–Nikšić **bus**, ask the driver to set you down by the village. During the summer it's best to visit as early or as late as possible in the day in order to avoid the crush of visitors.

There are **sleeping** quarters at the *konak* down at the lower monastery (☎020/811 133; €2 for a dorm bed – men and women sleep in separate dorms), though you should call in advance. Back down in Bogatići, there's the excellent, rustically styled *Koliba* **restaurant**, with seating arranged around a large wood-burning fire – smoked ham with melon, bean soup, Bosnian casserole (lamb and vegetables), roast lamb and *gibanica* are just some of the appetizing dishes on the menu.

St Basil of Ostrog

One of the Orthodox Church's most venerated saints, **St Basil** was born Vasilije Jovanović in the small village of Popovo Polje in Bosnia some time around 1610. He took his monastic vows in Tvrdoš, near Trebinje (today part of the Serbian Republic), before spending time at Cetinje Monastery and occasionally travelling to Mount Athos in Greece to further his education. He then returned to Bosnia to be consecrated as metropolitan of eastern Herzegovina, while simultaneously assisting in the renovation of numerous monasteries, which was at that time forbidden by the Turkish authorities. He briefly returned to Tvrdoš until it was eventually destroyed by the Turks. He then moved to **Ostrog**, founding the monastery in 1667 where he remained until his death in 1671. It was at Ostrog that Basil forged a reputation as a miracle-worker – more specifically as a healer of the mentally and physically afflicted. Tales of his ability to cure are legion, and it is for this reason that people of all faiths and persuasions have been making the pilgrimage to Ostrog for centuries. St Basil is buried in the monastery's Church of the Presentation.

Nikšić

Lying flat on a large plateau rimmed by distant mountains, **NIKŠIĆ** is Montene-gro's second largest town, counting a population of around 75,000. It's also the country's most important industrial centre, with a major steelworks, sawmills, bauxite mine and the country's main brewery, which produces the flavoursome, eponymously named Nikšićko beer. Set against this prevailingly industrial back-drop, it's little surprise that tourism plays little more than a walk-on part here, and tourist facilities are minimal. However, and while the town is palpably short on genuinely absorbing sights, it does possess a surprisingly attractive central core around the large main square. Moreover, it has an enviable location, midway between Podgorica and the Bosnian border, and within striking distance of the Durmitor Mountains. In July, the **Nikšić Guitar Festival** (Ⓦwww.niksicguitar-festival.com) is a fun, week-long event attracting an impressive international line-up of artists, partaking in concerts, seminars and competitions.

Originally a Roman camp called Anagastum, this name was transliterated to **Onogošt** some time in the twelfth century; at its centre it had a commanding for-tress, the remains of which are still visible. By 1355 the settlement had assumed the title Nikšić, before the Turks took over – it remained under their aegis until 1877, after Montenegrin independence. Following World War II, the town rapidly industrialized, though it also suffered more than most during the regional wars in the 1990s when inter-republic trade came to a standstill.

Arrival, information and accommodation

The large and modern **bus station** is a five-minute walk from the centre on Gorka Garčevića – there's a **left-luggage** office here (€1) too. The rail line between Nikšić and Podgorica is currently closed, though it is mooted to reopen before the end of 2009. There's currently no tourist office here but if you need **information**, pop over to the local tourist organization at Ivana Milutinovića 10 (Ⓣ040/213 262, Ⓔtoniksic@t-com.me) – they should also be able to furnish you with a town map. The **post office** is on Trg Save Kovačevića (Mon–Sat 7am–8pm) and there's **internet** access on the first floor of the Mex shopping centre on Njegoševa – though you'll probably have to ask to find it (daily 9am–9pm).

The town has two **hotels**. The better of them, the *Sindčel*, Danila Bojovića bb (Ⓣ040/212 591; ❹), is housed in an anonymous and rather ropey looking build-ing, but it has modern, spacious rooms with light-wood furnishings and wooden floors, plus TV and internet access. In contrast, the *Onogošt*, at Njegoševa 18 but actually accessed from Bulevar Nikole Tesla (Ⓣ040/243 608, Ⓔonogost@t-com .me; ❸–❹), is a superb example of the worst kind of socialist architecture (which is, oddly, part of the appeal). The rooms themselves are dated and spartanly fur-nished, but reasonably cheap.

The Town

The heart of the town is **Trg Slobode**, a large, open concrete square framed by a tidy ensemble of two-storeyed, pastel-coloured tenements, accommodating an assortment of shops and cafés. In the centre of the square stand two recent addi-tions: an oversized bronze statue of Prince Nikola on horseback and, directly opposite, a fountain ornamented with bird-like sculptures. Trg Slobode is bisected by **Njegoševa**, the main, partly pedestrianized north–south thoroughfare, which is transformed into a bustling, night-time *korzo* at sundown.

Walking west of Trg Slobode along Karađorđeva or Novaka Ramova will bring you to the bulky remains of **Bedem Fortress** (Trvđava Bedem). Situated along a

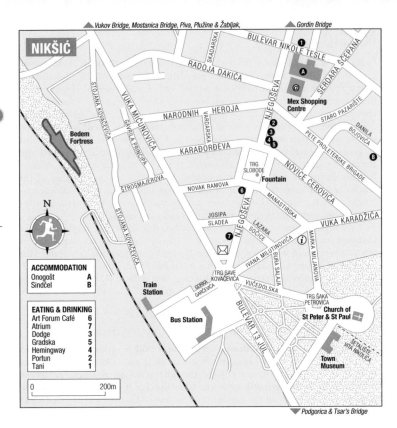

▲ Vukov Bridge, Mostanica Bridge, Piva, Plužine & Žabljak,   ▲ Gordin Bridge

NIKŠIĆ

BULEVAR NIKOLE TESLE

RADOJA DAKIĆA

SKADARSKA

STOJANA KOVAČEVIĆA

VUKA MIĆUNOVIĆA

GAVRILA PRINCIPA

NARODNIH HEROJA

VARDARSKA

NJEGOŠEVA

SERDARA ŠĆEPANA

❶
Ⓐ
@
Mex Shopping Centre

STARO PAZARIŠTE

DANILA BOJOVIĆA

❷
❸
❹❺

PETE PROLETERSKE BRIGADE

KARAĐORĐEVA

TRG SLOBODE
●Fountain

NOVICE CEROVIĆA

Ⓑ

ŠTROSMAJEROVA

NOVAK RAMOVA

❻

MANASTIRSKA

VUKA KARADŽIĆA

N

STOJANA KOVAČEVIĆA

JOSIPA SLAĐEA

NJEGOŠEVA

LAZARA SOČICE

IVANA MILUTINOVIĆA

ĐURA SALJAĐA

MARKA MILJANOVA

ⓘ

❼

✉

ACCOMMODATION
Onogošt   A
Sinđčel   B

▽

TRG SAVE KOVAČEVIĆA

VUČEDOLSKA

TRG ŠAKA PETROVIĆA

EATING & DRINKING
Art Forum Café   6
Atrium   7
Dodge   3
Gradska   5
Hemingway   4
Portun   2
Tani   1

Train Station

GORKA GARČEVIĆA

BULEVAR 13. JUL

Church of St Peter & St Paul ✚

Bus Station

ŠETALIŠTE VITA NIKOLIĆA

Town Museum

0   200m

▼ Podgorica & Tsar's Bridge

narrow, rocky ledge, the fortress has variously functioned as a Roman base camp, a medieval outpost, and then during the nineteenth century as a key Turkish fortification, which is when it last saw action. Although recent extensive reconstruction has quashed much of its historical charm, there are vestiges of the original fortification, notably around the central – and oldest – section, which would have once consisted of several platforms for cannons, sleeping quarters for the watchmen, and would also have functioned as a storage place for ammunition. Opening hours are erratic (meaning that it's more often than not closed), but the best time to visit anyway is for one of the open-air summer concerts that take place in the small amphitheatre located within the walls – check with the tourist organization to see what's on (see p.131).

The **town museum** (Muzej grad; Tues–Sat 9am–1pm & 5–8pm, Sun 9am–noon; €1) is located within one of King Nikola's former palaces – a long, rectangular and now very grubby building in the large park to the east of the centre. On show is the standard assortment of archeological bits and pieces and ethnographic paraphernalia. Constructed from huge blocks of grey-white stone, the neighbouring **Church of St Peter and St Paul** (Crkva Sv Petar i Sv Paul), built in 1900, is far too modern to be anything other than characterless; the cavernous, triple-nave interior is mostly bare, save for a high white-marble iconostasis.

The bridges of Nikšić

If you've got wheels, it's worth making an effort to track down some of the **stone bridges** that lie on the outskirts of Nikšić. A fifteen-minute walk north of Trg Slobode at the end of Njegoševa is the diminutive double-arched **Gordin Bridge**, built in 1902, quite some time prior to the large, belching brewery looming over it. A couple of kilometres west of town, in Kapino Polje on the road towards Trebinje, lies the **Vukov Bridge**, an elegant five-arched structure constructed on the orders of King Nikola and named after, hero of the Montenegrin epic poem, **The Mountain Wreath**, Vuk Micunović; now defunct, it stands alongside a more modern version. From here it's 4km (signposted) to the lovely **Mostanica Bridge**, an old Roman footbridge now largely concealed by thick clumps of trees and rock; a stream lazily flows underneath, while nearby stands a rather forlorn-looking stone chapel. Grandest of all the bridges, however, is the **Tsar's Bridge**, located 3km due south of town and named after Russian Tsar Alexander III, who financed its construction; it was eventually completed in 1896. Nearly 270m long and comprised of eighteen immaculately trimmed vaults, the road bridge spans a smooth, grassy field and part of the re-channelled Zeta River.

Eating and drinking

Options in Nikšić are extremely limited when it comes to eating, but one terrific **restaurant** is ℀ *Portun* (daily 8am–11pm), located through a passageway just off Njegoševa (next to the *Dodge* bar). A low, barn-like building with a dimly lit, rustic interior, it offers an outstanding menu including a fine selection of cheeses, fish (grilled squid, trout, eel and carp), stuffed kebabs and home-made sausages. There's also good draught beer and the service is top drawer.

While decent places to eat are thin on the ground, you'll have no such problem finding a suitable place to drink. Njegoševa, in particular, is run through with **cafés and bars**. On the southwestern corner of Trg Slobode, the *Art Forum Café* is a loungey place, with snug red and blue leather seating and lots of (very good) local artwork adorning the walls. A little further down is *Atrium*, a delightfully mellow little coffee-house with dark orange walls, wicker chairs and wood-framed mirrors. The more animated bars reside on the northern stretch of Njegoševa, such as *Dodge*, an outrageously loud venue dispensing big beats, while both *Hemingway* and *Gradska*, side by side just a few paces along, have pleasant terrace seating. Away from Njegoševa, check out the *Tani* café, a large, glass conservatory-style place opposite the *Onogošt* hotel on Bulevar Nikole Tesle. Expect all these places to stay open until midnight or 1am at least.

Plužine and around

From Nikšić, the main road spears north to the region's main settlement, **Plužine**, beyond which lies the marvellous **Piva Canyon** and the Bosnian border. Also not to be missed is the **Piva Monastery**, a short distance south of Plužine, with its wonderful seventeenth-century frescoes. There are buses from Nikšić as far as Plužine, but thereafter you will have to rely on your own transport.

Plužine

Fifty-nine kilometres north of Nikšić and close to the Bosnian border, **PLUŽINE** is a small, modern town sitting on a hillside overlooking the artificial Pivsko Lake (Pivsko jezero). Whilst there's little of real interest here, there is some accommodation and a very good restaurant, and it's also a good base from which to embark upon walks into the surrounding hills.

Buses from Nikšić drop off at the small **bus station** at the top of town, from where it's a five-minute walk down to the *Piva* **hotel** (☎040/271 129; ❸), an ageing establishment that's a bit ragged around the edges, but clean, bright and friendly enough. Close by is the *Sočica* **restaurant**, a lovely, stone cottage with a fine terrace from where you can sample some wonderfully tasty local trout and meat dishes such as lamb. The large, fenced-off stone building just down the slope was the former **headquarters of Tito's Partisans** (see p.170), which is surprisingly conspicuous given its strategic importance during World War II. It's been mooted that this will at some point reopen as a museum.

Piva Monastery

Around 7km south of Plužine, **Piva Monastery** (Manastir Pivski), celebrated for its remarkable frescoes, hoves into view. The monastery was originally located at the source of the Piva River, some 3km away and 100m below, but following the proposed construction of a hydroelectric plant on the site the decision was made to move it to its current position. It was an extraordinarily painstaking operation, entailing the removal of over one thousand fresco fragments and their replacement onto reconstructed walls. Begun in 1969 and completed in 1982, it was a job exceptionally well done.

At the heart of the complex stands the sixteenth-century **Dormition of the Mother of God Church** (Crkva Uspenje Bogorodice), outwardly austere but whose interior conceals a fine display of wall paintings as well as some beautifully crafted furnishings. The **frescoes**, more or less painted in three separate tiers, mostly date from the early seventeenth century; those on the lower level were the work of anonymous Greek artists, while the more sophisticated ones on the upper levels were completed by Father Strahinja of Budmilje and Kyr Kozma, the latter a renowned artist and woodcarver. One of the more interesting frescoes is that of the sixteenth-century Grand Vizier, Mehmet Pasha Sokolović, located on the southern wall just inside the entrance; it was Sokolović who commissioned the famous bridge over the River Drina in Višegrad, Bosnia, which was so vividly brought to life in Ivo Andrič's Nobel Prize-winning novel of the same name. Kyr Kozma was also responsible for the glittering gold-plated **iconostasis**, richly decorated with icons, which includes splendid paintings of St Sava and St Simeon Nemanja. The cross, meanwhile, was given to the church in exchange for ninety oxen, a not insubstantial price at that time. Take a look, too, at the furnishings, in particular the oversized chandelier, around which a dozen or so double-sided icons hang, and the splendid inlaid ivory doors between the narthex and nave.

Housed in the monastic residence is the **treasury**, whose cabinets are stuffed with bejewelled chalices, vestments, icons and holy lamps. Its most precious items, however, are a psalm from the Crnojević printing press (the first in the Balkans) dating from 1493, and a mitre given to the monastery by the Russian emperor, Alexander I, in the early ninteenth century. There is presently just one monk at Piva, the extremely welcoming Father Nikifor, who will quite happily guide you around the church and perhaps even invite you to join him for coffee.

There is no direct **transport** to the monastery but if you're travelling by bus, ask the driver to set you down at the main road, from where it's a five-minute walk along to the monastery.

△ Fresco at Piva Monastery

Piva Canyon and Soko Fortress

From Plužine, the E762 continues north for 25km through the **Piva Canyon** all the way to the Bosnian border. About 2km north of town, a bridge offers wide, open views of Pivsko Lake, beyond which a right turn marks the beginning of the long and winding mountain road across the Piva Plateau to Žabljak (see p.138), which peaks at the 1884-metre-high Prijespa Pass. For the first 15km or so, the road through the canyon runs parallel to the lake, passing through dozens of tunnels – some are more than 500m long and very dark – and shadowed by huge shafts of limestone rock and, to the east, snow-tipped peaks such as Veliki Vitao (2397m) in the Bioč mountain range. Crossing the dam at Mratinje – at 220m, it's one of the highest in Europe – the canyon narrows dramatically as the road tracks the course of the crashing **Piva River** all the way to the border, some 10km further ahead at **Šćepan Polje**. Here it joins with the Tara River to create the Drina, which flows into the heart of Bosnia.

Sited just above the border crossing point are the scant ruins of the fifteenth-century **Soko Fortress**, the one-time residence of Serb nobleman and former governor of Bosnia, Stjepan Vukčić, until it was destroyed by the Turks. Close by is the small **monastery complex**, its church completely bare, the only distinguishing features a smooth marble floor inlaid with the Montenegrin coat-of-arms and a marble iconostasis inlaid with floral symbols. From the top there are glorious views of the surrounding countryside and the ice-blue Drina River racing away into the Bosnian foothills. To access the fortress you must pass through the Montenegrin border control (not the Bosnian one, though you will need your passport), whereupon a tarmac road, which becomes a rough gravel track about halfway up, winds its way to the top of the hill and the fortress.

Durmitor

The almost completely mountainous **Durmitor** region is inland Montenegro's siren draw, a spectacularly wild and wonderful region of saw-toothed peaks, glacial lakes, deep canyons, and wide alpine pastures. Designated a **national park** in 1978 – it's the largest of the country's four national parks – and inscribed on the UNESCO World Heritage List in 1980, Durmitor is bordered by the Piva Canyon and Plateau to the west, and the Jezera Plateau to the east. In its western section, the park's boundaries embrace the many mingled peaks of the Durmitor Massif, a great shaft of limestone which numbers nearly fifty peaks that rise over 2000m, 27 of them reaching more than 2200m; **Bobotov kuk** is the highest at 2523m. The narrow finger that extends to the east incorporates the magnificent **Tara River Canyon**, whose eponymous river crashes through the heart of the gorge. Etymologically speaking, the name Durmitor is thought to derive from the Celtic *drumitor*, meaning "water from the mountain" which, given the preponderance of lakes within the park – fed by melted snow from the Durmitor Massif – seems wholly apt. The park harbours a wide range of flora – the high grassland areas in particular are richly carpeted in plant life – and fauna, the mountains sheltering brown bear, grey wolf and chamois, among others, as well as over 150 types of birdlife.

Durmitor's key resort, and the only settlement of any size in the region, is **Žabljak** which, though traditionally better known as the country's main **ski** centre, is no less busy a place during the summer months when walkers, hikers and adventure sports enthusiasts arrive here in large numbers. Indeed, Durmitor offers limitless possibilities for **outdoor pursuits** – in addition to skiing, climbing and hiking, whitewater rafting, kayaking and canyoning are increasingly popular on the Tara River. The Tara, richly sourced with trout and char, is also an attractive proposition for anglers during the fishing season, as are some of the mountain lakes.

Getting around without your own transport is not straightforward: relatively few **buses** serve the park, with just half a dozen or so a day from both Nikšić and Pljevlja to Žabljak.

From Nikšić to Žabljak

Seventeen kilometres north of Nikšić at Jasenevo Polje, a road branches off the main E762 towards Žabljak. From Nikšić, some half a dozen **buses** a day make the trip

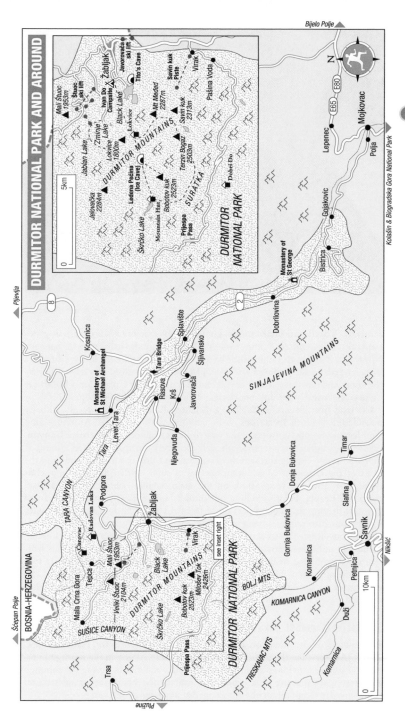

Kolašin & Biogradska Gora National Park

DURMITOR NATIONAL PARK AND AROUND

Inset map (top): DURMITOR MOUNTAINS / SURATKA area

Bijelo Polje

N

Mali Štuoc 1953m
Štuoc ski lift
Javorovača ski lift
Žabljak
Ivan Do
Campsite
Tito's Cave
Black Lake
Lokvice
Savin kuk Piste
Virak
Pašina Voda
Zminje Lake
Lokvice Lake
Lokvice 1800m
Mt Meded 2287m
Savin kuk 2313m
Jablan Lake
DURMITOR MOUNTAINS
Jelovačka 2284m
Ledena Pećina (Ice Cave)
Terzin Bogaz 2303m
SURATKA
Dobri Do
Bobotov kuk 2523m
Mountain Hut
Škrčko Lake
Prijespa Pass
DURMITOR NATIONAL PARK

0   5km

Main map

Pljevlja
8
Kosanica
Monastery of St Michael Archangel
Tara Bridge
Rasova
Krš
Splavište
Šijivansko
Javorovača
Monastery of St George
Bistrica
Gojakovic
Dobrilovina
2
Lepenec
E65 E80
Mojkovac
Polja

Šćepan Polje
BOSNIA-HERZEGOVINA
Tara
Lever Tara
TARA CANYON
Podgora
Radovan Luka
Njegovuda
SINJAJEVINA MOUNTAINS

Crkvovac
Tepca
Mala Crma Gora
Mali Štuoc 1953m
Žabljak
Black Lake
Virak
see inset right
Veliki Štuoc 2104m
DURMITOR MOUNTAINS
Bobotov kuk 2523m
Milošev Tok 2426m
BOLJ MTS
Gornja Bukovica
Donja Bukovica
Komarnica
Timar
Slatina
Šavnik

Trsa
Škrčko Lake
SUŠICE CANYON
Prijespa Pass
DURMITOR NATIONAL PARK
TRESKAVAC MTS
KOMARNICA CANYON
Petnjica
Nikšić

Duži
Komarnica

0   10km

Plužine

137

△ Komarnica Canyon

across the **Vojnik mountain range**, giving glorious views of Durmitor's magisterial peaks, before the road drops to **ŠAVNIK**, roughly the halfway point between Nikšić and Žabljak. A nothing little town, best known as the birthplace of former Bosnian-Serb leader Radovan Karadžić, planted at the bottom of a deep valley by the confluence of three rivers, Šavnik is the most unlikely place for a **hotel**, yet there is one, namely the dull but clean and modern *Šavnik* (☎040/266 227; ❹).

The road from Šavnik to Žabljak (a distance of 37km) climbs steeply, initially meandering beneath sheer rock walls bursting with waterfalls. Around 4.5km after leaving Šavnik, signs point the way to the magnificent **Komarnica Canyon**, whose jagged grey forty-metre-high walls lie barely 5m apart in places. Ahead of here, the valley cutting through the Treskavac and Bolj mountain ranges into the heart of the Durmitor Massif is an impressive sight, with 700-metre-high cliffs framing its yawning space. Back on the main Šavnik–Žabljak route, the road continues steeply, before levelling out onto a high, expansive plain. Be warned if you're driving that a good portion of this road is in a fairly parlous state, with many monstrous potholes lying in wait.

In various isolated spots across the plain are clusters of **stećci** (singular: *stećak*), medieval tombstones thought to have been constructed by the Bogomils, a Christian sect originating in Bulgaria that spread across the Balkans, particularly into Bosnia-Herzegovina. These large stone slabs take on various shapes – roofed sarcophagi, elongated cubes or high pillars – and are inscribed and decorated with figural (knights in armour, hunters, farmers) or floral (rosettes, vine leaves) motifs.

Žabljak and around

A sprawling resort town on the eastern fringes of Durmitor National Park, **ŽABLJAK** serves as the main springboard for winter skiing in the nearby mountains, as well as providing the ideal base for walks and climbs during the summer. As a result, it's the one place where you can solidly rely on being able to find somewhere to sleep, eat and be entertained at any time of the year.

A remote and largely agricultural settlement for centuries, the town merited little attention until World War II, when the **Partisans** based their headquarters here. Indeed, it became the focal point of resistance to the Fascist armies and was the site of savage fighting right up until its eventual liberation in 1943. The Italians and their allies, the Chetniks, made the local villagers pay heavily for the loyalty to the Communist cause, however, razing houses and rounding up and executing en masse.

Although tourism had already been established here in the 1930s, Žabljak only really emerged as the country's (and Yugoslavia's) number-one winter playground after the war, and has pretty much remained that way ever since. Its popularity as a summer destination has also grown in recent years, especially with exploitation of the potential of the nearby Tara River for adventure sports (see box, p.141). There's little to see or do in the town itself, but the beautiful **Black Lake**, just 3km outside of town, makes for a very popular short excursion.

Arrival and information

From the **bus station**, at the far eastern end of Vuk Karadžića, it's little more than a ten-minute walk to the main square, Trg Durmitorski Ratnika. This is more or less where most things of a practical nature are located, including the small **tourist information** hut (daily April–Nov 8am–8pm; Dec–March 8am–3pm), **post office** (Mon–Fri 7am–8pm) and a well-stocked supermarket (daily 9am–9pm). The **Durmitor National Park visitor centre** (Mon–Fri 9am–4pm) is sited just beyond the *Hotel Durmitor*, en route to the Black Lake, though the centre is used primarily as the park's administrative offices, and there's actually very little practical information to hand here. There's **internet access** (daily 9am–10pm) in the small chalet-type building next to the *Durmitor* restaurant. **Mountain bikes** can be rented from Summit Agency (☏052/360 082; April–Oct daily 9am–9pm), located 200m out along the road towards the Black Lake (€10 per day). For a list of the agencies offering activities on the Tara River and elsewhere, see the box on p.143.

Accommodation

Žabljak's **hotels** are a mix of large, package-oriented establishments still bearing the collective cheerlessness of Communist-era hospitality, and newer, privately run places offering somewhat superior facilities and happier service. That said, several of the town's hotels, such as the *Jezera*, located out on the road towards the Black Lake, the *Žabljak* and the *Planinka*, are either currently undergoing renovation or due to be renovated. **Private rooms** are widely advertised around

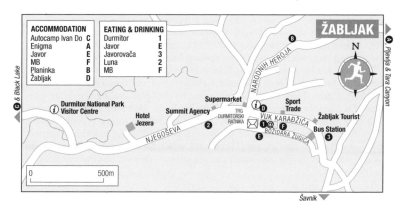

town, and there's a good chance you'll be met at the bus station by landladies offering such accommodation – expect to pay around €10–12; breakfast is not usually included, or even offered, but if it is, expect to pay a couple of euros extra. Žabljak's main **campsite**, *Autocamp Ivan Do* (T 069 041 749; May–Sept), is located out towards the Black Lake: around 200m beyond the Durmitor National Park visitor centre, a road leads uphill to the small site, which has electricity but cold water only. There are some terrific views out across the lake from here though.

Hotels

Enigma T 052/360 130, © hotelenigma@t-com .me. Located around 1.5km east of Žabljak on the road towards the Tara Bridge, this good-value place is the brightest of the town's hotels, with simply furnished but polished double, triple and quad rooms, some of which have electric hobs. Open May–Oct. ⑤

Javor Božidara Žugića 8 T 052/361 337, W www .durmitor.me. One of the town's more appealing options, this small and welcoming private place just behind the Opština has eight modern, clean and brightly furnished rooms. They've also got a couple of apartments sleeping four (€75), and a good little restaurant, too (see opposite). ⑥

MB Hotel Tripka Đakovića bb T 052/361 601, W www.mb-hotel.com. Tucked away just off Vuk Karadžić and midway between the bus station and the centre, this tidy, unassuming hotel has rather spartan but clean and comfortable rooms. ⑤

Planinka Narodnih Heroja 5 T 052/361 304, W www.primorje.me. The town's main ski hotel, which is due for renovation, currently has bog-standard rooms, fashioned in classic 1970s style with gaudy multicoloured furniture and tiny TVs. It is cheap though. ④

Žabljak Trg Durmitorski Ratnika T 052/451 612, © hmdurmitor@hotmail.com. Situated on the main square, this ugly building is in rather desperate need of a makeover, with flaking wallpaper and creaky furniture. Showering is an interesting experience, given that the boiler sits *in* the shower – mind your head. It's due for renovation, though. ⑤

The Black Lake

The easiest and most popular local excursion from Žabljak is to the delightful **Black Lake** (Crno jezero), which lies some 3km to the west of town and can easily be reached by either foot, bike or car via an asphalt road. En route, you may wish to pop your head in at the Durmitor National Park visitor centre (see p.139), where there's a small **museum** illustrating the park's flora and fauna. From the visitor centre, it's about a thirty-minute walk to the lake.

Lying in the shadow of the imposing 2287-metre **Mount Međed** ("Bear Mountain") and enveloped by thick forests of dark pine, the Black Lake is by far the largest of Durmitor's eighteen glacial lakes. It actually comprises two separate lakes, **Malo jezero** ("Small Lake"), 605m long and 49m deep, and **Veliko jezero** ("Big Lake"), 855m long and 24m deep, linked by a narrow sleeve (*struga*), which dries out in the summer, thus dividing them. The lake is fed by waters from numerous mountain streams, some permanent, some temporary, as well as from underground springs and karst wells on the steep slopes of Međed. Frozen for much of the winter, the lake reaches temperatures of 20°C during the summer, making it a popular **swimming** spot, while there are also **rowing boats** for hire (€5 per hour).

The best way to appreciate the lake is to walk around its 3.5-kilometre-long perimeter footpath, which curls under the tree line and then rises gently above the Malo jezero. From the *Katun* restaurant by the lakeshore, signs indicate various local hikes, including to the park's highest peak, **Bobotov kuk** (8hr return), and to **Zminje jezero** ("Snake Lake"; 1hr) and **Jablan jezero** ("Poplar Lake"; 2hr); for more on local hikes see the box on p.142. Walking past the restaurant, it's around 1km to **Tito's Cave** (Titova peć), which for a short time during World War II served as the Partisan leader's headquarters – there is, however, nothing to see there now.

Eating and drinking

Žabljak has a reasonable selection of **restaurants**, by far the best of which is
🌲 *Javorovača*, located in an isolated green spot just beyond the bus station at the
eastern end of town. Offering a wide selection of regional dishes, such as *jagnjetina
u mlijeku* (lamb boiled in milk) and *prebranac* (oven-cooked beans), in addition to
a range of smoked and grilled meat dishes, this cosy, rustically decorated restaurant is especially inviting on cold winter evenings. Elsewhere, the *Durmitor*, on
Božidara Žugića, is a fairly traditional sort of place, doling out plates of grilled
meat. In a similar vein, and just a five-minute walk along the road towards the
Black Lake, there's *Luna*, an alpine-chalet-type place with pine-panelled and bare-
brick walls; it's a popular spot with the locals. Alternatively, the restaurants in the
Javor and *MB* hotels are well worth a punt, particularly the former, which serves
generous portions of tasty domestic cuisine such as cheeses, smoked ham and sausages. **Drinking** takes place in a number of indistinguishable, low-key cafés in and
around the main square.

The Tara River Canyon

Durmitor's defining draw is the **Tara River Canyon** – a wild, sinuously twisting
river valley some 80km long and reaching depths of 1300m, it's Europe's longest
and deepest gorge. Cutting through the heart of the canyon is the 140-kilometre-
long **Tara River**, which tracks a course from the confluence of the Opasnica and
Veruša rivers, near Komovi in the southeastern corner of the country, through the
canyon to Bosnia-Herzegovina, where it converges with the Piva River to form
the Drina. The river is enormously popular with adventure-sports enthusiasts
thanks to its fast, foaming torrent, which commands thousands of rafters and fishing enthusiasts to its milky blue-green waters each summer (see box, p.143). For
the definitive view of the canyon's immense walls and floor, you should make a
beeline for **Ćurovac** (1626m), which lies near the village of Tepca, around 10km

△ Tara River

Outdoor activities in and around Durmitor National Park

Durmitor's mountains and rivers present some excellent possibilities to indulge in a wide range of active pursuits, most obviously **hiking**, **rafting** and **skiing**. The period between late April and September is the best time to hike and raft, while snow is pretty much guaranteed between December and early April.

Hiking

Durmitor is a hiker's wonderland, its valleys and mountains carved up by a well-worn nexus of waymarked paths and trails. The massif was a relatively late discovery for hikers and climbers, due to its relative inaccessibility up until the 1878 Berlin Congress, the point at which the region was finally liberated from the Turks. In fact, it wasn't until 1926, when the first groups of mountaineers ventured here, that successful attempts were made on some of the park's highest peaks, such as Bobotov kuk, Sljeme and Savin kuk.

Camping is permitted in several designated areas of the park, namely Lokvice, Zugica Luka, Radovan Luka, Škrčko, Sušica and Dobri do, though there are no facilities. The **best time of year** to hike is from June through to September, but bear in mind that the weather in the mountains can change with alarming rapidity whatever the time of year and so the usual provisos apply – bring sufficient provisions and appropriate clothing and equipment, particularly if you plan to do any high-altitude hiking. There is currently very little information available on hikes in Durmitor, and although the tourist office can advise, they have no literature. Branislav Cerović's *Durmitor and the Tara Canyon* has thoroughgoing descriptions of numerous **routes** in the Durmitor Massif, as well as a decent map – unfortunately it's out of print. Otherwise, you could try Rudolf Abraham's pocket handbook, *The Mountains of Montenegro* (see p.184), which outlines several hikes in the region.

One of the easiest and most direct **hikes** into the heart of the Durmitor Massif begins at the *Ivan Do* campsite (see p.140) and continues up to **Lokvice** (1800m; 2hr 30min), where there is a *katun* available for basic shelter as well as camping. From Lokvice there are numerous onward possibilities, including: a difficult hike across the narrow and very exposed ridge of **Međed** to **Terzin bogaz** (2303m; 5hr 30min return); an assault on the park's highest peak, **Bobotov kuk** (2523m; 8hr return), which affords by far the most spectacular views of the Durmitor; and a side-trip to **Ledena pećina** ("Ice Cave"; 3hr return), a small cave containing numerous ice stalactites and stalagmites – this last hike is also a popular day-trip from the Black Lake. If you fancy several days' continuous walking, you can complete a wonderful **circuit** of Durmitor (3 days) which tracks a route through Lokvice to Surutka and then takes in the beautiful **Škrčko jezero** – where there is a mountain hut (June–Sept; contact the tourist office in Žabljak for details) – before skirting the western side of the massif and descending to **Jablan jezero**. See p.192 for a glossary of hiking terms.

north of Žabljak and accessible by road – walking from Žabljak to Ćurovac takes just under two hours.

The Tara Bridge

Spanning the canyon at the point where the roads from Mojkovac, Pljevlja and Žabljak converge is the vertiginous **Tara Bridge** (Djurdjeviča Tara), one of the single most impressive feats of engineering to be found anywhere in Europe. The bridge was designed by Mijat Trojanović and built between 1937 and 1940; on completion it was easily the largest vehicular arch bridge in Europe. It's by no means the most beautiful piece of engineering, but the dimensions are

Rafting

Between late April and the beginning of October, the Tara River draws **rafting** enthusiasts from all over to its beautiful, fast-flowing waters, with the best time to raft during May or June following the winter snow melts. The standard half-day trip is the 15km run between **Splavište**, near the village of Šljivansko, and **Lever Tara**, just beyond the Tara Bridge, while a day-trip additionally takes in the section of river between Lever Tara and **Radovan Luka**, a further 25km or so back; hemmed in by the deepest part of the canyon, this is where the current picks up dramatically and the rapids become more frequent. Meanwhile, a two-day trip (which involves an overnight stay in a hut), extends all the way to **Šćepan Polje**, near the Bosnian border. The difficulty level of most of the route described rates a grade three (one being the easiest, six the most difficult).

A couple of **agencies** in Žabljak offer rafting, in addition to other activities: the Summit Agency (see p.139), and Žabljak Tourist (℡052/361 115, ✉office@mirotara .com; same opening months and times), near the bus station; the latter also has an office by the Tara Bridge (℡052/705 931). If you plan to do some rafting, you should ideally contact the agency at least one day in advance. Each raft can take up to eight people, in addition to the instructor; whoever you go with, expect to pay around €50 per person for a half-day trip, €100 for a day-trip and €200 for the two-day trip, which also covers transfers to and from the river, lunch, hut accommodation and all equipment – you just need to bring swimming gear and a towel. Rafting aside, other river-bound activities are still in their infancy.

Skiing

As Montenegro's main **ski resort**, Žabljak has a range of slopes to suit skiers of all abilities, including beginners, although facilities here veer strongly towards moderate to good skiers. The ski **season** usually starts around early December and can continue right through to mid-April. The main piste is at **Savin kuk** (3500m long), with two chair-lifts and three drag lifts, with others at **Štuoc** (2630m long) and **Javorovača** (800m long). **Snowboarding** is still in its infancy here, although there are facilities at Savin kuk. **Ski passes** are only available from the ski centres themselves; expect to pay around €15 for a day-pass and €75 for a weekly pass. There are several places in Žabljak where you can hire **ski equipment**, including Sport Trade, Vuk Karadžića 7, which also does repairs (skis and boot rental or snowboard €10 per day).

Other activities

Both Summit and Žabljak Tourist agencies (see above) offer **jeep touring** (approx €25 per person) through the Tara Canyon, while Žabljak Tourist also run **horseriding** (€15 per hour with guide or €30 for a full-day excursion with lunch). There's good **fishing** on the Tara River, too, with plentiful stocks of trout and grayling; licences (around €15) can be obtained from the National Park visitor centre (see p.139).

certainly impressive – 365m long, with the largest of the five arches spanning 116m, and some 160m high. In a somewhat unfortunate twist of fate, one of the bridge engineers, **Lazar Jauković**, joined the Partisans in 1942, but with the Italians closing in from Pljevlja, he was given the rather disagreeable task of dynamiting the central arch. And just to compound his bad luck, the poor fellow was captured just a few months later and executed here. At the southern end of the bridge, which was rebuilt in 1946, there are two stone **memorials**, one of which is dedicated to Jauković, and another to a young Partisan soldier killed in battle in 1941.

The Monastery of St Michael Archangel

Crossing the Tara Bridge, it's about 2km to a sign pointing the way to the **Monastery of St Michael Archangel** (Manastir Sv Mihaila Arhanđela), a dwarfish little church positioned on wooded slopes just above the Tara River – to get there from the main road, follow the bumpy gravel track for some 3km. The church originally dates from the fourteenth century, but has been renovated many times over, its most recent reworking having bestowed it with a shiny, silver, tin-like roof. Its cold, bare-brick interior is mostly devoid of ornamentation, save for a white marble iconostasis decorated with modern icons and a pair of wood-carved royal doors.

The Monastery of St George

Set in splendid rural isolation some 20km south of the Tara Bridge, at the tail end of the Tara Canyon, is the **Monastery of St George** (Manastir Sv Đorđe), also known as Dobrilovina Monastery after the village in which it's located. Laid to waste by the Turks on several occasions, the monastery church is a simple grey-stone structure dating from 1609, featuring a rudimentary-looking wooden belfry and a bare, barrel-vaulted interior, which is leavened slightly thanks to some partially preserved seventeenth-century frescoes. The living quarters (*konak*) are a relatively recent addition. Unfortunately, and unlike the majority of Montenegro's monasteries, visitors are not actively encouraged; however, even if you don't manage to view the church (you'll need to ask one of the sisters if they can open it for you), it's worth making the effort to get here just for the delightfully serene setting.

Pljevlja

First impressions of **PLJEVLJA**, some 40km north of the Tara Bridge, are unlikely to be particularly favourable: on the surface, it's a grimy cityscape of large factory buildings, smoking chimneys and classic socialist architecture. Yet parts of the centre preserve a highly distinctive Ottoman character, which is writ surprisingly large in numerous mosques and Turkish-style tenements, rendering the town worthy of a linger.

Some history

Initial human settlement in the area can be traced back to the Ice Age, with evidence coming from several caves sited close to present-day Pljevlja. The discovery of some substantial items from Stone-, Bronze- and Iron-Age sites nearby points to continued high level of later human activity in the region. Later, between the first and fourth centuries AD, the Romans started building their own city on the ruins of an existing Illyrian one near the modern-day suburb of Komine, just outside Pljevlja. This site – supposedly the second-largest Roman city in Montenegro after Doklea, near Podgorica (see p.106) – has since simply been referred to as **Municipium S**, the letter S being the first (and only identifiable) letter of the name of this city. The destruction of Municipium S coincided with the arrival of Slav tribes in the sixth century; they established the city of Breznica, which formed part of the medieval Serbian state of Raška.

In 1462, the Ottomans arrived, renamed the city **Taslidža** ("Rocky Place"), and set about establishing churches, mosques and religious schools. Following the transfer of the regional seat of the all-important Sandžak of Hercegovina (Sandžak was the Turkish term for Ottoman administrative provinces) from Foča in Bosnia

The Great Outdoors

Montenegro's abundant mountains, forests, hills, lakes and rivers offer huge potential to indulge in a wide range of outdoor pursuits, from hiking the high peaks of Durmitor National Park to tackling the slopes in Žabljak, or tracking birds on Lake Skadar. Those seeking an adrenaline rush can try their hand at rafting on the raging Tara River or sea kayaking around the beautiful Bay of Kotor. Whatever your activity of choice, the permutations for adventure are endless.

Scaling the peaks

Whilst Montenegrins are not the keenest hikers themselves, during the spring and summer their countryside offers some of the finest and most unspoilt **walking** and **hiking** terrain in Europe, with trails to suit all abilities. Hut to hut walking is still in its infancy as mountain refuges are few and far between, so most hikes are best done as day excursions. For the majority of hikers and climbers, the main destination is the **Durmitor** region, an enticing mix of wide-open pastureland, glacial cirques and lakes and sheer-sided peaks, many of which reach over 2000m. Second only to Durmitor in terms of profile is the alluring **Bjelasica** mountain range in eastern Montenegro, an undulating tract of slightly more gentle, rounded tops, which incorporates the thickly forested **Biogradska National Park** with its signature lake. At the country's southeastern corner, running the length of the Albanian border, are the stunning **Prokletije Mountains**, a heavily glaciated region manifesting a majestic wreath of jagged peaks, including the country's highest, Maja Kolata (2528m). For the slightly less energetic there's more moderate, but no less enjoyable, walking in the limestone massif of **Orjen**, on the border with Bosnia-Herzegovina, and **Lovćen National Park**, which affords magnificent views down to the Bay of Kotor.

Mountain huts, Durmitor National Park ▲

Skiing in Žabljak ▼

Hitting the slopes

Heavy snows are pretty much guaranteed in Montenegro's mountainous interior every winter, and Montenegrins certainly make the most of them. Although the **skiing** here is nowhere near as advanced or as challenging as in the Alps or the Pyrenees, Montenegro's handful of resorts are well appointed and comfortable, while the spectacular scenery, thinner crowds and lower prices add considerably to their appeal; moreover, the season usually runs well into April. The main resort is **Žabljak**, on the edge of Durmitor National Park, where the dramatically set pistes offer runs to suit all abilities; it's also the site of the country's only **snowboarding** facility. **Jezerine**, just outside Kolašin in the Bjelasica, is Montenegro's second ski resort, which though small has excellent new facilities.

Birdwatching

Montenegro's lakes, wetlands and mountains provide myriad opportunities for observing a wonderful range of winged fauna. As the largest body of water in the Balkans, **Lake Skadar** is a key site for any serious naturalist. Hundreds of thousands of water birds winter here or stop over during the spring and autumn migrations – unique and colourful pageants that feature species as diverse as the great and pygmy cormorant, glossy ibis, whiskered tern and the lake's signature bird, the magnificent Dalmatian pelican. With rich stocks of carp and eel, amongst other species, there's also terrific **fishing** here in the summer months. The coast, too, boasts some fine birdwatching sites – notably the **Ulcinj saltpans** and the expansive wetlands adjoining **Buljarica** beach – while in the mountains, especially the **Tara Canyon** in Durmitor National Park, ornithologists can track numerous species of birds of prey, including eagles, buzzards and griffon vultures.

Water adventure

Be it lake, river or sea, Montenegro's waters offer some exciting possibilities for those looking for adventure. Adrenaline junkies make a beeline for the Tara River,

▲ Dalmatian pelican

▼ Fishing on Lake Skadar

▼ Sea kayaking in the Bay of Kotor

Hiking in Durmitor ▲

Parasailing at Budva ▼

Top 5 hikes

▶ **Grbaja Valley** Strike into the heart of the awesome Prokletije Mountains with this easy-to-moderate hike from the *Radnički* mountain hut up to Volušnica (1879m) and beyond to Popadija on the Albanian border. See p.159.

▶ **Bobotov kuk** One of the most challenging hikes in Durmitor is the ascent to its highest and most exalted peak, Bobotov kuk (2523m), best approached from the beautiful Black Lake. See p.142.

▶ **Biogradsko Lake to Razvršje** Bjelasica's many picturesque hikes include this excursion from Biogradsko Lake to Razvršje (2033m), a reasonably strenuous round-trip of around seven hours. See p.150.

▶ **Orjen Massif** Enjoy this fabulous karst landscape with a terrific (and very straightforward) hike from Herceg Novi up to the Vratlo Pass and onwards to Subra (1679m), from where there are fantastic views down to the Adriatic. See p.52.

▶ **Durmitor circuit** For a more strenuous workout tackle this three-day circuit around Durmitor's highest peaks via the scenic Škrčko and Jablan lakes. See p.142.

carving through the spectacular canyon of the same name, where the thrashing torrent is perfect for **whitewater rafting**. The coast, too, has much to offer in the way of genuine thrills and spills. **Sea kayaking** is a great way to explore the gorgeous coves and inlets of the Bay of Kotor, while there are plenty of other water-borne activities available in the multitude of beach resorts ranged along the coast. Swimming aside, of course, there are opportunities for **parasailing**, **jet-skiing** and **windsurfing** (also possible on Lake Skadar), or you can just have a bit of fun bouncing about on an inflatable banana boat or rubber ring.

to Taslidža in 1575, the city prospered further – indeed, its status at the time was equal to that of Mostar (in Bosnia), the Sandžak's chief economic and cultural centre. Unlike much of the rest of the country, the town did not accede to Montenegro following the Congress of Berlin in 1878, and was instead annexed by the Austrians, under whose auspices it remained until 1913. Occupied in World War II, first by the Italians, then by the Germans, the town was the scene for the **Battle of Pljevlja** on December 1, 1941, one of the bloodiest scraps on Montenegrin territory during the war. Though the Partisans were unsuccessful in their attempt to retake Pljevlja, their efforts nevertheless resulted in the deaths of some one thousand Axis forces, as against around two hundred and fifty Partisans.

Arrival, information and accommodation

Pljevlja's **bus station** is a ten-minute walk from the main street, Kralj Petra I. There's **internet** access at Elipsa (Mon–Sat 11am–midnight, Sun noon–8pm), which is inside the sports complex, a five-minute walk north of the centre on Ada (island).

Pljevlja has a fair smattering of **accommodation**, the best of which is the *Hotel Gold* (☎052/323 102, ✉goldpv@t-com.me; ❺), a ten-minute walk from the centre at the end of Marka Miljanova, where slick, airy rooms are complemented by good service and a generous breakfast. Immediately next door, the quiet *Garni* (☎067 501 774; ❸) has simple, plain and very cheap rooms, though breakfast is not available here. A third, though rather less appealing, option is the *Hotel Pljevlja* (☎052/323 140, ✉recepcija@hotelpljevlja.t-com.me; ❹), housed in a weird, triangular-shaped building opposite the mosque on Kralj Petra I. Still bearing the classic stamp of socialist-era hospitality, its careworn rooms are painted a ubiquitous brown colour, but it is central and pretty cheap.

The Town

Pljevlja's main attraction is the **Hussein-Pasha Mosque** (Hussein Pašina džamija), prominently sited on the main street, Kralj Petra I, and named after its designer, the Turkish dignitary Hussein-Pasha Bojanić. Built between 1585 and 1594, it's arguably the most striking of all Montenegro's Islamic monuments, a beautifully proportioned marble building with walls peppered with colourful patterns and topped by a low dome; note, too, the diminutive wooden balcony. The interior is no less richly decorated, painted with vivid floral motifs in the style of the great Persian-Arabic frescoes – this is most apparent on the dome ceiling, the prayer niche (*mihrab*), pulpit (*mimber*) and the wooden gallery (*makfil*). The mosque also holds numerous old manuscripts and printed books in both Arabic and Turkish, which can be viewed upon request. The **minaret**, 42m high, is one of the highest in the Balkans, and features some unusual stalactite-like formations around its upper gallery. Across the small park opposite the mosque, the Hall of Culture – currently undergoing extensive renovation – will eventually house the **town museum**; when it opens, expect to see a comprehensive display of archeological artefacts garnered from the numerous sites located around Pljevlja.

The other major sight in the vicinity of the town is the **Monastery of the Holy Trinity** (Manastir Sv Trojice), located 3km north of the centre amidst thick woodland above the source of the Breznica River. It's a most pleasant walk to the monastery – head along Ivana Milutinovića, then left up Njegoševa, from where it's well signposted – and also accessible by car (a taxi will cost €2–3). Enclosed on two sides by large balustraded living quarters (*konak*), the modest-sized **church**, overlooked by a sturdy, grey-brick bell tower, was built piecemeal during the sixteenth century. The frescoes on its interior walls, painted by Father Strahija of Budimilje, were completed at the tail end of that century; the most interesting are those depicting the

Serbian Nemanjić dynasty, but look out too for a dazzling icon of Mary and Child. The monastery's **treasury** holds a valuable collection of icons, in addition to numerous reliquaries, some beautifully cut medieval embroidery and several illuminated manuscripts, some of which were made in the monastery's own scriptorium.

Eating and drinking

The town's best **restaurant** is *Tri Šešire* ("Three Hats") at Njegoševa 26 (daily 9am–1am), which offers all the traditional grilled-meat dishes at very cheap prices; it's a bit of a local's retreat (the menu is in Cyrillic only), hence very smoky, but there is a small terrace to eat out on. To get here walk along Ivana Milutinovića then left up Njegoševa, just past the sign for the monastery – the restaurant is the salmon-coloured building near the top of the road. On the same numerical theme, for **drinking** try *Četiri Sobe* ("Four Rooms"), just off Kralj Petra I on Tršova, a colourful pub-style gaff staging live music most evenings.

Bjelasica and around

An enticing mix of lofty peaks, lush valleys and rolling green hills, the **Bjelasica mountain range** is second only to Durmitor in terms of its superb natural heritage, while there's also some marvellous hiking and skiing to be enjoyed here. Located at the heart of Bjelasica is **Biogradska Gora National Park**, a lovely, relaxing spot with a beautiful lake and wonderfully diverse array of flora and fauna. Bjelasica is easily accessed from both the mountain resort of **Kolašin**, which is especially popular with skiers visiting nearby **Jezerine**, and rather more low-key **Mojkovac**. The region's foremost cultural monument is the **Morača Monastery**, which manifests some outstanding Byzantine-era architecture and artwork.

Kolašin and around

Attractively sited at the foot of Bjelasica, the small town of **KOLAŠIN** is, after Žabljak, the country's most important mountain resort, with the nearby **mountains** providing skiing and some terrific hiking opportunities. It's also one of the more accessible towns in inland Montenegro, thanks to its position on the rail line and on the main E80 road from Podgorica to Bijelo Polje in the north of the country. Founded by the Turks in the seventeenth century, the town was severely damaged during World War II, hence its mostly modern, rather faceless appearance. However, it's a friendly little place and there are plenty of tourist facilities here, including a good stock of hotels and restaurants.

Arrival and information

From the **train station**, it's a 1.5km walk downhill west to the centre, while the **bus station** (such as it is – it's due to be completely renovated) is more conveniently sited at the entrance to town on Junaka Mojkovačke Bitke. The very good **tourist office** is housed in the large wooden building in between the *Hotel Lipka* and Trg Borca (June–Sept & Dec–Feb daily 8am–4pm; March–May, Oct & Nov Mon–Fri 8am–4pm; ℗020/865 110). As well as providing information on the town, this is also the place to come to find out about Biogradska Gora National Park and Bjelasica, for both of which maps are also available; it also has **bikes** for rent (€10 per day). For **organized activities** in the local area, contact the *Vila Jelka* (see opposite), which offers a good programme of outdoor excursions, such as hiking, mountain biking, horseriding and whitewater rafting on the Tara; see also

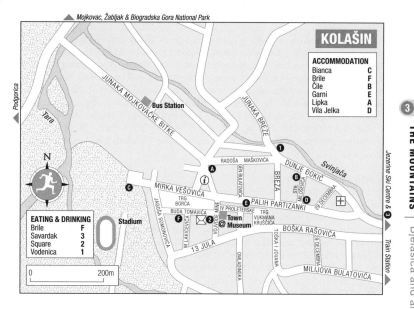

KOLAŠIN

ACCOMMODATION

Bianca	C
Brile	F
Čile	B
Garni	E
Lipka	A
Vila Jelka	D

EATING & DRINKING

Brile	F
Savardak	3
Square	2
Vodenica	1

the box on p.150. The **post office** (Mon–Fri 7am–8pm) is on the south side of the main square, and there's **internet** access on the first floor of the Cultural Centre (Dom Kultura) next to the museum (Mon–Fri 7am–8pm).

Accommodation

As befits its status as a key mountain resort, the town rates some pretty good accommodation possibilities, including two of the country's finest **hotels**, which largely cater to the winter-skiing fraternity – both of these (the *Bianca* and *Lipka*) increase their rates substantially over the Christmas and New Year period. Aside from the hotels, there is a smattering of **private accommodation** (€10–15), which the tourist office can advise on.

Bianca Mirka Vešovića bb ☎020/863 000, Ⓦwww.biancaresort.com. This imposing structure, shaped like a mountain lodge, is the town's main ski hotel, boasting wonderfully appointed rooms designed with stone and pine wood, and beautifully offset with soft orange and white furnishings. Facilities include a super basement pool and a first-rate spa centre with sauna, solarium, Turkish bath and fitness suite. ➒

Brile Buda Tomovića 2 ☎069 015 249, Ⓦwww.brile.info. Although better known for its restaurant (see p.148), this quiet place has a handful of modestly sized, spartanly furnished rooms – it's nothing special, but reasonably priced. ➎

Čile Strahinje Miloševića bb ☎020/865 039, Ⓦwww.zlatnido.com. Peaceful, family-run hotel on a residential street just a short walk from the centre, offering nine basic rooms and three marginally larger apartments. ➍

Garni IV Proleterske bb ☎020/865 454. Once you've got past the smoky bar, which also functions as the reception, you'll find this sister hotel to the *Brile* has seven fairly reasonable if slightly care-worn rooms. The street itself, lined with the town's main cafés and bars, can get pretty noisy. ➍

Lipka Mojkovačka 20 ☎020/863 200, Ⓦwww.hotellipka.com. One of Montenegro's classiest hotels, this is not dissimilar to the *Bianca* (though not nearly as expensive), with warm, alpine-style, wood-panelled rooms, sumptuous beds and sparkling bathrooms equipped with wonderfully large showers. It also has a spa centre. ➑

Vila Jelka Strahinje Miloševića bb ☎020/865 150, Ⓦwww.vilajelka.me. Personable little pension with simple, clean rooms. Its proprietors also run the *Eco Katun Vranjak* on Bjelasica (see p.151) and organize various tours and excursions in the region (see opposite). ➎

The Town

There's little in Kolašin in the way of conventional sights, save for the dusty little **town museum** (Mon–Fri 9am–1pm & 5–8pm; free), housed in the pink building at the eastern end of the large main square, **Trg Borca**. A somewhat random collection, it comprises exhibitions on the Partisans and King Nikola, in addition to a small display of ethnographic wares and a gallery exhibiting old photos of Kolašin prior to World War I. The square itself, part concrete, part grass, is marred by a hideous concrete-and-glass building housing the town's administrative offices – that aside, it's dotted with busts of national heroes killed during World War II, including a woman, Jelica Mašković, who was just 18 when killed at Kupress in Bosnia in 1942.

Eating and drinking

For a truly authentic **dining** experience head to *Savardak* (℡069/051 264; call for opening times, which vary), a couple of kilometres out on the road towards Bjelasica; housed inside a teepee-style, straw-clad hut, this cosy place has just a handful of simple wooden tables and knocks up national specialities such as *cicvara* and *kačamak*, as well as meat-heavy grills. In a similar vein there's *Vodenica*, at Junaka Breze 1, an oversized house that looks a bit old-fashioned and gloomy on the inside, but it's very friendly and serves tasty grilled-meat dishes in generous portions. Around the main square, there's the restaurant at the *Brile* hotel (see p.147), an understatedly smart establishment serving grilled and roast meats, *sarma*, goulash and moussaka, and the oddly named *Square*, next to the post office, which offers the full gamut, from salads and pizzas to fish and steak, as well as cooked breakfasts. The majority of drinking takes place in the smoky **cafés and bars** along IV Proleterske, none of which particularly excite.

South of Kolašin: the Morača Monastery

From Kolašin, the main E80 road descends through the lovely Morača Valley, its walls rising sheer above and the eponymous emerald-green river falling further below in the deepening gorge. This road is both quite narrow and poorly surfaced in parts, so care should be taken if driving, particularly at night or if it's raining.

As the valley begins to widen, the **Morača Monastery** (Manastir Morača) hoves into view, squatting by the roadside like a gatehouse to the lower valley beyond. Pitched on a small plateau amidst perfectly manicured lawns just a stone's throw from the rushing Morača River, the monastery was founded in 1252 by Stefan, grandson of the great Serbian ruler, Stefan Nemanja. Despite having undergone piecemeal reconstruction over the centuries, the main **Church of the Assumption** (Crkva Uspenje Bogorodice) is deceptively simple – a single-nave building with a large narthex on its western side. There is, however, much to admire, both artistically and architecturally. This is initially manifest in some fine Romanesque detail, notably the main entrance whose smoothly cut portal is plastered with a couple of odd-looking bas-reliefs of Christ on the Cross and Christ with Mary. Another Romanesque portal separates the nave and narthex, framing a set of beautiful, intricately patterned, inlaid double doors.

The church's **frescoes** are quite superb. The few original works that date from the founding of the church, located in the sanctuary, show scenes from the life of Ilija (the Prophet Elija), gently coloured in the flowing yet monumental style of the court painters. The remaining wall paintings are mostly sixteenth and seventeenth century: on the western facade and the eastern wall of the narthex are works by Georgije Mitrofanović, a monk from the ancient Serbian Orthodox monastery of Hilandar on Mount Athos in Greece, while the renowned Serbian artist Kyr Kozma completed the scenes depicting the life of Stefan in the small chapel next to the narthex. The richly carved **iconostasis**, topped by an enormous gold cross, comprises a set of royal doors, on either side of which are icons representing various saints, including St Sava, founder of the Serbian Church. The nave also holds the stone sarcophagus of Stefan. The much smaller **Church of St Nicholas** (Crkva Sv Nikole), dating from 1635, sits just across the way, and also features frescoes by Kozma, with cheerfully colourful scenes relating the events of the eponymous saint's life.

Buses from Kolašin to Podgorica (roughly every 30–45min) pass by the monastery and you can ask to be set down here. However, you may have to wait a while for the next one to come along, and even then you'll have to rely on the benevolence of the driver to stop and pick you up.

Biogradska Gora National Park

Some 15km north of Kolašin on the road to Mojkovac, a small bridge crosses east over the Tara River, the road beyond which leads after 5km to the main entrance to **Biogradska Gora National Park** (May–Oct; €2). Covering an area of 54 square kilometres across the central part of the Bjelasica mountain range in between the Lim and Tara rivers, Biogradska Gora is the smallest of the country's four national parks, designated as such in 1952, having been placed under special protection by King Nikola as long ago as 1878. It boasts a wonderfully diverse

Hiking and skiing in Bjelasica

While it may not possess the high peaks of the Durmitor, there's some lovely **hiking** to be had throughout the Bjelasica mountain range, with a series of well-marked paths and trails crisscrossing this green and delightfully picturesque landscape. A particular appeal of walking here is the mountains' accessibility, with easy access via any number of towns that ring Bjelasica, such as Berane, Kolašin and Mojkovac. The best time to hike is from May to September. There's also good, though not particularly challenging, **skiing** here, the season running from early December through to mid-April.

Hiking

From **Mojkovac**, one of the best hikes is the fairly straightforward one south to **Biogradsko Lake**, via Bjelojevice and the *Laništa katun* (1405m; 3–4hr), while another (circular) tour takes in the **Brskovo Valley** via the *Džambas* (℡050/472 221; 1438m) and *Brskovo* (℡069 642 310; 1199m) huts, a moderately easy hike of around six hours. This latter trail gives you the opportunity to stop overnight at one of the huts, useful if you plan to extend this walk and combine with another, longer trail, for example from *Džambas* to **Mt Turjak** (1912m) or from *Brskovo* to **Mt Bjelogrivac** (1970m), from where you can reach the Siško Lake (see below).

A pleasant walk from **Berane** on the eastern fringes of Bjelasica begins at the Đurđevi Stupovi Monastery (see p.156), from where a part-tarmac, part-gravel track ascends through a lovely valley to the hamlet of **Crni Vrh** and then on towards **Siško Lake** (via *Katun Strmenica*; 6hr) which lies just inside the national park. From here you can continue to **Mt Razvršje** (2033m), whereupon the trail descends steeply to the Biogradsko Lake. There are also several trails from the lake itself, the most enjoyable of which is a circular route via **Mt Bendovac** (1774m), from where there are fabulous views back over the lake, and Mt Razvršje, a fairly strenuous round-trip of some six

spectrum of flora and fauna, including red and roe deer and some 150 types of bird, such as eagle and buzzard, as well as more than two hundred species of plant, many endemic (see p.178). Its most celebrated natural assets, however, is its five **glacial lakes** – by far the largest of which is Biogradsko – and a large expanse of **virgin forest**, one of the very few surviving ancient woodland areas in Europe. Although the majority of visitors come to the park to enjoy the lake and its surrounds, there's some excellent **hiking** to enjoy within and just beyond the park boundary (see box, above), and also marked trails for **mountain biking** too. Note that there is no public transport to the park.

From the park's main entrance, the road continues steeply uphill, concluding at the **Biogradsko Lake** (Biogradsko jezero), a shimmering body of deep-blue water ringed by thick banks of pine and fir. It's encircled by a three-kilometre-long pedestrian path, which should take no more than a leisurely hour or so to walk. **Boats** can be also hired on the lake (€5 per hour).

There's a small **visitor centre** (daily 9am–5pm) by the lake, in fact little more than a souvenir shop, as well as a **restaurant** (daily 10am–7pm), serving soups, salads and grilled meats, though you're better off bringing your own picnic to enjoy under the high trees shading the lakeshore. If you wish to stop over, there are simple log-cabin **bungalows** available (€20 for the bungalow), each sleeping two people, while it's also possible to pitch your tent here (€5 per tent).

to seven hours. Another very scenic hike, taking in two of Bjelasica's highest peaks, namely Zekova Glava (2117m) and Troglava (2072m), begins at the hamlet of **Raskrs-nica** (located near the Jezerine Ski Centre and accessible by car) in the park's south-ern periphery, passing by the *Eco Katun Vranjak* (T020/860 150; ❸), where there are over a dozen huts for hire, and the *Bjelasica* mountain hut on the way.

Most **mountain huts** are usually open between May and September, but it's always worth ringing in advance just to check. You might want to consider getting hold of the *Mountains of Bjelasica* **guidebook**, produced by the local tourist organization, which outlines numerous routes throughout the range, and the 1:60,000 *Bjelasica and Komovi* **map**; both are available from the tourist office in Kolašin.

See p.192 for a glossary of hiking terms.

Skiing

Most visitors to Kolašin come to ski at the nearby **Jezerine Ski Centre**, on the slopes of the **Bjelasica Mountain** some 9km east of Kolašin. Montenegro's second-largest ski centre after **Žabljak**, it's relatively small but modern, with 15km of trails, one chairlift and three drag lifts, and also offers night-skiing. Although snowfall is fairly reliable here, cannons make up for any shortfall in the white stuff, and it's generally good value for money: a **day-ski pass** costs around €20, a **three-day pass** around €50 and a **night-ski pass** (7–10pm) around €10. **Lessons** cost around €60 for five hours' tuition. There's good, modern **equipment for hire** at the resort, with the complete kit available for around €15 a day. **Ski scooters**, which can only be hired with a guide, cost €50 for thirty minutes, €80 for an hour. There's a pretty good restaurant here too, where you can tuck into wholesome roast-meat dishes around a large open fire. Note that the road from Kolašin to Jezerine is badly potholed in places, so take care if driving.

Mojkovac

Sitting in a small valley at the intersection of the roads south to Podgorica, west to the Tara Canyon and north to Bijelo Polje, **MOJKOVAC** is a dusty little crossroads town that once represented one of the country's most important silver, lead and zinc mining centres. Indeed Serbia's first coins were minted here during the reign of King Uroš in the middle of the thirteenth century, hence the name – Mojkovac literally translates as "my minted money". Mojkovac was also the setting for the eponymous **battle** on the nights of January 6 and 7, 1916, when a small Montenegrin army of 6500 troops, led by General Janko Vukotić – a large statue of whom stands in the main town square – defeated its numerically superior, 14,000-strong Austro-Hungarian enemy.

Mojkovac's mines and industrial plants have long shut down, and the town is instead now trying to reinvent itself as a base for both hikes in Bjelasica and rafting on the nearby Tara River, though development is very much in the formative stages. While there's really no reason to make a special visit to Mojkovac, there are good onward bus and train connections and a couple of **accommodation** possibilities here, should the need arise. Situated at the southern entrance to the town, near the junction of the road to the Tara Canyon, the *Palas Hotel* (T050/472 508; ❹) is an ugly building concealing clean, though rather spartan and weary-looking rooms; much better is the *Dulović*, on the main town square, Trg Ljubomira Bakoča (T050/472 710; ❹), which has seven fresh, clean and modern rooms.

△ Biogradsko Lake

Bijelo Polje

Thirty kilometres from Mojkovac, and just 25km shy of the Serbian border, **BIJELO POLJE** is easily the largest town in northern Montenegro, though it harbours a still very modest population of less than 20,000. As part of the geographical Sandžak region, the town has long retained a significant Muslim community, which today accounts for nearly half of its population. Its Muslim history is also visible in the numerous mosques in town and the surrounding countryside, though its Christian heritage is manifest in several other important ecclesiastical buildings.

Arrival, information and accommodation

The town's **train station** is 2km along the main road heading north out of town; your only options to get into town are to walk or get a taxi (around €3) from the rank outside. The **bus station** is centrally located at the top of Slobode, the town's main road. As yet, there's no tourist office in town, but you can consult the local **tourist organization** (℡ 069 653 054, ⓔ bizniscentarbp@t-com.me) if you'd like information on any aspect of the town, though it is tricky to find: using the defunct *Bijela Rada* hotel as a reference point, cross the road, walk north for about 50m and then turn right before the clothing shop; it's the tall, salmon-coloured building next to the car park. The **post office** (Mon–Fri 7am–8pm) is at Tomaša Žižica 2, and there's **internet** access inside the Cultural Centre, the lime-green building on the west side of Trg Slobode.

The main town **hotel**, the *Bijela Rada*, was closed at the time of writing, which for the time being leaves the *Motel Durmitor* (☎050/488 111; ❸), a dour but inexpensive roadside haunt rather inconveniently sited at the southern entrance to town on Rakonje.

The Town

Bijelo Polje revolves around leafy **Trg Slobode**, a busy pedestrianized square, in the centre of which is a moving stone **memorial** to the forty-seven victims, a number of whom were from the town, of Montenegro's worst ever train crash, which occurred in Bioče, just north of Podgorica, in 2006. The town has more than its fair share of religious monuments, none older or more important than the **Church of St Peter and St Paul** (Crkva Sv Petar i Paul) on Kneza Miroslava. Held within a low stone wall, this stumpy little structure was founded by the Serbian Nemanjić dynasty in the twelfth century, around the same time as the town was founded. Save for the forty-metre-high white-painted belfry, the church exterior is all bare, though there are splashes of colour inside, including a layer of frescoes in the nave – itself separated from the narthex by a fine, high stone portal. The church's most precious work of art is the so-called *Miroslav Gospels*, an illuminated manuscript on parchment dating from the twelfth century, and named after the Serbian king Stefan Nemanja's brother. If you wish to view it, ask the priest by the stand of cards and candles just inside the entrance.

Housed in a building once occupied by Italians during World War II, the **town museum** (Mon–Fri 8am–4pm; free), on Radnička, keeps a ragbag assortment of items, from archeological bits and bobs (glass vases, pottery and the like) to old

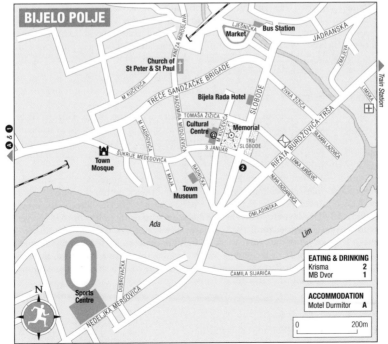

▼ Church of St Nicholas & Mojkovac

coins, household furnishings and wartime artefacts, including a section of a British warplane that crashed in nearby Bistrica during World War II. There's also a nod to the local Muslim community with displays of Turkish smoking pipes, coffee pots and costumes. It's actually a fairly entertaining little collection, though let down somewhat by the lack of any English captioning. About 200m from the museum is the main town **mosque**, originally built in 1741 but brought to its existing site, piece by piece by hand in just two days from the village of Jabučno some thirty kilometres away.

On the opposite side of town, across the wide, rushing River Lim, stands the fourteenth-century **Church of St Nicholas** (Crkva Sv Nikole), an unusual, squat-looking structure with a two-tiered roof and high cupola. Inside, a rather grand iconostasis, topped with a gold cross, frames a set of wooden royal doors, while some fresco fragments adorn a section of the nave walls.

Eating and drinking

Eating possibilities in Bijelo Polje are fairly sparse, the best place being *MB Dvor* (daily 11am–11pm), south of town on Rakonje, just 400m from the *Motel Durmitor*; pizza and pasta line up alongside Montenegrin specialities like Njeguši steak and oven-baked lamb in milk. Otherwise, there's *Krisma*, a popular, well-stocked bakery opposite the town hall on Trg Slobode, doling out sweet pastries and good fresh coffee, and a bunch of terrace cafés further along the square.

Berane and Rožaje

Montenegro's two easternmost towns, **Berane** and **Rožaje** are isolated, poor places, with little tourism infrastructure to speak of as yet. That said, the former is possessed of some important ecclesiastical sights and makes a good base for forays into the Bjelasica Mountains (see p.150), while the latter, attractively positioned in the Ibar Valley, sits close to the border with **Kosovo**, which makes a side-trip to **Peč** and the outstanding **Dečani Monastery** more than feasible.

Berane and around

Positioned on the eastern fringe of the Bjelasica mountain range, **BERANE** is typical of many settlements in this part of the country, a remote, downtrodden place rarely visited by outsiders. Berane's modest status, and today largely modern appearance, belies a colourful historical past, however, and there are some historically noteworthy sites in the vicinity of town.

During medieval times, Budmilja, as the town and region was then known, was of key political, economic and religious importance within the Serbian state of Raška, as evidenced by the presence of several monasteries hereabouts, most importantly Đurđevi Stupovi. The town was overrun by the Turks in 1455, under whose aegis it remained until 1912 (despite several uprisings in the nineteenth century). It was then at the centre of fierce fighting between Partisans and Chetniks during World War II, at the end of which it assumed the name **Ivangrad**, in tribute to the prominent Partisan member, Ivan Milutinović – a title it retained until 1992 when it changed to its current name.

The Town

There's not a lot of interest in town itself, but it's worth popping over to the **Polimski Museum** (Polimksi muzej; Mon–Fri 9am–4pm; free) at Miloša Mališića

From Rožaje, a minor mountain road climbs south up to the border at Lučanski Stanovi, before a snaky descent to **Peč**, some 45km distant. Crossing the border is a formality, just so long as you have your passport (and visa, if required – visa requirements are the same as for Montenegro), with few, if any, delays likely. The second largest town in Kosovo, Peč (Pejë in Albanian) is a lively, chaotic place, its highly distinctive Turkish character manifest in the many Ottoman-era houses and dusty streets. It became important in the fourteenth century when the patriarch of the Serbian Orthodox Church made it his permanent residence, which it remains to this day. For this reason, Peč is regarded by Serbs as their spiritual seat – not surprisingly, the town was at the centre of inter-ethnic unrest during the war in Kosovo in 1999. If you wish, or need, to stay here, there's decent budget **accommodation** at the *Hotel Dona* (℡049/690 857; ❸) on Rruga Besnik Lajqi, near the train station on the east side of town. Note that the euro is also the currency used in Kosovo.

Twelve kilometres to the south of Peč, just beyond the village of Dečani itself – it's well signposted from the village, but you will need your own transport to reach it – stands the magnificent **Dečani Monastery** (Manastir Dečani), one of the most important of all holy Serbian shrines, in a shallow valley surrounded by a thick forest of pine and chestnut trees. That the monastery has survived at all is something of a miracle, having withstood various wars and pillaging raids through the centuries, most recently during the 1999 conflict: a mortar attack in 2007 emphasized its vulnerability and it remains under UN protection, so you will require your passport to enter. The **Ascension of Our Lord Church** (Crkva Vaznesenje Gospodnje; Mon–Sat 11am–1pm & 4–6pm, Sun 7am–6pm) was built by a Franciscan monk from Kotor named Fra Vid between 1327 and 1335, upon the orders of the Serbian king Stefan Uroš III Dečanski, though its completion was overseen by his son, Emperor Dušan, following the former's death in 1331. Beautifully proportioned, the church exterior manifests smooth, alternating bands of creamy lilac and reddish-purple-coloured marble, and doors and windows embellished with some sublime stone-carved ornamentation. Above the western entrance is a tympanum with a relief of Christ between two angels and the signs of the zodiac, above which is a representation of George slaying the dragon and, on the southern door, a fine relief of the Baptism of Christ.

The cathedral-like interior is an exquisite blend of Romanesque and Gothic, while the scale of its **frescoes** – more than a thousand – is quite possibly the most complete anywhere in the countries of the former Yugoslavia. The bright and airy narthex, architecturally resplendent with soaring octagonal pillars topped with floral and zoomorphic motifs, is a veritable portrait-gallery of Serbian kings, the most impressive of which is a splendid artistic rendition of the Nemanjić family tree (St Sava stands bottom left, Stefan Dečanski on the right-hand side of the third row, and Emperor Dušan top middle). By way of contrast, the nave is high and dark, though the frescoes here are no less clear or precise – in particular, look out for a superb *Tree of Jesse* on the western wall, a rare depiction of Christ with a sword on the pillar to the right as you enter, and a fresco of Dečanski on the wall to the left of the wood-carved Baroque iconostasis. The oldest of the icons, meanwhile, is the early fourteenth-century *Holy Mother of God* on the altar screen, in front of which lies Dečanski's richly carved marble sarcophagus.

3, which relays Berane's colourful history to pleasing effect. The archeological collection is especially impressive, holding weapons, tools and ceramic ornaments, including jewellery and some exquisitely carved figurines, garnered from the Neolithic and Illyrian periods, as well as Roman antiquities from the ancient Budmilja military camp. Look out, too, for an intriguing chain-mail tunic, weighing nearly

20kg and thought to date back to the time of the Crusaders, as well as some fresco fragments retrieved from Celije Monastery (see below).

Sited near a disused airstrip two kilometres north of town, but well signposted, is Berane's most important ecclesiastical monument. Founded in the thirteenth century by Prvoslav, son of Stefan Nemanja's brother, Tihomir, **Đurđevi Stupovi Monastery** (Manastir Đurđevi) remains the greatest legacy from the Budmilja era. With a handsome white-brick exterior, it is slightly unusual in form: long and narrow, it's topped with two towers, one square and one octagonal, with a striking red-coloured relief of St George slaying the dragon just above the entrance. The cold, grey interior betrays little in the way of ornamentation, the walls mostly bare save for some fresco remains in the apse.

Practicalities

The **bus station**, on Dušana Vujoševića, is just a five-minute walk from the centre of town with Berane's one **hotel**, the agreeable, oddly named *Hotel S* close by on Mitropolita Pajsije (☎051/232 031; ③), whose simple, comfortable rooms are complemented by cheery, helpful service. The **post office** is just off the main town square at Crnogorska brigade 5 (Mon–Fri 7am–8pm) and there's **internet** access just below the hotel. The terrific little *Dva jelena* ("Two Deers") **restaurant**, a block behind the *Hotel S* on Sveti Save, is easily the best place to eat in town, serving up traditional Montenegrin dishes and good wine in rustic, welcoming surrounds. Elsewhere, pavement **cafés** consume the entire stretch of the main pedestrianized street, Mojsija Zečevića.

Around Berane: Celije Monastery

Wedged between steep-sided cliffs by a babbling river in the village of **KALUDRA**, some 8km south of Berane, lies a much less heralded monastery than Đurđevi Stupovi. Likewise founded by the Nemanjić family, this one in the fourteenth century, **Celije Monastery** (Manastir Celije) was so named after the nearby caves ("celije") once inhabited by its monks. The church was more or less completely destroyed by the Turks, before the Partisans literally built a road over the site during World War II – its latest reincarnation dates only back to 2001, as testified by the freshly painted icons decorating the interior. You'll need your own transport to get here: cross the main town bridge, pass beyond the defunct *Hotel Berane* and follow the road towards and into the gorge.

Rožaje

From Berane, it's a lovely thirty-kilometre drive through the green and lush Ibar Valley to the small market town of **ROŽAJE**, squeezed into a tiny pocket of the country within a stone's throw of the Kosovan border. Smaller and even more isolated than Berane, Rožaje grew up around a Turkish fortress in the late seventeenth century and has retained a large Muslim population ever since. In March 1999, the town was the first stop for thousands of Kosovars fleeing the war in Kosovo, most of whom were dispersed to other parts of the country, and specifically Ulcinj on the coast (see p.85). Indeed, while there's little reason to specifically venture here, it does provide one of the few convenient gateways into neighbouring Kosovo. The sturdy **Ganić Tower** (Ganića kula) on Trg Crnogorske brigade is now occupied by the **town museum** (Mon–Fri 8am–4pm; free), housing items of Turkish crockery and traditional local textiles.

Buses stop just a five-minute walk south of the centre on the main (E65) through road. If you find yourself in need of **accommodation**, make for the first-rate *Rožaje Hotel* (☎051/342 382, ✉hotelrozaje@t-com.me; ③), a large, shiny, glass building on the main town square, Maršala Tita, with fabulously large and sunny, elegantly furnished rooms – there's also a pool, sauna and massage salon. It's also easily the best **place to eat** in town, classy yet informal, with an above-average (albeit meat-heavy) menu that includes schnitzels, smoked sausages and roast lamb as well as Montenegrin dishes such as *sarma*. There's more accommodation 5km back out of town on the road towards Berane, in the shape of the cheap *Motel Grand* (T 069 465 539; ❸), which keeps simply furnished but clean and modern rooms, as well as a restaurant. Apart from the *Rožaje Hotel*, drinking options include the bunch of **cafés** that cluster around Maršala Tita, one of which, *Café Tajson*, is an appealing, loungey haunt with good coffee and beer. There's a **post office** (Mon–Fri 7am–8pm) just off Maršala Tita, and **internet** access in the small Sofico shopping centre opposite the hotel.

Plav and around

Wedged into a small, mountainous corner of the country some 45km south of Berane, the small town of **PLAV** (which means "blue") was once one of Montenegro's most popular summer destinations. During the 1990s, a sharp decline in visitor numbers, due to the ongoing wars in the region, combined with a major influx of displaced persons from Kosovo (many of whom have stayed) at the end of the decade, resulted in a downturn in the town's fortunes. Yet some fascinating architecture, beautiful lakes and the town's proximity to the stunning **Prokletije Mountains**, means that, while it may be in its infancy, tourism is ripe for development here. A good time to be here is during the town's major annual event, the **Lim Regatta**, a fast and furious whitewater-rafting competition, which takes place on the eponymous river.

The Town

Plav was established in 1619 by Turkish aristocrats, and the town's Islamic legacy is writ large in its mosques. The oldest of these, simply called the **Old Mosque** (Stari džamija), sits on a small rise at the junction of Čaršijska and Racina, the town's two conjoining through-streets. Affording lovely views over Plav Lake and across to the Visitor Mountain, it's an atmospheric little shrine, part wood, part brick, with a slim wood-shingled minaret and wooden gazebo in the garden. In stark contrast, the modern **Sultanija Mosque** (Sultanija džamija), just 50m away across the roundabout, is a crude, grey-brick structure with a towering stone minaret. Built in 1909, it has experienced a rather chequered history, having been confiscated by the authorities in 1924 and then used variously as a military warehouse, school and police station, before being returned to the Islamic community.

At the top end of Čaršijska is the **Prnjavdrska Mosque** (Prnjavdrska džamija), which is almost identical in both size and structure to the Old Mosque, but possessed of a stone gazebo. A few paces away stands the chunky stone-block **Režepagića Tower** (Režepagića kula), built in the seventeenth century originally as a dwelling but which later served as a defensive lookout.

The town's main draw is **Plav Lake** (Plavsko jezero), a large, oval expanse of water from whence the River Lim springs, continuing all the way to the Serbian border. On warm summer days bathers flock to the lake, but if you don't fancy a swim, there are other water-bound activities you can participate in: kayaks and paddleboats are both available for hire, each costing around €3 per hour – the main jetty is reached via a road opposite the bus station which winds down past the defunct *Jezero* hotel.

Practicalities

The **bus** station is on the main through street, Racina, from where nothing in town is more than a ten-minute walk away. In the absence of a tourist office, you should consult the very helpful HRID Mountaineering Association (℡069 424 984, ⓔpskhrid@t-com.me), whose office is near the bridge on Čaršijska (no number), for **information**. They can also organize a number of local **activities**, such as four-wheel-drive excursions, mountain biking and paragliding, and can provide hiking guides. The **post office** (Mon–Fri 7am–3pm) is by the roundabout next to the Old Mosque. Following the closure of the main lakeside *Jezero* hotel, there's presently very limited **accommodation** in Plav, with options restricted to the very small and simple *Djerdan Hotel* (℡051/252 503; ❹), just across from the bus station, or a **private room** (❸), which you can book through HRID. Most of the town's eateries (there are no restaurants as such) and **cafés** are congregated at the southern end of Racina, which is also where the majority of night-time drinking takes place.

Gusinje and around

Nestled in the shadow of the Prokletije (see opposite), just 11km southwest of Plav, is **GUSINJE**, a friendly, straggling village spotted with lots of stone-built

△ The Prokletije

houses. Once more populous than Plav, it, too, has more than its fair share of religious monuments, including the **Vizier's Mosque** (Vizier džamija), constructed in 1626, and nearby, both Orthodox and Catholic **churches**. The former, a boxy white structure standing alone in a small field next to its detached belfry, dates from the eighteenth century, while the latter is more modern and rather ungainly. In the centre of the village, a sign points the way to **Ali Pasha Springs** (Ali Pašnici izvor) and the hamlet of **VUSANJE**; after about 3km the road forks, the right turn taking you to the springs, where there's a beautifully sited and well-regarded restaurant, *Vodenica*, though it has been closed for a couple of years and no one appears to know whether it will open again – regardless, it's a wonderfully idyllic spot. Turning left at the fork brings you to Vusanje, around 7km ahead, and the thirty-metre-high **Skakavice** ("Grasshopper") **Waterfall**, from which the close-up views of the Prokletije are simply magnificent. From here you can take a walk up the gorgeous Ropojana Valley (see below).

For **accommodation** in Gusinje, there's the simple *Motel Galerija* (☏051/256 493; ❸), some 500m from the centre of the village in the direction of Plav. Note that there is no public transport from Plav to Gusinje, so unless you have your own wheels you will have to hitch a lift – alternatively, the walk itself is extremely pleasant.

The Prokletije Mountains

A wild and rocky region of deep glacial valleys, sharp cliffs and saw-toothed peaks, the glorious **Prokletije** (Bjeshket e Nemuna in Albanian) is one of the most remote and least-visited mountain areas in Europe. Translated as the "Accursed Mountains" – evocatively brought to life in Robert Carver's book of the same name – this formidable alpine spine straddles the border with Albania for some 50km, though the Montenegrin share of the Prokletije represents by far the smaller part of the massif. Montenegro's highest peak, **Maja Kolata** (2528m), which trumps Bobotov kuk in Durmitor by just 5m, resides here; Prokletije's highest peak, Maja Jezerces (2694m), is on the Albanian side.

There's fantastic **hiking** in these mountains, with the best approaches from the **Grbaja Valley**, a narrow, 10km-long glacial valley which begins a short way southwest of Gusinje. Most walks start from the *Radnički* **mountain hut** located deep inside the valley – if you wish to stay here check first with the HRID Mountaineering Association in Plav (see p.157) to see whether it's open. A fairly easy half-day hike is up to **Volušnica** (1879m), which can be extended (by about two hours) to include Popadija on the Albanian border. More challenging, and slightly longer, is the hike to **Krošnja** (2165m), from where it's possible to continue to the needle-sharp peaks of the **Karanfili** ("Carnation"; 2490m), though this latter part is much more difficult and very exposed in places. A more straightforward but no less beautiful walk is along the adjacent **Ropojana Valley**: beginning in Vusanje (see above), follow the flat track all the way to the Jezerce Lake, which sits in a large basin at the head of the valley, on the other side of which is the Albanian border – this eleven-kilometre round-trip should take no more than four hours. The HRID Mountaineering Association in Plav can advise on hikes in the region and provide guides if required.

Travel details

Trains

Bijelo Polje to: Bar (5 daily; 3hr 45min); Kolašin (5 daily; 1hr); Mojkovac (5 daily; 40min); Podgorica (5 daily; 2hr 45min); Virpazar (5 daily; 3hr 20min).
Kolašin to: Bar (5 daily; 2hr 45min); Bijelo Polje (5 daily; 1hr); Mojkovac (5 daily; 30min); Podgorica (5 daily; 1hr 45min); Virpazar (5 daily; 2hr 30min).
Mojkovac to: Bar (5 daily; 3hr 15min); Bijelo Polje (5 daily; 40min); Kolašin (5 daily; 30min); Podgorica (5 daily; 2hr 15min); Virpazar (5 daily; 3hr).

Buses

Berane to: Bijelo Polje (12 daily; 45min); Kolašin (every 45min–1hr; 1hr 30min); Mojkovac (every 45min–1hr; 50min); Plav (4 daily; 1hr 15min); Rožaje (7 daily; 30min).
Bijelo Polje to: Berane (9 daily; 45min); Kolašin (Mon–Fri 6 daily, Sat & Sun 3; 1hr 20min); Mojkovac (9 daily; 40min); Pljevlja (2 daily; 1hr 45min); Podgorica (Mon–Fri 6 daily, Sat & Sun 3; 2hr).
Danilovgrad to: Nikšić (every 20–30min; 40min); Podgorica (every 20–30min; 20min).
Kolašin to: Berane (every 45min–1hr; 1hr 30min); Bijelo Polje (Mon–Fri 6 daily, Sat & Sun 2; 1hr 20min); Mojkovac (every 45min–1hr; 40min); Pljevlja (5 daily; 2hr 45min); Podgorica (every 30min–1hr; 1hr 20min).

Mojkovac to: Berane (every 45min–1hr; 50min); Bijelo Polje (hourly; 40min); Kolašin (every 30min; 35min); Pljevlja (9 daily; 2hr); Podgorica (every 30–45min; 1hr 45min).
Nikšić to: Budva (every 45min–1hr 15min; 1hr 45min); Herceg Novi (every 45min–1hr 15min; 2hr 15min); Kotor (every 45min–1hr 15min; 2hr 15min); Plužine (5 daily; 1hr 20min); Podgorica (every 20–30min; 1hr); Risan (6 daily; 1hr); Tivat (6 daily; 2hr 15min); Žabljak (6 daily; 2hr).
Plav to: Berane (3 daily; 1hr 15min).
Pljevlja to: Bijelo Polje (2 daily; 1hr 45min); Kolašin (4 daily; 2hr 45min); Mojkovac (8 daily; 2hr); Žabljak (4 daily; 1hr 15min).
Rožaje to: Berane (6 daily; 30min).
Žabljak to: Nikšić (6 daily; 2hr); Pljevlja (5 daily; 1hr 15min); Podgorica (6 daily; 3hr).

International trains

Bijelo Polje to: Belgrade (3 daily; 5hr).
Kolašin to: Belgrade (3 daily; 6hr).
Mojkovac to: Belgrade (3 daily; 5hr 30min).

International buses

Bijelo Polje to: Belgrade (8 daily; 6hr 30min).
Kolašin to: Belgrade (8 daily; 7hr 30min).
Mojkovac to: Belgrade (8 daily; 7hr).
Žabljak to: Belgrade (2 daily; 7hr 30min).

Contexts

Contexts

History

Montenegro's history, like that of all those countries that once constituted Yugoslavia, is complex. It has been ruled over by a succession of invaders and occupiers, from Illyrians and Romans to Venetians and Ottomans, all of whom have had a hand in shaping the country's cultural, religious and political landscape. It then spent much of the twentieth century enmeshed in a fraught and complex Yugoslav federation, which imploded spectacularly in the 1990s, culminating in a succession of wars throughout the region. In 2006, Montenegro became the last of the original six Yugoslav republics to gain its independence.

Illyrians, Greeks and Romans

Although recorded history of the area now covered by Montenegro begins with the arrival of the Romans, the discovery of inhabited ice caves in the vicinity of Pljevlja and jewellery around Berane suggests that this territory was already settled in the **Paleolithic** and **Neolithic** eras. The late Iron Age (fifth century BC onwards) coincided with the arrival of the Illyrian tribes – an Indo-European people who had already established themselves along the eastern Adriatic seaboard. The Illyrians were a diverse confederation of tribes scattered throughout the region, such as the Pirustae in northern Montenegro, the Ardiaei around the territory of Lake Skadar, the Olchiniatas from Ulcinj and the Docleates and Labeates near Podgorica; their main fortress and capital, meanwhile, was Risan. Whilst little is known about their lifestyle, the numerous hill forts that they built indicated a high level of violence and warfare.

Around the same time, the Illyrians were joined by colonies of **Greeks**, who established trading centres in places such as present-day Budva and Ulcinj. Although their influence was largely restricted to the coastal areas, by the third century BC it was extensive enough to provoke a backlash from the Illyrians. A confederation of tribes led by King Agron, and later his widow Queen Teuta (who reigned from 231 to 228 BC), succeeded in driving them from just about everywhere. However, progressive incursions by **Celtic** peoples meant that the Illyrians had little time to consolidate these gains.

The coast was also an obvious target for **Roman** expansion, using as their pretext defence against Illyrian piracy, and the second and first centuries BC saw repeated warfare between the two sides, culminating in 9 AD with the Roman annexation of the region by Tiberius. In 10 AD, the Romans established the province of **Dalmatia**, which incorporated most of present-day Montenegro as well as much of Croatia, with the capital at Salona, near Split. Their main trading centres were largely confined to the coastal cities and provincial strongholds, such as Stari Bar, Birziminium (on the site of present-day Podgorica) and what is now known simply as Municipium S, just outside Pljevlja, though programmes of road building and tax collection extended throughout the territory. Whilst there's relatively little to show for their presence, there remain some vestiges, notably extensive ruins at Doklea, near Podgorica, and some superbly preserved mosaics in Risan.

Emperior Diocletian's division of the territories in 285 AD into the two new provinces of Dalmatia and Praevalitana was a major cause of the fragmentary development of the region. When the Roman Empire split into the two rival empires of Rome and Byzantium (the latter with Constantinople – Istanbul – as its capital), a division that would later result in a crucial split between the Eastern Orthodox and Roman Catholic churches, the territory that would be come Montenegro found itself sitting astride a cultural and religious divide: the western part – in a line that run roughly from Budva to Belgrade – fell under the influence of the western emperor, the eastern section now ruled from the east.

The Slavs

The disintegration of the Roman Empire in the fifth century coincided with the Age of Migration, a time of huge population shifts throughout the region, and a series of invasions of Montenegrin lands by semi-nomadic peoples from Central Europe and Asia. First up were the Germanic **Goths**, then the Asiatic **Huns**, whose demise was sealed by the death of Attila in 453. These were followed in the sixth century by the **Avars**, a powerful Turkic tribe. Whereas the inhabitants of the (largely walled) coastal towns managed to repel attacks, inland settlements were repeatedly pillaged and destroyed.

The Avars were followed in the seventh century by the **Slavs** who, it's thought, had originally occupied the lands north of the Danube in present-day Ukraine, though it was from here that they were driven by Avar and Bulgar tribes. However, unlike most of the other barbarian tribes, they had no real homeland to return to and settled permanently in the territory of the future Yugoslavia, henceforth becoming the dominant ethnic group in the region. The Slavs comprised three disparate groups: the Slovenes, who settled in the north; the Croats in the west; and the Serbs, who settled in the south, which included the present-day territory of Montenegro. Whilst they originally shared a fairly common language and, to an extent, an identity, their distinct patterns of settlement meant that each soon forged very different dialects, while the mountainous nature of the terrain they occupied ensured a degree of isolation from one another; as a consequence, they developed differently. Of the three, the Serbs had a particularly strong social structure, known as *zadruga*, whereby extended families, governed by a local chief (*župani*), held land and oversaw common social responsibilities.

Whilst enjoying a relative amount of freedom, the Slavs remained very much under Byzantine suzerainty. Eager to expand their influence, the Byzantines enforced one of the most important cultural changes amongst the South Slavs in the ninth century, when two Thessaloniki-based missionaries, Cyril and Methodius, were entrusted with the task of creating an alphabet suited to the needs of the Slav language. They created the Glagolithic script, on the basis of which, St Clement, a disciple of Cyril, devised a simplified version known as **Cyrillic**, named in honour of his mentor. The script remains very much in use to this day, not only in Montenegro but in Serbia, Bulgaria and Russia.

The Middle Ages: medieval dynasties

By the end of the ninth century, the various Serb tribes had organized themselves into more coherent units, the first of which emerged in **Raška**, in (today's) southwestern Serbia, just north of Kosovo. A century later, a second Slav state, **Duklja** (also known as Doclea), was established, encompassing most of the territory of modern-day Montenegro, and so named after the Illyrian tribe that once inhabited the region. Its first ruler, Jovan Vladimir, was succeeded by his nephew, Stefan Vojislav, whose greatest achievement was to wrestle the state free from Byzantine control following victory against a powerful Byzantine army at Tudjemili, near Bar, in 1042. Duklja's high point – albeit short-lived – came under the patronage of Vojislav's son, Mihailo, who contrived to expand his territory, and later (in 1077) received the royal crown from the pope, and towards the end of the century, his son, Bodin, who successfully petitioned for an archdiocese at Bar; at one stage, he even managed to exercise a degree of control over Raška and parts of neighbouring Bosnia. By this time, Dukla had become known as **Zeta**, hitherto a *župan* (municipality) within Duklja itself. By the time of Bodin's death sometime around 1101, however, Zeta was beginning to weaken, owing to civil wars and incessant family feuding, and by the end of the twelfth century had been completely usurped and reduced to vassal status by its former rival, Raška. This coincided with the beginning of a golden period in Serbian medieval history under the Nemanjićs.

The Nemanjić dynasty

By the end of the twelfth century, Byzantine pressure on Raška had relented and a dominant family had emerged. Named after **Stefan Nemanja** a Serb nobleman born in Ribnica (modern-day Podgorica) in 1109, the **house of Nemanjić** went on to rule the Serb lands for some two centuries – during which time it spawned some ten monarchs – becoming by far the most powerful medieval state in the Balkans. Having annexed Zeta in 1190 and installed his eldest son, Vukan, as its governor, Nemanja moved on to acquire further territories in present-day Kosovo and Macedonia. Following his death in 1199, he was succeeded by his second son, also called Stefan – titled Stefan the First-Crowned (*Prvovenčani*) – who continued Nemanja's process of state-building, aided by his younger brother, **Sava**, who established an independent **Serbian Orthodox church** in 1219 and, as the church's first archbishop, became the most venerated of all Serbian saints. The inclusion of Zeta within the Orthodox jurisdiction was particularly significant, given that many of the coastal towns, such as Kotor and Bar were, at that time, heavily under the influence of the Catholic Church.

During their tenure, the Nemanjić rulers were responsible for the construction of some of the greatest Orthodox monastic churches, including Morača in Montenegro, Mileševa and Studenica in Serbia, and the magnificent Dečani Monastery near Peć, Kosovo. The construction of Dečani was overseen by Dušan (Uroš IV, 1331–55); the ninth ruler, Dušan was also the architect of some distinguished military feats, including the plunder of much of Bulgaria's territory in Macedonia, and victories over the Turks at Thessaly and Epirus in Greece, earning him the sobriquet "Dušan the Mighty". His successor, Uroš V (1355–71), or "Uroš the Weak", abjectly failed to consolidate the gains made by Dušan, and his ineffectual leadership resulted in the fragmentation of the empire's various districts, and the ensuing Ottoman advance through the Balkan peninsula. With this, the Serbian empire fell into rapid decline, with, as it turned out, Uroš being the last of the Serb medieval kings.

The Ottomans and Venetians

The collapse of the Serbian empire paved the way for Zeta to reassert its autonomy, which it did initially under the aristocratic **Balšić** family (possibly descendants of Serb-Albanians) in 1356. The Balšići however clashed repeatedly with the **Venetians**, who by this time had assumed a significant presence along the Adriatic, which they were dominate for several centuries; the Balšići took the sea ports of Budva and Bar, and later Ulcinj, from the Venetians, though their repeated attempts to acquire the latter's stronghold of Kotor came to nothing.

Throughout this period an even greater threat was emanating from the east, however. From the mid-fourteenth century, the fate of the Balkan countries was increasingly determined by the spread of the **Ottoman empire** of the Seljuk Turks, who emerged from Anatolia and spread inexorably northeast. A heavy defeat of the Serbs at the Maritsa River (in modern Bulgaria) in 1371 was compounded by an even more comprehensive beating at the Battle of Kosovo Polje in 1389, a defeat so heroic that it has attained mythological status for Serbians.

In the meantime, the Balšići had been ousted by the rival **Crnojević** family, in 1435, during whose reign the first references to **Montenegro** (Crna Gora) were made. Having formed a small semi-independent principality in Cetinje in 1482, their leader, **Ivan Crnojević**, established a court, built a monastery and then proceeded to wage a ceaseless guerrilla campaign against the Turks throughout the last years of the fifteenth century. However, they too were eventually forced out, fleeing to Venice (on whose side they had fought in battles against the Turks at Lake Skadar) as the Ottomans consolidated their hold. With the departure of the Crnojevići, the Ottomans finally held sway over much of the country, though the inhospitable, mountainous nature of the terrain meant that they could achieve little more than collect basic taxes and were forced to accept, albeit grudgingly, a degree of autonomy for the leaders of the local communities. Despite this, as elsewhere throughout the Balkans, Ottoman occupation left an indelible mark on the Zetan lands, especially in provincial centres such as Podgorica, Pljevlja and Bijelo Polje, where local communities were converted to **Islam**.

This was not the case along the coast, however, where Venice had reasserted control, reclaiming some of those towns it had previously lost to the Balšići, such as Bar, Budva and Ulcinj. The coast also attracted other would-be occupiers, notably the **Bosnians**, whose king, Tvrtko, ruled Herceg Novi, from its foundation in 1382 (save for a brief Spanish interregnum) through to 1482, when it fell to the Ottomans. Kotor, meanwhile, had spells under the rule of both the Austro-Hungarian king, Ludovic, and Tvrtko before placing itself under Venetian suzerainty in 1420.

Despite the obvious turmoil of the fourteenth and fifteenth centuries, it was a time of considerable cultural advancement in what was to become Montenegro: monasteries were constructed, including island churches on Lake Skadar; *scriptoria* (monastic libraries) were established in places like Bijelo Polje and Morača; and southeastern Europe's first printing house was set up in Cetinje. Meanwhile, along the coast, and especially in Kotor, a rich cultural and artistic community developed alongside thriving trades, such as goldsmiths, blacksmiths and carpenters.

The sixteenth to eighteenth centuries

In the early sixteenth century, the demise of the Crnojevići marked the emergence of a theocratic state, with rulers elected from Cetinje Monastery and known as **prince-bishops**, or *vladikas*, who bore responsibility for both the state and the church. This link ensured a degree of stability over the following three centuries. The society that developed on Montenegrin lands during the sixteenth and seventeenth centuries was, in large part, conditioned by the complex mountainous terrain: within what were essentially a collection of geographically autonomous areas, a pattern of tribal organization emerged, whereby social communities or clans were more or less able to control life within their own territories. Moreover, the deep local bonds that had been forged and maintained over the centuries ensured that, when united, these clans represented a significant military force – to the extent that the Montenegrins invariably managed to hold their own in the ongoing hostilities with the immeasurably superior Ottoman forces. With the exception of the coastal towns under Venetian control, this pattern of tribal organization extended to cover most of the country by the end of the eighteenth century.

The elective process of the *vladikas* was superseded in 1697, with the election of **Danilo Petrović**, the first in a long line of rulers from the all-powerful Petrović clan. He won the right to transfer power from uncle to nephew, thus establishing a hereditary theocracy. Danilo's period of rule saw notable successes, particularly in uniting Montenegrin tribes and clans against Turkish rule. He also paid a visit to Peter the Great in 1715, securing a strong alliance with Orthodox Russia against the Turks since the Russians too were keen to see the Ottomans driven out.

Following the relatively passive reigns of succeeding *vladikas*, Sava and Vasilije, the rule of the next prince-bishop (following the bizarre interlude of Sćepan the Small, see box, p.70), **Petar I Petrović Njegoš**, was altogether different in character. Ordained in 1785, Petar was a charismatic, courageous and highly educated man – he spoke Italian, French, German and Russian – and became much venerated for his successes in battle against the Turks, most famously at Martinići, on the Bjelopavlići plain, and Krusi, near Podgorica, in 1796. His period as *vladika* was marked by new legislation and the creation of various state organs, albeit with substantial financial aid from Russia.

The nineteenth century and independent sovereignty

At the beginning of the nineteenth century, attention switched from the interior to the coast. After the fall of the Venetian Republic in 1797 to **Napoleon**, and the splitting of its territory between France and Austria, Dalmatia, which included the Gulf of Kotor, passed into Austrian hands. Napoleon then vanquished the Austrians in 1806 (although his forces still had to contend with a determined Montenegrin–Russian alliance which secured this part of the coast in 1806–07), thereafter creating a quasi-ethnic state stretching from Graz (in Austria) to the Gulf of Kotor, known as the **Illyrian provinces**. Napoleon's disastrous defeat at the hands of the Russians in 1815, and the subsequent collapse of the French Empire, spelt an end to French rule, and at the Congress of Vienna, Dalmatia (and the Gulf of Kotor) was returned to the Hapsburgs, under whose jurisdiction it would remain until the end of World War I.

Petar II Petrović Njegoš

Following his death in 1830, Petar I was succeeded by his nephew, **Petar II Petrović Njegoš** (see box, p.121), who would not only go on to become an even greater ruler than his uncle, but would also come to be regarded as the single most important figure in Montenegrin history. This owed as much to his standing as the country's pre-eminent poet as it did to his impact on Montenegro's social and political life – indeed his epic, *Gorski Vijenac* ("The Mountain Wreath"), remains to this day the single most important literary work throughout all the ex-Yugoslav lands and is often cited as one of the catalysts for the nationalist and liberationist ideologies that were soon to emerge in Montenegro. Although Montenegro had increased its share of territory and gained a greater amount of autonomy by the time of Njegoš's accession, it still remained in thrall to Ottoman rule. However, fired by Njegoš's literary brilliance and astute leadership, the territory underwent a period of significant political, social and cultural advancement, with the creation of governmental bodies, including a senate and police force, and cultural institutions such as schools and libraries. Upon one visit to Russia, he returned with a printing press – no mean feat at that time – while he also oversaw the publication of Montenegro's first periodical, *Grlica* ("Turtle Dove").

Njegoš died in 1851 and was succeeded by his nephew, **Danilo II** who broke ranks with theocratic tradition and decided to secularize the office, taking the title of prince. The high point of his otherwise authoritarian reign was a momentous routing of the Turks at the **Battle of Grahovo** in 1858, just two years before he was assassinated in somewhat mysterious circumstances in Kotor.

Prince Nikola Petrović and Montenegrin independence

Following Danilo's death, his nineteen year-old nephew, **Nikola Petrović** (see box, p.114), was hastily summoned from Paris, where he was studying, and designated the new prince. He immediately set about building upon the administrative and cultural reforms started by Njegoš, establishing one of the first schools for girls in the Balkans, in Cetinje, and improving communications, which included the opening of the first post office and an extensive programme of road and rail construction. Nikola's personal life was no less fruitful: he sired three sons and nine daughters, many of whom were married off into European aristocratic families.

Military reform was also on the agenda, and Nikola created a cavalry corps and mountain artillery unit, and acquired larger stocks of ammunition and more modern weaponry. This move was clearly vindicated by the ensuing victories over the Ottomans, such as the catastrophic defeat they suffered at the **Battle of Vučji Do** in 1876 which, like the Battle of Grahovo some twenty years earlier, further loosened their grip on power. The subsequent involvement of close neighbour, Serbia, as well as Russia, in a revolt against the Ottomans was to prove decisive, and when European powers met at the **Congress of Berlin** in 1878 to reorganize the countries of the Balkans, Montenegro, like Serbia, was finally granted its **independence**. With this, it acquired huge swathes of territory and many towns, including Podgorica, Nikšić and Bar, the last-named finally giving Montenegro its long-desired access to the sea.

In the years following independence – a period of hitherto unknown stability – an increasingly autocratic Nikola continued with his programme of legal, educational and cultural reforms, the most significant of which was the inauguration of the country's own currency (the perper), alongside the creation of a national bank and the introduction of the country's first constitution in 1905. Independence also brought closer international relations, and a number of diplomatic missions were established in Cetinje, including those of Russia, the United States and Britain. In 1910, Nikola elevated Montenegro from the status of principality to kingdom, in doing so declaring himself king, amidst much pomp and ceremony.

World War I and the creation of Yugoslavia

Though Serbia and Montenegro had achieved independence in 1878, the Ottoman presence continued in Macedonia, to the south, and under the leadership of King Peter I of Serbia, a League for the Liberation of the Balkans from Turkey was formed, with Montenegro, Bulgaria and Greece involved. This led, in 1912, to the first, short **Balkan War**, which resulted in the Turks being forced to cede both Macedonia and today's region of Kosovo to Serbia. A subsequent falling out over control of Macedonia between Bulgaria and the other allies sparked the second Balkan War, in 1913, which again saw Serbia further strengthened; Montenegro, for its part, gained more territories on the Albanian and Kosovan borders. Following the **assassination of Archduke Franz Ferdinand** in Sarajevo in June 1914, Austria-Hungary declared war on Serbia, setting off a chain of reactions that led to the outbreak of **World War I** within a month.

For its part, Montenegro was dragged into a war on two sides of the country, initially invading Albania, and then, in conjunction with Serbia, declaring war on Austria-Hungary. The odds were of course heavily stacked against the two Slav states, and by the beginning of 1916, Austro-German forces had captured Cetinje and the entire country had capitulated. It remained under Central Power control until the end of the war – King Nikola, meanwhile, had already fled to Italy.

During the war, in April 1915, the so-called **Yugoslav committee** was formed, initially based in Paris and later moving to London. Comprised mainly of nationalist politicians from Croatia, it lobbied Allied forces to ensure that any future peace settlement made provision for the inclusion of a pan-Slavic state in the western Balkans. Despite initial reservations, this was ratified by the Allies at the **Corfu Declaration** of 1917. Montenegro was not represented, but in 1918 a group of local Serbophiles formed the Podgorica Assembly, who believed that Montenegro's future lay as a single state with Serbia. As the Central Powers began to collapse, Serb, Croat and Slovene politicians convened in Zagreb in October 1918 to create the National Council, its aim to declare independence from the Austro-Hungarians. Little more than a month later, on December 1, 1918, the **Kingdom of Serbs, Croats and Slovenes** came into existence, its territories uniting Serbia, Croatia and Slovenia with Montenegro, Macedonia and Bosnia-Herzegovina, with Alexander Karađorđević as prince-regent for his ageing father, Petar I.

Unsurprisingly, Montenegro's loss of independence, just forty years after gaining it, engendered widespread anger and resentment and was a major blow to national self-esteem. In January 1919, a ferocious **national uprising** against Serb rule began in the traditionally royalist centre of Cetinje, though aside from bringing outside attention to their struggle, it ultimately came to nothing, ending in a heavy defeat for the rebel forces. With this, and the death of Nikola – his reputation heavily stained – in Cap d'Antibes, France, on March 1, 1921, the royalist movement was all but over.

Meanwhile, the **1921 Vidovdan Constitution** had established a parliamentary constitutional monarchy for the kingdom, with control firmly established centrally in its capital Belgrade and, following Petar I's death, Karađorđević as its head of state wielding almost absolute power. For Montenegrins, this ensured that the interwar period was, for the most part, a period of repression and overall impoverishment. Things deteriorated further when, in 1929, the constitution was dissolved and a royal dictatorship imposed; the Kingdom of Serbs, Croats and Slovenes was then recast as **Yugoslavia**, ostensibly to foster greater Slav unitarism, but in reality it was a disaster for all non-Serbs. The constitution also made provision for a reorganization of the kingdom, splitting it into nine provinces – thereby rendering the country's previous borders redundant – with Montenegro, along with parts of southern Dalmatia and Herzegovina renamed **Zetska banovina**. One organization however remained determinedly opposed to a unitary Yugoslav state: the **Communist Party of Yugoslavia** (KPJ), which, from the time of its formation in 1919 until the mid-1930s, had remained a largely underground movement with much of its activity supervised by Moscow. With **Josip Broz Tito**'s appointment as its leader in 1937, however, the KPJ was reshaped into a more disciplined movement, purged of those who didn't follow the party line.

World War II

It was some eighteen months after the start of World War II that Yugoslavia became embroiled, by which time much of Continental Europe had fallen under the sway of the German–Italian Axis. Under pressure from Hitler, Prince Paul, who had assumed the regency in 1934 following the assassination of his cousin, King Alexander, initially aligned Yugoslavia with the Axis, whom he saw as protection against the Bolshevik threat. Following mass demonstrations, there was a military-led revolt, however, which saw Prince Paul exiled; Yugoslavia then renounced the decision just a few days later. In retaliation Germany blitzed Belgrade and sent land forces into Yugoslav territory. Within eleven days the whole country had capitulated. Yugoslavia was then carved up between the two major Axis powers, with the territory of Montenegro, along with the entire Adriatic coast, occupied by Italy. In response to this, **resistance groups** immediately took up arms: key amongst these were the pro-Serb, anti-Communist **Chetniks**, under the command of the former Royal Yugoslav Army colonel Draža Mihailovič, who remained loyal to the Kingdom of Yugoslavia's government-in-exile, and the **Yugoslav Partisan resistance**, organized by the KPJ with Tito as its chief military commander. This second group, whose ultimate goal was to establish a Communist state once the war was over, drew support from all backgrounds and beliefs, and was by far the most effective of the resistance groups.

Throughout 1942–43, the Partisans engaged in constant fighting, not just against the occupying forces but also against their rival organizations, in particular the Chetniks, who themselves had collaborated with the Italians in essence because they saw the Partisans as the principal threat to their plans for a Serb-dominated, monarchist Yugoslavia. Montenegro's difficult, often impenetrable terrain was a particularly effective operating base for the Partisans because of its strong tradition of guerrilla warfare. The territory still bore witness to some of the most savage fighting of the war, however, and the Partisans suffered some of the heaviest reverses.

By 1943, with so many German divisions tied up in Yugoslavia, the Allies had little option but to choose to support one of the resistance groups. In May, during the Gemans' brutal **Fifth Offensive** against the Partisans, six officers from the British-led **Special Operations Executive** (SOE), led by Captain William Deakin, were parachuted onto the Durmitor plain straight to a meeting with Tito at his headquarters on the Black Lake near Žabljak. Deakin concluded that the Partisans were the group likely to inflict the greatest damage upon the Axis forces and a military mission was attached to Tito's headquarters, in order to provide intelligence for the Partisans. Deakin was later succeeded in the SOE mission by Brigadier Fitzroy Maclean, former diplomat and friend of Churchill. Despite massive losses during the Fifth Offensive – estimated at more than six thousand troops plus several thousand civilians – the Partisans' position was further strengthened by the surrender of the Italians in September (from whom they seized substantial quantities of arms), which in turn dramatically reduced the effectiveness of the Chetniks; and though the Germans took over control, their position was significantly weakened across the Balkans. By 1944, the Partisans had acquired the full support of both the British and Americans, who pressured the government-in-exile to accept Partisan rule. Tito moved to establish a provisional form of government, the **Anti-Fascist Assembly for the National Liberation of Yugoslavia** (AVNOJ), which laid down the principles for the eventual Yugoslav state. Together with the Allied forces, the Partisans played a major part in forcing an Axis retreat from the Balkans, and with Russian assistance in October 1944 they liberated Belgrade, thereafter assuming control of the entire country.

The second Yugoslavia: Tito and socialism

Following the émigré government's acceptance of Tito as de facto leader and the Partisans as the official army, elections were held in November 1945. Although they were ostensibly democratic, the political climate was such that the only party truly represented was the **People's Party**, an organization dominated by the Communists (KPJ), making the result something of a foregone conclusion. Their first act was to abolish the monarchy, following which, on November 29, 1945, came the foundation of the **Socialist Federal Republic of Yugoslavia**; Montenegro was one of the six constituent members, alongside Serbia, Croatia, Slovenia, Bosnia-Herzegovina and Macedonia; each state had its own administration but was ultimately under the full control of the party, directed by Tito himself. Although it was forced to cede some of the territory it had gained at the end of the Balkan wars – namely the lands within Kosovo (which itself became an autonomous region within Serbia) – Montenegro simultaneously acquired the strip of coast from just north of Bar all the way up to and including the Gulf of Kotor, an area it had long coveted and a significant gain. Podgorica, which had taken an immense pounding from Allied forces during the war, was renamed **Titograd** and proclaimed the capital of Montenegro, though there was less than enthusiastic support for this amongst royalist sympathizers from Cetinje, many of whom were still in thrall to the idea of independence.

The postwar years: split with Russia and Titoism

Although in the early postwar years, the Soviet Union and Yugoslavia were officially allies, by 1947 a rift between them had begun to emerge. Stalin saw Tito as a threat, and grew increasingly incensed at what he saw as Tito's independent interpretation of Marxist-Leninist doctrine. Tito himself resented Stalin's attempts to dictate to him, reasoning that Yugoslavia had liberated itself largely on the back of its own efforts and had no Soviet occupation forces in the territory. Stalin appealed unsuccessfully to Yugoslav Communists to overthrow their leader, but Tito continued to refuse to kowtow to the Soviets, and widened his policy of **non-alignment** to include international relations, forming closer ties to the West and enhancing his standing both at home and abroad. These political and ideological differences reached a critical stage the following year, culminating in Yugoslavia's expulsion from **Cominform**, the Soviet-controlled organization of European Communist parties. Of all the Yugoslav republics, Montenegro had historically the strongest ties with the Soviet Union (and pre-1917 Russia) and it was here that the split was felt most acutely. Rebellions broke out throughout the republic, which were unceremoniously quashed and dissenters were imprisoned or even executed; indeed, those party members suspected of collaborating with Stalin (known as Conformists) were immediately purged and packed off to prison camps, such as the notorious Goli Otok ("Bare Island") in the Adriatic. It was estimated that around a third of the Communist Party membership in Montenegro – including some of the highest-ranking officials – eventually aligned themselves with the Soviets, a level of support far beyond that anywhere else in Yugoslavia.

Following the split there was an almost immediate, albeit largely cosmetic, change in name of the Communist Party, to the **Yugoslav League of Communists**; at the same time each republic was granted a greater degree of autonomy than had hitherto been the case. Yugoslavia's expulsion from Cominform also presented Tito with an opportunity to fashion his own alternative brand of Communism, one that featured a mix of socialist and capitalist ideals. In contrast to the Soviet model, which was based on central planning, it aimed at far greater decentralization of power. Indeed, the basic tenet at the heart of **Titoism**, as it was known, was a system of workers' self-management, whereby greater power was vested in the hands of the workers. Testament to this was the popular slogan, "Factories to the Workers!".

The 1960s and 1970s

Yugoslavia in the 1960s was characterized by economic **liberalization**. There was greater exposure to market forces – and in particular access to Western European markets – than in the rest of Eastern Europe, while Yugoslavs were given permission to work in the West. Living conditions and education standards improved. Many problems remained, however: World War II had left Yugoslavia, and particularly Montenegro, in a desperate state, with towns flattened, much of the infrastructure obliterated and a largely displaced population, and the task of reconstruction was huge. In keeping with Tito's policy of redistributing the country's wealth amongst the least developed republics in the federation, Montenegro, along with Kosovo, received a relatively disproportionate share of the national funds. In turn this gave rise to a large degree of resentment amongst the richer republics, particularly Croatia and Slovenia, who complained that their own development was being stifled as a result. Montenegro in particular received significant capital-intensive development, with money pumped into mining, hydro-electrical projects and industrial plants.

It was partly for these reasons of economic self-interest that the majority of Montenegrins wholeheartedly embraced the concept of Yugoslavism, certainly more so than the inhabitants of any of the other republics. That, combined with the republic's (for the most part) unswerving loyalty both to the Communist Party and to Tito himself, ensured a level of contentment unmatched elsewhere across the federal construct. Moreover, Montenegrins displayed little, if any, enthusiasm for the liberal movements that began to emerge in the other republics – particularly Slovenia, Croatia and Serbia – in the mid-1960s.

In the 1970s, old arguments about decentralization and the need for greater autonomy within the federation began to re-emerge. The **1974 Constitution** made provision for such autonomy, not only allowing each republic to be more accountable for its own internal affairs, but also permitting them the right to initiate their own legislation. Although the economy in Montenegro could hardly be said to be flourishing at this time, **tourism** was beginning to play an increasingly important role, the beautiful, unspoilt Montenegrin coast attracting holidaymakers from east and west, and even the rich and famous – politicians and movie stars alike – many of whom were entertained by Tito himself. A massive **earthquake** in 1979 (see box, p.85) caused severe damage to the coastal region, though the effect on the local tourist industry was relatively minor and rebuilding swift. This didn't, however, prevent further sniping from the richer republics which, having being asked to contribute funds for reconstruction, complained that, once again, the Montenegrins were coming in for special treatment. The latter half of the decade was marked by economic stagnation, enormous foreign debt, record levels of inflation and spiralling unemployment. But most importantly, this period was marked by growing nationalist sentiments throughout the federation and the brewing of ethnic tensions, which escalated dramatically following **Tito's death** on May 4, 1980.

The 1980s: the rise of Milošević

The 1974 Constitution had laid down plans for a system of **power sharing** to be adopted on Tito's death. Thus, a collective eight-man presidency, comprising the six republics plus the autonomous Serbian provinces of Kosovo and Vojvodina, was installed, with the chairmanship to be rotated yearly from republic to republic. In Kosovo, tensions begun to escalate between Serbs and the majority Albanian population who demanded their own republic. Riots in 1981 were followed by draconian anti-Albanian measures, though these were merely a foretaste of what was to come.

In 1987, one **Slobodan Milošević**, an ambitious Serbian Communist Party apparatchik born of Montenegrin parents, entered the fray. Having vanquished his former friend and mentor, Ivan Stambolić, at the Central Committee of the Serbian League of Communists, he replaced him as President of Serbia in 1988. Milošević begun to engage in a succession of speeches aimed at stirring up Serbian nationalist sentiment – most memorably in June 1989, on the six-hundredth anniversary of the battle of Kosovo Polje, where he uttered the now infamous words, "No one will dare beat you again!" His main pretext for his nationalist rhetoric was the growing unrest in Kosovo, where he implemented a heavy-handed crackdown on the Albanians, including abolishing many of the province's political institutions and drastically reducing its cultural autonomy. Significantly, though not surprisingly, Milošević's actions in Kosovo received much support amongst the political elite in Montenegro, which itself had a sizeable Albanian minority living within its borders. Milošević also seized upon growing disenchantment within Montenegro to orchestrate what effectively amounted to an administrative coup, subsequently dubbed the **Anti-Bureaucratic Revolution**. With the economy in decline, and a leadership widely perceived to be weak and ineffectual, a series of statewide demonstrations took place, the most pronounced of which were in Titograd and Nikšić, where there were violent clashes between steelworkers and the police. The state leadership tended its resignation in January 1989, and a band of fresh young Communists was installed, led by a Milošević protégé, **Momir Bulatović** as new Montenegrin president, and **Milo Đukanović**, who at 29 became Europe's youngest prime minister. Having also stripped both Kosovo and Vojvodina of their autonomous status, and with his supporters now in control of the Montenegrin leadership, Milošević now had control of half of the eight republics.

Within months, the fall of the Berlin Wall had precipitated a chain of events that convulsed Eastern Europe, and the scene was set for Yugoslavia's own spectacular implosion.

The break-up of Yugoslavia

At the fourteenth (and, in the end, final) Congress of the Yugoslav League of Communists in January 1990, Slovene calls for independence for the respective Communist parties, were swiftly rejected by the Serbs, prompting a walkout by the Slovene delegation. The Croatians followed, effectively spelling the end for the party. In the multi-party elections that followed throughout Yugoslavia in 1990, the Montenegrin League of Communists won comfortably, thereafter renaming themselves the **Democratic Party of Socialists** (DPS), and in doing so effectively aligning themselves with Milošević's newly formed Socialist Party of Serbia (SPS).

The Slovenes voted for full independence in a referendum in December 1990, and the Croatians, led by the Croatian Democratic Union (HDZ) party and its bullish leader, Franjo Tuđman, followed suit the following May. Both nations then declared their independence in June 1991, prompting the short Ten-Day War in Slovenia and an escalation of fighting that had started earlier in the year between Croats and Serbs (who, with Milošević's tacit support, wanted their autonomous region within the country) in Serb-dominated areas of Croatia. The Serb-dominated Yugoslav army (JNA) then joined the fray with an assault on Dubrovnik; officially Montenegro had had no involvement, but it is clear that the JNA was not short of support from Montenegrin paramilitaries and reservists who were involved in the shelling of Dubrovnik from their positions in the hills above.

Following a UN-brokered ceasefire in Croatia, and the other republics having seceded, in March 1992 a referendum was hastily arranged in Montenegro to determine whether Montenegrins wished to remain in union with Serbia. More than 95 percent of Montenegrins (in an admittedly low turnout) voted to maintain the relationship, giving rise to the creation of a two-member **Federal Republic of Yugoslavia** (FRY), each with its own president and legislature – effectively, this was the third Yugoslavia. In the subsequent Montenegrin presidential and parliamentary elections of December 1992, both the president, Bulatović, and the ruling DPS, with Đukanović still prime minister, consolidated their grip on power.

By this time, attention had shifted away from Croatia to Bosnia-Herzegovina, whose declaration of independence sparked the third and bloodiest conflict of the Yugoslav break-up. Despite the intensity of the Bosnian war, Montenegrins, both politicians and civilians alike, had little appetite for getting involved, and, aside from the actions of a few reservists who had been involved in the siege of Dubrovnik and some incursions into eastern Bosnia, the republic took little part in the war. However, Montenegro's union with Serbia meant that it, too, was subject to the **economic sanctions** imposed upon the federation in April 1992; indeed, the impact of these sanctions arguably hit Montenegro harder, its tourism-dependent trade drying up overnight. The war in Bosnia continued to savage effect for the next three years.

Political split and NATO bombings

In 1997, a critical split emerged within the ruling DPS, with Đukanović on the one hand intent on recasting both himself and his party as political liberals and allies of the West, and Bulatović on the other a keen advocate of preserving the union with Serbia; in the event, Bulatović left to create the pro-Serbian **Socialist People's Party** (SNP), effectively a clone of Milošević's own Socialist Party. This internal split also marked a distinct cooling in the relationship between the two republics, especially once Đukanović's new political and economic direction, which included adopting the Deutschmark as Montenegro's official currency in 1999 (later switched to the euro), became clear. Đukanović received growing support from Western governments who had long since grown weary of Milošević's recalcitrance. In the subsequent republican elections of May 1998, Bulatović was comprehensively defeated by Đukanović, who thereafter assumed the presidency.

Around the same time, the seemingly intractable problem of Kosovo took centre stage; escalating violence throughout 1998, with reprisals on both sides, came to a head in early 1999 when, following the massacre of ethnic Albanians at Račak, Milošević refused to accept NATO peacekeeping troops in Kosovo – in effect on Serbian territory, something neither he nor the Serbian population would possibly countenance. Following the collapse of diplomatic talks, on March 24 **NATO** began a **bombing campaign** against Yugoslavia. Mainly because of the republic's refusal to side with Serbia, NATO indicated that it would avoid hitting targets in Montenegro if at all possible, but it wasn't entirely immune, and during an attack on a bridge at Murino, near Berane, six lives were lost, including those of three children. Montenegro's biggest problem, however, was **refugees**, large numbers of whom streamed across the border from Kosovo – according to NATO to escape Serbian persecution, according to Serbs to escape NATO's bombs – into towns with significant Albanian populations, such as Plav, Rožaje and, particularly, Ulcinj, which saw its population more than double. The bombing campaign continued for 77 days, yet again leaving the country facing enormous political and economic turmoil.

The road to independence

By now Milošević – now President of Yugoslavia (a position he had created for himself as the constitution barred him from standing for a third term as President of Serbia) – was an international outcast. He was finally toppled in the 2000 federal elections (though he only admitted defeat after the army refused to support his requests for back-up against pressure from demonstrations), and replaced as federal president by **Vojislav Koštunica**, who formed an interim coalition government. Whilst this was clearly welcomed in all political circles, it placed Đukanović in a slightly awkward situation: with Milošević deposed, the international community now believed that the two republics, both now with democratically elected governments, could and should work more closely together. Moreover, Western governments were wary that any attempts by Montenegro to push ahead with independence might once again inflame the situation in Kosovo, which was still extremely fragile, and encourage separatist groups in unstable areas such as Macedonia and Bosnia to pursue their own agendas.

▲ Independence celebrations in Podgorica

It was too late to turn back the clock, however, and in 2002 the two republics agreed on a new, looser state union (the Belgrade Agreement), which was formally proclaimed in February 2003. With this, the country assumed the rather unwieldy title of **Serbia and Montenegro** (SCG), once and for all putting Yugoslavia to bed. The federal system was, therefore, abandoned and state sovereignty transferred to the two member states. Part of the new constitution also made provision for either republic to hold a referendum for independence. In the meantime, and following victory in the parliamentary elections in October 2002, Đukanović had stood down from the office of presidency to become prime minister, with his own candidate, **Filip Vujanović**, annointed his successor as president.

Predictably enough, a **referendum** on independence duly took place in Montenegro on May 21, 2006. In a turnout of 86.5 percent, 55.5 percent voted in favour of a break with Serbia, and 44.5 percent against, a much closer call than many expected and one which demonstrated quite clearly the strength of pro-Serbian feeling that remained amongst the populace. But with widespread support from the international community, and amid jubilant scenes in Podgorica and elsewhere throughout the country, Montenegro **declared its independence** on June 3, 2006.

Montenegro today

Montenegro's first **multi-party elections** as an independent nation took place in September 2006, with Đukanović's **Coalition for a European Montenegro** alliance, comprising his own Democratic Socialist Party and the Social Democratic Party, as well as a host of representatives from the country's many ethnic groups, emerging as the comfortable victors. This has enabled him to continue his programme of economic and social modernization, which includes combating high inflation and rising unemployment. The first presidential elections since independence took place two years later, in April 2008, and saw Vujanović comfortably hold his position with more than fifty percent of the vote.

With a declining industrial base, the economy is, and will continue to be, heavily reliant on **tourism**. Following the traumas and upheavals of the past fifteen years or so – during which for some years foreign visitor numbers dropped to almost negligible levels – there has been a sharp upturn in tourists visiting the country in recent years, the majority of whom spend most of their time along the stunning Adriatic coastline. Here, too, there has been considerable foreign investment, particularly from Russia, and the coastal strip has become something of a hotspot for foreign property developers. Not before time, however, attention is turning to the currently underdeveloped inland regions of the north, with ecotourism high on the agenda.

On the international front, one of the key issues dominating the political agenda is the country's prospective membership of the **European Union**, an organization to which most Montenegrins aspire. Whilst the accession process has undoubtedly picked up speed since the split with Serbia, there is as yet no definite timescale, though the country is unlikely to join any time before 2012.

Flora and fauna

Montenegro has an abundance of spectacular flora and fauna, its vast tracts of karst limestone mountains and alpine meadows rich in **plant** species, whilst its large swathes of forest, as well as these same mountains, shelter extensive populations of both **mammals** – including bears and wolves – and smaller animals, including a diverse range of **reptiles, amphibians** and **fish**. Montenegro also possesses some of the most exciting **birdlife** in the Balkans, its myriad lakes and wetlands – notably Lake Skadar – providing outstanding opportunities for keen birders. With the exception of migrating birds, the best time to see animals in their natural habitat and the blossoming plant life and is between May and September.

Flora

In common with other mountain regions throughout the Balkans, **Durmitor** harbours a wide range of flora. The massif is primarily covered by a mixture of broadleaf and coniferous trees, the lower slopes (to around 800m) characterized by oak, ash and hazel, the upper reaches (around 1200m upwards) cloaked in pine, silver fir, spruce, beech and birch. Above here, the higher, rockier mountain slopes (from around 1700m) are covered with thick clusters of dwarf pine, known locally as *klek*, beyond which, in the higher alpine zone, there's grass, lichen, moss and ultimately bare rock. The park also contains one of Europe's last remaining virgin black pine forests. The high grassland areas are richly carpeted in plant life, the dominant flowers being bellflower, violet, gentian and occasionally edelweiss, while snowbells are very common on the melting snowfields; endemic species include white and yellow saxifrage, trefoil and figwort. Between July and October, there are also plentiful supplies of blueberries on the lower slopes and wild strawberries in the forest glades.

Lovćen National Park is similarly rich in flora. The lower slopes are dominated by oak and hornbeam, while above about 1000m there is a forest zone of eastern beech, which has leaves like western beech but branches that slant upwards. Other tree species include Montpelier maple, Turkey oak, whitebeam, ash and hazel. The mountain meadows are rich with a wide range of plants, the most noticeable being the bright-blue globe thistle, several species of pinks and many types of bellflower. Although early summer is the best time for plants, there are still many flowers that bloom well into late July and August. The most significant feature of **Biogradska National Park** is its dense virgin forest, consisting mostly of beech and fir trees, some of which exceed fifty metres in height. Otherwise, the park and the surrounding Bjelasica Mountains share much in common with the flora of both Lovćen and Durmitor.

Coastal vegetation is typically Mediterranean, primarily consisting of pine, holm oak and cypress, alongside wild olive and maquis, a high, dense evergreen shrub vegetation, which is the result of degradation of the original forest. There's plentiful colour here, too, with flowers such as mimosa, oleander, wisteria and bougainvillea ranged along the coast. **Lake Skadar**, too, can boast a wealth of plant life, especially during spring when the vast areas of marshland come alive in a profusion of floating plants, notably yellow and white lilies, water plantain and duckweed. Unique to the lake is the *kasaronja*, an edible, chestnut-like plant that requires rain in order to bear fruit. The most common of the emergent water plants include reed, reedmace and water mint, while large clusters of white willow line much of the lake's edge.

Birds

Montenegro has a fantastic array of winged fauna, with more than enough to satisfy the most demanding of birders. The most significant birding region is **Lake Skadar**, which is not only the largest lake in the Balkans – around a third of its area is in Albania – but it's one of the most important stopovers for migrating birds anywhere in Europe. Among the many unusual and exciting water birds here are the great cormorant, pygmy cormorant, glossy ibis and white and little egret, though the lake's star turn is the magnificent Dalmatian pelican. Possessed of a greyish-white plumage, this rare and elegant bird is the largest of the pelicans, with a wingspan of some 3m, though it is, sadly, a species in decline. Whiskered terns quarter the shoreline in places, and there are many waterfowl in the winter: coots and moorhens are abundant along the water's edge while little grebes and black-necked grebes are both much in evidence. The woods along the shore and the extensive reed swamp provide good habitat for small birds. Among the warblers you might see are the moustached, wood and cetti, while in the breeding season large numbers of red-rumped swallows flicker over the water's surface catching mosquitoes. Dedicated birders time their visit to the area over two seasons – from the end of March to early June and late July to early October – though the lake is worth a visit at pretty much any time of the year.

The same applies to Montenegro's other wetlands, which are dotted along or close to the coast. The largest of these is the **Ulcinj saltpans**, east of Ulcinj itself, where one can see a similar array of birdlife – including more cormorants and pelicans, though on a much smaller scale – in addition to a few flamingos in summer, while at **Đsasko**, a small but wild freshwater lake a little further inland, there's a good variety of swamp birds; you may also just catch sight of storks and herons here. Further up the coast, the extensive area of wetland adjoining **Buljarica** beach is home to pygmy cormorants, olive-tree warblers and Syrian woodpeckers, amongst others.

Away from the lakes and wetlands, the most worthwhile place to see birds are inevitably the **mountains**. More than one hundred and fifty types of birds have been catalogued in **Durmitor** alone, including several birds of prey, amongst them various species of eagle, the common kestrel, buzzard and griffon vulture. Similar birds of prey can be seen in parts of **Lovćen National Park**, too. On the mountain tops and higher crags smaller birds include alpine accentors, swifts, choughs, wallcreepers and snowfinches, together with common black redstarts and water pipits; here, too, you'll come across some birds usually associated with more northerly regions, such as the shore lark. At the tree line, three-toed woodpeckers can be found, together with ring ouzels, while on open, stony hillsides, you'll find the distinctive rock partridge. The **mountain forests** are home to the very shy capercaillie, hazel grouse and black grouse, while the lower coniferous forests shelter nutcracker, wood warbler, cross tit and crossbill, to name but a few.

Brown bear cub

Animals

Given the country's relatively small size, Montenegro harbours a fairly healthy population of large carnivore species. While it's difficult to establish exact figures, there is a small number of **brown bears** (probably no more than a hundred or so), mostly restricted to the Durmitor region and further east around the Bjelasica and Prokletije ranges. Given their general aversion to humans, it's unlikely, however, that you'll encounter these animals, and whilst it's not unusual for bears to take prey such as red deer, cattle or sheep, they are more apt to feast on wild fruit, such as plums and apples. Likewise, the more remote mountain areas are also home to a limited population of both **grey wolves** and **lynx**, though these are even more elusive creatures and very rarely seen. Other large mammals you're more likely to see roaming the forests include **chamois**, which can sometimes be seen in small herds just above the tree line in mountain areas, as well as **wild boar** and **red** and **roe deer** in the lowland forest areas. White and golden martens, polecats, otters and weasels are also fairly widespread at lower altitudes, as are several species of bat, particularly in the Biogradska National Park.

Montenegro has a significant **reptilian** presence, with a particularly healthy population of **snakes**, the commonest being the grass snake, found around the margins of woodlands and river banks in the mountains. The most venomous species, however, is the horned viper (known locally as *poskok*), a greyish-brown specimen with a dark zigzag pattern along its back, which mainly occurs in dry, rocky mountainous areas, while the common viper (or adder) is more widespread, mainly in hilly areas. Other non-venomous species include the impressively large whip snake and the intriguingly named worm and cat snakes. The warm climate and Mediterranean-type shrubby vegetation and rocky shores of the southern part of the country are also suitable for a wide variety of **lizards**, notably the exotic-looking Balkan green lizard, the Balkan wall lizard, Turkish

▲ Brown bear cub

gecko and endemic (to the Adriatic) species such as the Dalmatian algyroide and sharp-snouted rock lizard, alongside the more everyday species like the sand lizard.

The most frequently seen **amphibian** is the alpine newt, primarily distributed throughout the highland lakes of Durmitor and Bjelasica. It's not uncommon, either, to see the black and orange coloured fire salamander in woodland areas, particularly during or just after rainfall, while large numbers of green and marsh frogs, as well as the European green toad, inhabit the lowlands and marshier areas around Lake Skadar.

Montenegro's lakes, rivers and streams harbour impressive **fish** stocks, nowhere more so than Lake Skadar, where up to forty species have been catalogued; the most common fish caught are crucian carp, common carp, bleak and eel, all of which find their way onto many a local menu, typically grilled or smoked. The country's river systems, in particular the Tara and Morača, have healthy levels of brook trout and Arctic char, as well as the much sought-after grayling.

There's plenty here, too, for **butterfly** lovers. The most common species found at lower altitudes, usually in open woodland or grassy places, include the southern swallowtail, little tiger blue and the Grecian copper, while both the Balkan clouded yellow and Balkan copper are more usually found amongst meadows at higher elevations, typically from around 1000m upwards. The best time to view butterflies is June and July. Dragonflies frequent Lake Skadar and the lakes and tarns of Durmitor and Bjelasica in great numbers throughout the summer.

Books and literature

Unfortunately, there's a real dearth of books about Montenegro in the English language, in every genre. What recent titles there are – mainly travelogues, historical and political publications – tend to revolve around the other countries of the former Yugoslavia, particularly Serbia, Croatia and Bosnia. For such a small country, Montenegro's literary heritage is surprisingly strong, however, though there's very little available in the way of translation. Titles marked ✶ are particularly recommended.

Literature

The first publication written within the borders of modern-day Montenegro dates back to some time in the late twelfth century, when the *Chronicle of the Priest of Duklija* (or *Kingdom of the Slavs*) was composed by an anonymous Catholic priest from Bar. The development of a specifically Montenegrin literature first began in the fifteenth century with the introduction of southern Europe's first printing press at Cetinje Monastery in 1493. The printing house was founded by the Zetan ruler, Durad IV Crnojević; the following year it published (in Cyrillic) the first South Slav book, *Oktoih* ("The First Voice"), which comprised five volumes of psalms The next significant written works, in the eighteenth century, were the domain of Orthodox spiritual leaders, most important of whom was Bishop Vasilije Petrović, whose *Istorija o Cernoj Gori* ("A History of Montenegro"), published in Moscow in 1754, chronicled life in Montenegrin lands under their various medieval rulers.

Subsequent members of the Petrović clan were responsible for the first real heavyweight literary works, initially **Prince-Bishop Petar I Petrović Njegoš**, whose poems – such as *Pohvala Karadjordju* ("Poems to Karageorge") and *Sinovi Ivanbegovi* ("The Sons of Ivan-Bey") – recalled and paid deference to the times of the former rulers, the house of Crnojević. Petar I was succeeded by his nephew, **Petar II Petrović Njegoš** (see box, p.121) who, though arguably the country's most influential-ever leader, is known above all else as its outstanding literary figure. Despite a prolific output, his defining work remains *Gorski Vijenac* ("The Mountain Wreath"), an epic poem concerned with the struggles of the Montenegrins – indeed it's still widely regarded as the most important piece of literature to come out of any of the countries of the former Yugoslavia. The last of the Petrović dynasty, **King Nikola** (see box, p.114), was himself was no slouch when it came to writing, producing a string of short stories and novels, as well as plays such as *Balkanska Carica* ("The Balkan Empress"), which was first staged in Cetinje in 1888 – though relatively little was actually published. Other significant nineteenth-century scribes included **Marko Miljanov** (see p.107), whose work focused on the lives and times of the Montenegrin people, and **Stefan Mitrov Ljubiša** (see p.74), a native of Budva whose repertoire ranged from cultural and political treatises to folk literature and poetry.

The most prominent twentieth-century Montenegrin writer was Tito's onetime deputy, and later dissident, **Milovan Djilas**, whose extensive output (*The New Class*, *Conversations with Stalin*, *Life without Justice* and *Memoir of a Revolutionary*, to name just a few) recall his life in the Partisans and his subsequent fall from grace in the postwar order – his publications earned him several lengthy stints in prison during the 1950s and 1960s. One of Djilas' last books, *Tito: Story from Inside*, shed further, critical, light on the Yugoslav leader's regime (see below). The other significant literary figure of the postwar period was Podgorica-born **Borislav Pekić**, a prolific novelist whose works, such as *Vreme ÐCuda* ("The Time of Miracles") and – later – the brilliantly titled *Kako upokojiti Vampira* ("How to Quiet a Vampire"; see below), saw him fall foul of the authorities and exiled to London, where he died in 1992. Pekić also wrote more than twenty film scripts, one of which, *Dan četnaesti* ("The Fourteenth Day"), represented Yugoslavia at the 1961 Cannes Film Festival.

Books

The number of books dedicated to the break-up of Yugoslavia is vast, yet in just about all cases the coverage of Montenegro is scant – not itself particularly surprising given that the country played a largely peripheral role in the wars. You'll find some reference to Montenegro in the following titles, and they are all excellent reads in their own right: Misha Glenny, *The Fall of Yugoslavia*; Laura Silber and Alan Little, *The Death of Yugoslavia*; John Allcock, *Explaining Yugoslavia*; John Lampe, *Yugoslavia as History*; Tim Judah, *The Serbs and Kosovo: War and Revenge*; Dejan Djokić, *Elusive Compromise: A History of Interwar Yugoslavia*.

Fiction

Borislav Pekić *How to Quiet a Vampire* (Northwestern University Press). Montenegro's foremost postwar novelist draws on his own experiences as a

political agitator (and prisoner) in this sobering tale of a former Gestapo officer trying to come to terms with his totalitarian past.

History and politics

Živko Andrijašević & Serbo Rastoder *The History of Montenegro* (Montenegro Diaspora Centre). Fairly comprehensive though somewhat rambling history of the country, beginning with the medieval dynasties and winding up in 2003. It's nowhere near as lucid as Elizabeth Roberts' book (see below) but it does include some fine images and photographs.

Neil Barnett *Tito: Life and Times* (Haus Publishing). Although not overly extensive, this concise and illuminating portrait of the Yugoslav president is a study of both Tito's historical legacy and his complex private life; it also features some excellent photographs.

Milovan Djilas *Tito: the Story from Inside* (Weidenfeld & Nicolson). The

Montenegrin Djilas was postwar Communism's first and most famous dissident, and in this fascinating account he details the struggles for power within the Partisan movement, alongside a detailed portrait of Tito and his regime.

Fitzroy Maclean *Eastern Approaches* (Penguin). Politician, diplomat, soldier and traveller, Maclean recounts his many daring adventures in this absorbing autobiography, including his time as leader of the British mission to the Partisans in Yugoslavia during World War II. His tales of time spent in the prewar Soviet Union and with the SAS in North Africa are no less entertaining.

Elizabeth Roberts *Realm of the Black Mountain: A History of Montenegro* (Hurst). One of the very few books available on the history of Montenegro, this is an excellent, authoritative and highly readable account of the country's turbulent past. Beginning with detailed coverage of its earliest inhabitants and the medieval dynasties, it continues with an illuminating and thorough-going assessment of the twentieth century, concluding with Montenegrin independence.

🏃 **Bato Tomašević** *Life and Death in the Balkans* (Hurst). This sympathetic and superbly accomplished memoir begins with the author's life as a young boy in German-occupied Cetinje, then follows his time as a Partisan and subsequent experiences living in postwar Yugoslavia. As much historical narrative as memoir, Tomašević also provides illuminating insight into the country's struggles right up to the NATO bombing campaign in 1999 and Milošević's subsequent downfall.

Heather Williams *Parachutes, Patriots and Partisans* (Hurst). This interesting though occasionally heavy-going read examines the political and military activities of the British-led Special Operations Executive (SOE), of which Fitzroy Maclean was part, and its relationship with the Partisans during World War II.

Travel and travelogues

Rudolf Abraham *The Mountains of Montenegro* (Cicerone Press). Useful pocket-sized guide detailing a number of hikes throughout the country's mountain regions, including Durmitor, Bjelasica, Lovćen, Orjen and Prokletije. It also contains some good illustrated maps.

🏃 **Rebecca West** *Black Lamb and Grey Falcon* (Canongate). A classic of twentieth-century travel writing, this remarkable, complex and voluminous, book (originally published in 1942) chronicles West's repeated visits to Yugoslavia in the 1930s, where her travels took her to several towns of Montenegro's eastern interior, as well as Podgorica, Skadar, Cetinje and Budva. Interweaving social and political observations with historical narrative, the author's prose is unmatched, if occasionally overly romantic in places.

Language

Language

Montenegrin

Montenegrin (Crnogorski jezik, or in Cyrillic Црногорски) is a Slavic language, part of the Indo-European family of languages. Until recently it was generally recognized as a variant of Serbian, with the addition of more Turkish-based words. Since 2004, however, the Montenegrin government has fostered the idea of Montenegrin as a separate language, and in the 2007 Constitution it was proclaimed as the new country's national tongue. A standard form to be taught in schools has yet to be agreed but one major change is that the Latin alphabet is increasingly preferred to Cyrillic, which is associated with the Serbian-dominated past. Whilst any attempt to speak Montenegrin will be appreciated, generally speaking there will be little call for it as the standard of English throughout the country is pretty high. Indeed, English has supplanted Russian as the main second language, while some people also speak Italian or German.

Pronunciation

Pronunciation is quite easy to grasp as all words are pronounced phonetically (i.e. every letter is pronounced and never silent), with every letter representing a single sound. There are a few consonants that might cause difficulty – these do however have an equivalent in English. They are as follows:

c "ts" as in "cats"

č "ch" as in "chocolate"

ć a softer version of "č"; similar to the "t" in "future"

đ "j" as in "June"

dž is a harder version of "đ", similar to "j" in "job"

g always hard, as in "get"

j "y" as in "yogurt"

r always rolled; fulfils the function of a vowel in words like *prst* (finger)

š "sh" as in "shoe"

ž "s" as in "pleasure"

The digraphs, lj and nj, are essentially single letters and pronounced thus:

lj "lli" in "million"

nj "ni" in "onion"

The **stress** in Montenegrin is placed either on the first or second syllable depending on whether the word has more or less than three syllables.

Basic terms and phrases

da	yes	zašto?	why?
ne	no	koliko?	how much?
kada?	when?	veliko	large
gde?	where?	malo	small

The Cyrillic alphabet

Montenegrin can be written in two different alphabets: Cyrillic (ћирилица) and Latin. You will find most signs in Latin script, though train timetables still often seem to be in Cyrillic.

Cyrillic	Latin	Cyrillic	Latin
А	A	Н	N
Б	B	Њ	NJ
В	V	О	O
Г	G	П	P
Д	D	Р	R
Ђ	DJ	С	S
Е	E	Т	T
Ж	Ž	Ћ	Ć
З	Z	У	U
И	I	Ф	F
Ј	J	Х	H
К	K	Ц	C
Л	L	Ч	Č
Љ	LJ	Џ	DZ
М	M	Ш	Š

više	more	Crnogorka	Montenegrin (person – female)
manje	less		
dobro	good	kako se zoveš?	what is your name?
loše	bad	zovem se...	my name is...
jeftino	cheap	odakle ste?	where are you from? (polite)
skupo	expensive		
otvoreno	open	odakle si?	where are you from? (familiar)
zatvoreno	closed		
toplo	hot	ja sam iz . . .	I am from . . .
hladno	cold	Velike Britanije	Great Britain
sa/bez	with/without	Engleske	England
govorite li engleski?	do you speak English?	Škotske	Scotland
ne razumijem	I don't understand	Velsa	Wales
ne znam	I don't know	Severne Irske	Northern Ireland
kako se ovo kaže na crnogorskom?	How do you say this in Montenegrin?	Irske	Ireland
		Amerike	the US
Crna Gora	Montenegro	Kanade	Canada
Crnogorac	Montenegrin (person – male)	Australije	Australia
		Novog Zelanda	New Zealand

Greetings and civilities

dobar dan	hello/good day	kako si?	how are you? (informal)
ćao!	hi!/bye!	dobro, hvala	fine, thanks
kako ste?	how are you? (polite)	gdje si?	How's it going? (literally: "where are you?")

što činiš?	What's new? (literally: "what are you doing?")
dobro jutro	good morning
dobro veče	good evening
laku noć	good night
do viđenja	goodbye
molim	please
hvala (lijepo)	thank you (very much)

nema na čemu	you're welcome
izvinite	excuse me
oprostite/izvinite	sorry
izvolite	here you are
hajdemo!	let's go!
požuri!	hurry up!

Accommodation

imate li (jednokrevetnu /dvokrevetnu) sobu?	do you have a (single/double) room?
sobe	rooms
apartman	an apartment
privatnu sobu	a private room
sa . . .	with . . .
francuskim ležajem	a double bed
tušem/kadom	a shower/bath
pogledom na more	a sea view
mogu li pogledati sobu?	can I see the room?
imate li nešto jeftinije?	do you have anything cheaper?
noćenje i doručak	bed and breakfast

pun pansion/ polupansion	full board/half-board
imam rezervaciju	I have a reservation
mogu li rezervisati sobu?	can I book a room?
slavina/svijetlo/ telefon/televizor/ klima/ključ ne radi	the tap/light/ telephone/TV/ air conditioning/key doesn't work
gdje je najbliži autokamp?	where's the nearest campsite?
autokamp	campsite
šator	tent
prikolica	caravan
vreća za spavanje	sleeping bag

Directions and getting around

kuda?/gdje je?/gdje se nalazi . . . ?	where is . . . ?
najbliža banka	the nearest bank
najbliži hotel	the nearest hotel
ovdje	here
tamo	there
lijevo	left
desno	right
pravo	straight on
natrag	backwards
gore	above; upstairs
dolje	below; downstairs
sjever	north
jug	south
istok	east
zapad	west

izgubio sam se	I'm lost (m)
izgubila sam se	I'm lost (f)
je li to blizu?	is it nearby?
koliko je daleko?	how far is it?
polazak	arrival
odlazak	departures
u koliko sati polazi voz/autobus/trajekt?	what time does the train/bus/ferry leave?
kada polazi sledeći autobus/trajekt/ voz za . . . ?	when does the next bus/ferry/train leave for . . . ?
ima li zakašnenja?	is it running late?
jednu kartu za . . . molim	a ticket for . . .please
u jednom pravcu	single
povratnu kartu	return

mogu li rezervisati sjedište?	can I reserve a seat?	ulaz	entrance
zabranjeno pušenje	no smoking	izlaz	exit

Shopping

gdje mogu da kupim . . . ?	where can I buy . . . ?	poštanske marke	postage stamps
kupaći kostim	bathing costume	razglednice	postcards
baterije	batteries	sapun	soap
cigarete	cigarettes	toalet papir	toilet paper
upaljač	cigarette lighter	pastu za zube	toothpaste
vadičep	corkscrew	peškir	towel
hranu	food	prašak za veš	washing powder
šibice	matches	koliko košta?	how much does it cost?
telefonsku karticu	phonecard	to je skupo	that's expensive

Numbers

jedan	1	dvadeset i jedan	21
dva	2	trideset	30
tri	3	četrdeset	40
četiri	4	pedeset	50
pet	5	šezdeset	60
šest	6	sedamdeset	70
sedam	7	osamdeset	80
osam	8	devedeset	90
devet	9	sto	100
deset	10	dvjesta	200
jedanaest	11	trista	300
dvanaest	12	četiristo	400
trinaest	13	petsto	500
četrnaest	14	šesto	600
petnaest	15	sedamsto	700
šesnaest	16	osamsto	800
sedamnaest	17	devetsto	900
osamnaest	18	hiljadu	1000
devetnaest	19	dve hiljade	2000
dvadeset	20	milion	million

Times and dates

dan	day	utorak	Tuesday
nedelja	week	srijeda	Wednesday
mjesec	month	četvrtak	Thursday
godina	year	petak	Friday
danas	today	subota	Saturday
sutra	tomorrow	neđelja	Sunday
juče	yesterday	praznik	holiday
prekosutra	the day after tomorrow	januar	January
prekjuče	the day before yesterday	februar	February
ujutro	in the morning	mart	March
popodne	in the afternoon	april	April
naveče	in the evening	maj	May
rano	early	juni	June
kasno	late	juli	July
koliko je sati?	what time is it?	avgust	August
sat	hour	septembar	September
minuta	minute	oktobar	October
deset sati	10 o'clock	novembar	November
deset i petnaest	10.15	decembar	December
deset i po or	10.30	proljeće	spring
pola jedanaest		ljeto	summer
petnaest do	10.45	jesen	autumn
jedanaest		zima	winter
ponedjeljak	Monday		

General terms

aerodrom	airport	dvorac	castle
amam	Turkish bath	dvorište	courtyard
ambasada	embassy	džamija	mosque
apoteka	pharmacy	gaj	grove
autobuska stanica	bus station	galerija	gallery
bazen	swimming pool	garderoba	left-luggage office
benzinska stanica	petrol station/	grad	town
	gas station	gradska kuća	town hall
bioskop	cinema	groblje	graveyard
bolnica	hospital	Jadransko more	Adriatic Sea
brdo	hill	jezero	lake
bulevar	boulevard	kafana	inn or tavern
bunar	well	kafić	café
centar	centre	kaštel	castle, fortress
crkva	church	katun	shepherd's mountain hut
dvor	palace, court	kolosijek	platform

191

korzo	evening promenade	rijeka	river
kuća	house	riznica	treasury
luka	port	rt	cape
magistrala	highway running the length of the Adriatic coast	sahat kula	clocktower
		samoposluga	supermarket
		selo	village
manastir	monastery	šetalište	walkway, promenade
mol	pier	stadion	stadium
more	sea	stari grad	(i) old town; (ii) castle
most	bridge	staza	path
muzej	museum	suncobran	umbrella
obala	shore, quayside	sveti	saint
oluja	storm	toranj	tower
opština	town hall	trajektna luka	ferry terminal
optičar	optician	trg	square
ostrvo	island	turist biro/turistički informativni centar	tourist office
palata	palace		
nacionalni park	nature reserve	tvrđava	fortress
park	park, public garden	ulica	street
pećina	cave	uvala	bay
pijaca	market	varoš	central residential quarter of an old town
plaža	beach		
policijska stanica	police station	vrata	gate, door
poljana/polje	field, square	vrh	peak
poluostrvo	peninsula	vrt	garden
pošta	post office	zaliv	bay, gulf
pozorište	theatre	željeznička stanica	train station
prodavnica	shop	zemlja	country
put	road, way	zidine	walls
restoran	restaurant	zvonik	belltower, campanile

Hiking terms

dolina	valley	sklonište	shelter
gora	massif	smjer	fixed route
izvor	spring	stijene	cliff
kamen	rock	šuma	forest
klizavo	slippery	vodopad	waterfall
planinarski dom	mountain hut	vrata/prijevoj	pass

Food and drink terms

Basic terms

čaša	glass	pladanj	platter
doručak	breakfast	pohovani	fried in breadcrumbs
hrana	food	poslastičarna	patisserie
gotova jela	main dishes	prijatno!	bon appetit!
jelovnik	menu	prženo	fried
kašika	spoon	račun	bill
konoba	inn, tavern, folksy restaurant	restoran	restaurant
		ručak	lunch
kuvano	boiled	savardak	alpine lodge-style restaurant
na ražnju	spit-roasted	šoljica	cup
na roštilju/na žaru	grilled	tanjir	plate
nazdravje!	cheers!	večera	dinner
nož	knife	viljuška	fork
pečeno/u pećnici	baked	živjeli!	cheers!
pekara	bakery		

Basic foods

biber	pepper	omlet	omelette
burek	greasy pastry, usually filled with cheese	pašteta	paté
		pavlaka	sour cream
hleb	bread	pekmez	jam
jaje	egg	pirinač	rice
jogurt	yoghurt	sa	tomato sauce
kajmak	thick sour cream	salata	salad
kifla	breakfast pastry, croissant	šećer	sugar
maslac	butter	sir	cheese
masline	olives	sirće	vinegar
maslinovo ulje	olive oil	so	salt
med	honey	umak	sauce
mlijeko	milk		

Starters (predjela)

kobasica	sausage	ovčji sir	sheep's cheese
kozji sir	goat's cheese	punjene paprike	stuffed peppers
kulen	spicy paprika-flavoured pork and beef salami from eastern Croatia	sir iz ulja	hard yellow cheese with a piquant rind, kept under vegetable or olive oil
mladi sir	creamy cottage cheese	šunka	ham
Njeguški pršut	home-cured ham similar to Italian prosciutto	supa	soup
		vrat	cured pork neck

For a detailed account of popular Montenegrin dishes and local specialities, see pp.30–32.

Vegetables (povrće) and pasta (tjestenine)

ajvar	spicy relish made from puréed aubergines, peppers and tomatoes		kupus	cabbage
bijeli luk	garlic		luk	onion
blitva	spinach-like leaves of mangel-wurzel (eaten with fish)		mlinci	torn sheets of baked pasta dough
			njoki	gnocchi
đuveč	ratatouille-style mixture of vegetables and rice, heavily flavoured with paprika		paradajz	tomato
			pasulj	beans; also bean soup
			patlidžan	aubergine
gljiva	mushroom		ren	horseradish
grašak	peas		repa	turnip
mladi luk	spring onion		spanać	spinach
kiseli kupus	sauerkraut		šampinjoni	champignon mushrooms
krastavac	cucumber, gherkin		šargarepa	carrot
krompir	potato		špargla	asparagus
kukuruz	corn on the cob		tartufi	truffle

Meat (meso) and poultry (živina)

Bečka šnicla	Wiener schnitzel		piletina	chicken
bubrezi	kidneys		pljeskavica	hamburger-style minced-meat patty
ćevapčići/ ćevapi	grilled mincemeat rissoles		pršut	ham
ćuretina	turkey		ražnjići	pieces of pork grilled on a skewer; kebab
govedina	beef			
gulaš	goulash		salama	salami
guska	goose		sarma/japrak	cabbage leaves/grape leaves stuffed with meat and rice
jagnjetina	lamb			
jetra	liver		slanina	bacon
koljenica	pork knuckle		šnicla	escalope of veal or pork
kotlet	cutlet, chop		svinjetina	pork
pančeta	bacon		teletina	veal
papci	pigs' trotters		žablji bataci	frogs' legs
patka	duck		zečetina	rabbit

Fish (riba) and seafood (morski plodovi)

bakalar	cod (often dried)		girice	small fish like whitebait, usually deep-fried whole
barbun	mullet			
brancin	sea bass		grdobina	frogfish
cipal	golden grey mullet		hobotnica	octopus
crni rižoto	squid risotto		inćun	anchovy
dagnje	mussels		jastog	lobster

194

jegulja	eel
kapica	clam
kovač	John Dory
krap	carp
lignje	squid
list	sole
lubin	sea perch
orada	gilthead sea bream
oslić	hake
ostrige	oysters
pastrmka	trout
rak	crab

riblja salata	literally "fish salad" (usually a mixture of octopus, squid and mussels)
riblji paprikaš	fish stew
sardele	anchovies
sipa	cuttlefish
škampi	scampi
škarpina	groper, sea scorpion
školjkewe	scallops
skuša	mackerel
štuka	pike
trilja	striped or red mullet
zubatac	dentex

Desserts (deserti)

baklava	baklava
kolač	cake
krempita	cream cake or custard slice
krofna	doughnut
kroštule	deep-fried twists of pastry
palačinke	pancakes

pita s jabukama	apple pie
sladoled	ice cream
štrudla s makom	poppy-seed cake
štrudla s orasima	walnut cake
torta	gateau
voćna salata	fruit salad

Fruit (voće)

ananas	pineapple
banana	banana
borovnica	blueberry
dinja	melon
grožđje	grapes
jabuka	apple
jagoda	strawberry
kivi	kiwi

kruška	pear
kupina	blackberry
lubenica	watermelon
malina	raspberry
narandža	orange
šljiva	plum
višnja	cherry

Drinks (pića)

bambus	red wine and cola
bijelo vino	white wine
čaj	tea
crno vino	red wine
đus	orange juice
kafa	coffee
led/s ledom/ bez leda	ice/with ice/ without ice
limunada	lemonade
loza/lozovača	grape brandy
medovača	honey-flavoured brandy
mineralna/	mineral water

kisela voda	
obična voda	still water
orahovača	walnut-flavoured brandy
pelinkovac	bitter, wormwood-based aperitif
pivo	beer
šampanjac	sparkling wine
rakija	brandy
roze	rosé wine
šljivovica	plum brandy
sok	juice
špricer	white wine and soda
topla čokolada	hot chocolate

viljamovka **pear brandy**
vino **wine**

voda water
vodka vodka

L

LANGUAGE | Food and drink terms

Travel
store

Small print and index

Publishing in 1982, the first Rough Guide – to Greece – was a student scheme that became a publishing phenomenon. Mark Ellingham, a recent graduate in English from Bristol University, had been travelling in Greece the previous summer and couldn't find the right guidebook. With a small group of friends he wrote his own guide, combining a highly contemporary, journalistic style with a thoroughly practical approach to travellers' needs.

The immediate success of the book spawned a series that rapidly covered dozens of destinations. And, in addition to impecunious backpackers, Rough Guides soon acquired a much broader and older readership that relished the guides' wit and inquisitiveness as much as their enthusiasm, critical approach and value-for-money ethos.

These days, Rough Guides include recommendations from shoestring to luxury and cover more than 200 destinations around the globe, including almost every country in the Americas and Europe, more than half of Africa and most of Asia and Australasia. Our ever-growing team of authors and photographers is spread all over the world, particularly in Europe, the USA and Australia.

In the early 1990s, Rough Guides branched out of travel, with the publication of Rough Guides to World Music, Classical Music and the Internet. All three have become benchmark titles in their field, spearheading the publication of a wide range of books under the Rough Guide name.

Including the travel series, Rough Guides now number more than 350 titles, covering: phrasebooks, waterproof maps, music guides from Opera to Heavy Metal, reference works as diverse as Conspiracy Theories and Shakespeare, and popular culture books from iPods to Poker. Rough Guides also produce a series of more than 120 World Music CDs in partnership with World Music Network.

Visit www.roughguides.com to see our latest publications.

Rough Guide travel images are available for commercial licensing at www.roughguidespictures.com

A Rough Guide to Rough Guides

Published in 1982, the first Rough Guide – to Greece – was a student scheme that became a publishing phenomenon. Mark Ellingham, a recent graduate in English from Bristol University, had been travelling in Greece the previous summer and couldn't find the right guidebook. With a small group of friends he wrote his own guide, combining a highly contemporary, journalistic style with a thoroughly practical approach to travellers' needs.

The immediate success of the book spawned a series that rapidly covered dozens of destinations. And, in addition to impecunious backpackers, Rough Guides soon acquired a much broader and older readership that relished the guides' wit and inquisitiveness as much as their enthusiastic, critical approach and value-for-money ethos.

These days, Rough Guides include recommendations from shoestring to luxury and cover more than 200 destinations around the globe, including almost every country in the Americas and Europe, more than half of Africa and most of Asia and Australasia. Our ever-growing team of authors and photographers is spread all over the world, particularly in Europe, the USA and Australia.

In the early 1990s, Rough Guides branched out of travel, with the publication of Rough Guides to World Music, Classical Music and the Internet. All three have become benchmark titles in their fields, spearheading the publication of a wide range of books under the Rough Guide name.

Including the travel series, Rough Guides now number more than 350 titles, covering: phrasebooks, waterproof maps, music guides from Opera to Heavy Metal, reference works as diverse as Conspiracy Theories and Shakespeare, and popular culture books from iPods to Poker. Rough Guides also produce a series of more than 120 World Music CDs in partnership with World Music Network.

Visit www.roughguides.com to see our latest publications.

Rough Guide travel images are available for commercial licensing at www.roughguidespictures.com

Rough Guide credits

Text editor: Edward Aves
Layout: Dan May
Cartography: Miles Irving
Picture editor: Emily Taylor
Production: Vicky Baldwin
Proofreader: Jennifer Speake, Diane Margolis
Cover design: Chloë Roberts
Photographer: Paul Whitfield
Editorial: **London** Ruth Blackmore, Andy
Turner, Keith Drew, Alice Park, Lucy White, Jo
Kirby, James Smart, Natasha Foges, Róisín
Cameron, Emma Traynor, Emma Gibbs, Kathryn
Lane, Christina Valhouli, Monica Woods, Mani
Ramaswamy, Alison Roberts, Harry Wilson,
Joe Staines, Peter Buckley, Matthew Milton,
Tracy Hopkins, Ruth Tidball; **New York** Andrew
Rosenberg, Steven Horak, AnneLise Sorensen,
April Isaacs, Ella Steim, Anna Owens, Sean
Mahoney, Paula Neudorf, Courtney Miller; **Delhi**
Madhavi Singh, Karen D'Souza
Design & Pictures: **London** Scott Stickland,
Diana Jarvis, Mark Thomas, Nicole Newman,
Sarah Cummins; **Delhi** Umesh Aggarwal, Ajay
Verma, Jessica Subramanian, Ankur Guha,
Pradeep Thapliyal, Sachin Tanwar, Anita Singh,
Nikhil Agarwal

Production: Rebecca Short, Vicky Baldwin
Cartography: **London** Maxine Repath, Ed
Wright, Katie Lloyd-Jones; **Delhi** Rajesh
Chhibber, Ashutosh Bharti, Rajesh Mishra,
Animesh Pathak, Jasbir Sandhu, Karobi Gogoi,
Amod Singh, Alakananda Bhattacharya, Swati
Handoo, Deshpal Dabas
Online: **London** George Atwell, Faye Hellon,
Jeanette Angell, Fergus Day, Justine Bright, Clare
Bryson, Aine Fearon, Adrian Low, Ezgi Celebi,
Amber Bloomfield; **Delhi** Amit Verma, Rahul Kumar,
Narender Kumar, Ravi Yadav, Debojit Borah,
Saurabh Sati, Rakesh Kumar, Ganesh Sharma
Marketing & Publicity: **London** Liz Statham,
Niki Hanmer, Louise Maher, Jess Carter, Vanessa
Godden, Vivienne Watton, Anna Paynton, Rachel
Sprackett, Libby Jellie; **New York** Geoff Colquitt,
Katy Ball; **Delhi** Ragini Govind
Manager India: Punita Singh
Reference Director: Andrew Lockett
Operations Manager: Helen Phillips
PA to Publishing Director: Nicola Henderson
Publishing Director: Martin Dunford
Commercial Manager: Gino Magnotta
Managing Director: John Duhigg

Publishing information

This first edition published April 2009 by
Rough Guides Ltd,
80 Strand, London WC2R 0RL
345 Hudson St, 4th Floor,
New York, NY 10014, USA
14 Local Shopping Centre, Panchsheel Park,
New Delhi 110017, India
Distributed by the Penguin Group
Penguin Books Ltd,
80 Strand, London WC2R 0RL
Penguin Group (USA)
375 Hudson Street, NY 10014, USA
Penguin Group (Australia)
250 Camberwell Road, Camberwell,
Victoria 3124, Australia
Penguin Group (Canada)
195 Harry Walker Parkway N, Newmarket, ON,
L3Y 7B3 Canada
Penguin Group (NZ)
67 Apollo Drive, Mairangi Bay, Auckland 1310,
New Zealand

Cover concept by Peter Dyer.

Typeset in Bembo and Helvetica to an original
design by Henry Iles.

Printed in China

© Norm Longley 2009

No part of this book may be reproduced in any
form without permission from the publisher except
for the quotation of brief passages in reviews.

216pp includes index

A catalogue record for this book is available from
the British Library

ISBN: 978-1-85828-771-3

The publishers and authors have done their best
to ensure the accuracy and currency of all the
information in **The Rough Guide to Montenegro**,
however, they can accept no responsibility for
any loss, injury, or inconvenience sustained by
any traveller as a result of information or advice
contained in the guide.

1   3   5   7   9   8   6   4   2

Help us update

We've gone to a lot of effort to ensure that the
first edition of **The Rough Guide to Montenegro**
is accurate and up to date. However, things
change – places get "discovered", opening hours
are notoriously fickle, restaurants and rooms raise
prices or lower their standards. If you feel we've got it
wrong or left something out, we'd like to know,
and if you can remember the address, the price,
the hours, the phone number, so much the better.

Please send your comments with the subject
line "**Rough Guide Montenegro Update**"
to ©mail@roughguides.com. We'll credit all
contributions and send a copy of the next edition
(or any other Rough Guide if you prefer) for the
very best emails.
    Have your questions answered and tell others
about your trip at
©community.roughguides.com

Acknowledgements

A massive thanks to Ed, for his brilliant and enthusiastic editing, not to mention his incredible patience during the course of writing this book; Monica Woods and Mani Ramaswamy for their continued support; and Martin Dunford for his enthusiasm in helping to get this project off the ground. Huge thanks are also due to Milan Jovanović for compiling the language section, and Danica Ćeranić at the Montenegrin Tourist Board in Podgorica for her continued assistance; Jack and Hayley Delf in Herceg Novi, Matt Lane in Herceg Novi, Jim Costa and Milica Medenica in Ulcinj, Jovan Martinović in Cetinje, Tatjana Krgušić in Bijelo Polje, Saša and Olja in Podgorica; Jelena Vukovič in Novi Sad; and Jon Bousfield, for beers and a place to stay. Most of all, thanks to Tim for being a sterling friend; and Luka, my little inspiration.

Cameron, Emma Traynor, Emma Gibbs, Kathryn Lane, Christina Valhouli, Monica Woods, Mani Ramaswamy, Alison Roberts, Harry Wilson, Joe Staines, Peter Buckley, Matthew Milton, Tracy Hopkins, Ruth Tidball; **New York** Andrew Rosenberg, Steven Horak, AnneLise Sorensen, April Isaacs, Ella Steim, Anna Owens, Sean Mahoney, Paula Neudorf, Courtney Miller; **Delhi** Madhavi Singh, Karen D'Souza
Publishing Director: Martin Dunford
Commercial Manager: Gino Magnotta
Rough Guides Ltd,
80 Strand, London WC2R 0RL
345 Hudson St, 4th Floor,
New York, NY 10014, USA
14 Local Shopping Centre, Panchsheel Park,
New Delhi 110017, India
Distributed by the Penguin Group
Penguin Books Ltd,
80 Strand, London WC2R 0RL
Penguin Group (USA)
375 Hudson Street, NY 10014, USA
Penguin Group (Australia)
250 Camberwell Road, Camberwell,
Victoria 3124, Australia
Penguin Group (Canada)
195 Harry Walker Parkway N, Newmarket, ON,
L3Y 7B3 Canada
Penguin Group (NZ)

Please send your comments with the subject line "**Rough Guide Montenegro Update**" to mail@roughguides.com. We'll credit all contributions and send a copy of the next edition (or any other Rough Guide if you prefer) for the very best emails.
Have your questions answered and tell others about your trip at

We've gone to a lot of effort to ensure that the first edition of **The Rough Guide to Montenegro** is accurate and up to date. However, things change – places get "discovered," opening hours are notoriously fickle, restaurants and rooms raise prices or lower standards. If you feel we've got it wrong or left something out, we'd like to know, and if you can remember the address, the price, the hours, the phone number, so much the better.

Photo credits

All photos © Rough Guides except the following:

Introduction
p.7 Eating under the clocktower, Herceg Novi © Scott B. Rosen/DRR.Net
p.8 National celebrations © Diomedia/Alamy
p.10 Sheep walking through the snow, Durmitor © Diomedia/Alamy

Things not to miss
04 Kayaking © Florian L'Hostis
12 Boka Nights festival, Kotor © Courtesy of Montenegro Tourism Board
17 *Catovići Mlin* restaurant, Morinj © Courtesy of Montenegro Tourism Board

Coastal life colour section
Petrovac Beach © Diomedia/Alamy
Pržno Beach © Nicholas Pitt/Alamy

The Great Outdoors colour section
Skiing © Ted Levine/zefa/Corbis
Dalmatian pelican © blickwinkel/Alamy
Kayaking © Keith Hare-Brown

Black and whites
p.63 Boys playing cards, Kotor Old Town © Andy Kerry/Axiom
p.78 Pržno © Jon Arnold Images Ltd/Alamy
p.176 Independence celebrations © Sipa Press/Rex Features
p.180 Brown bear cub © Sygma/Corbis

SMALL PRINT

Selected images from our guidebooks are available for licensing from:
ROUGHGUIDESPICTURES.COM

Index

Map entries are in colour.

H

I

K

L

M

N

O

P

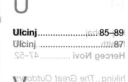